Urban Planning/My Way

From Baltimore's Inner Harbor
to Lower Manhattan and Beyond

By
David A. Wallace, AICP

Planners Press
American Planning Association
Chicago, Illinois
Washington, D.C.

To Paul Ylvisaker and the Ford Foundation,
Wallace Roberts & Todd, LLC, and Joan Dulles Wallace,
patient sponsors all.

Contents

Introduction

The most exhilarating moments in a planning consultant's life are those when you have been pursuing a big job in a tough, competitive situation, and the prospective client calls to tell you that you have won. You have been selected over all the others. Your efforts to analyze and understand the people and the problem, to propose the right methods to produce what is wanted and needed within budget and time constraints, and to show why you are the right personality and your firm has the skills and creativity for the assignment have paid off. You have been searching for and have literally found, or created a key to a kingdom—a kingdom not as in domain, but as in realm, the realm of people and possibilities. And that's what planning is all about. Break out the champagne, the key is the catalyst for opening the way to the problem's resolution.

My definition of planning: As I have practiced it, planning is an action-oriented, problem-solving process. The process starts with problem definition. Within every complete problem definition, a realm of possible actions lies before you. The search for the right combination of possibilities for a particular client is a search for the key that will open the realm to the solution. The key can be an idea, a concept, and often is a specific project which, when acted on by the client, leads to a successful resolution to the problem.

My belief that all planning, including physical planning, is a problem-solving process is consistent with my attitude toward life. "Pragmatism claims that human thinking and acting, from the least sophisticated to the most sophisticated, are driven by the need to respond to problems: All thought and action are provoked by a tension between ourselves as needy organisms, on the one side, and on the other the environment that must satisfy those needs. We think and act to reduce that tension."[1] This is the conceptual framework for planning as I see it.

Within this framework, and in simpleminded terms, action-oriented planning is a process that begins with a description, in clients' value terms, of a current situation. The values give us a measure of what the client likes and doesn't like about the situation. This is the problem definition. We can then determine alternative courses of action, those short-term goals that are within the realm of possibility and can be taken to correct what is wrong, thus modifying the current situation. The client can then select that course or combination of actions that most nearly achieves the goals and act on them. If we have found the key to the kingdom properly and opened the realm of possibilities, we can help the client implement the actions.

In the process the client must be involved from start to finish. Workshops, charrettes, vision and so-called value planning are important tools to ensure that the client is part of the process and internalizes the conclusions.

And if we've found and used the key to the kingdom successfully and the selected course of action has been acted upon, over time a new situation evolves that includes the intended (and unintended) consequences of the original and intervening actions. The original situation has changed, a new problem must be defined, and the process of planning repeated.

All of the above sounds bare and abstract but is borne out again and again by my professional planning experience. When I first went to Baltimore in 1957, the downtown area was under rapid decline, a situation that needed focused and dramatic action. A self-fulfilling prophecy of decline was under way. After initial analysis, the problem was understood and defined to community leaders—the clients. Alternative possible actions were outlined, and the 22-acre Charles Center redevelopment project in the heart of the central business district was seen as the key to the kingdom, the catalytic action necessary to turn the situation around and reverse the self-fulfilling prophecy. As Charles Center was developed over the ensuing years, the community was persuaded that downtown's future was achievable. The project set in motion the opportunity for the Inner Harbor's revitalization that in turn has spawned the rebirth of much of the central area of Baltimore. This has taken 40 years, with many intervening cycles of growth and planning steps and actions. And today Charles Center is under intense revitalization. The process is being repeated.

The Baltimore experience was the major one of my professional life. In addition, planning for Lower Manhattan, for New Jersey's Hudson River waterfront, for Atlantic City, for downtown Norfolk, Virginia, and for the New Orleans Central Area illustrates the same principles and conclusions.

Let me introduce myself. I am an architect, urban designer, and city planner by profession. I was born in Chicago, brought up in Philadelphia, and trained in architecture at the University of Pennsylvania's Graduate School of Fine Arts (now called the School of Design). Following five years in the U.S. combat engineers during World War II, and several after the war as an itinerant architectural designer, I became a registered architect in California in 1947, and increasingly became interested in the contextual problems of the individual buildings on which I worked. Initiated into the problems of race and poverty by my mother, who was a prominent Philadelphia social worker, influenced by six months in the army at World War II's end serving as a defense council for black and Hispanic soldiers on a General Courts Martial, and involved in studying slum problems during a year in Los Angeles working for America's most prominent black architect, Paul R. Williams, I became preoccupied by the issues of race and city planning.

With the GI Bill as financing, a wife to help support me, I entered Harvard's Graduate School of Design in 1948 where I studied planning and wrote a doctoral dissertation on the influence of planning and redevelopment policies on the segregation of African-Americans in Chicago.[2] A short stint teaching at the University of Chicago led to four years back in Philadelphia as the chief of planning and development for the city's redevelopment authority. My family and I moved to Baltimore in early 1957.

From then until recently I have been continuously involved in planning and design of central city urban redevelopment projects and suburban regional growth management programs, at first in and around Baltimore, then increasingly in other cities around the country. For the first five of those years my family and I lived in Baltimore's Roland Park section while I was director of the Greater Baltimore Committee's Planning Council. I prepared plans for downtown Charles Center's redevelopment and various related projects that triggered revitalization of the Central Business District. Toward the end of the five years, I began a part-time practice on the side as an architectural and urban design consultant for projects in Toronto, Canada; Trenton, New Jersey; and Washington, D.C.

My Harvard University mentor, G. Holmes Perkins, had become dean of the University of Pennsylvania's Graduate School of Fine Arts and my dissertation supervisor at Harvard, William L.C. Wheaton, was the chairman of Penn's Department of City and Regional Planning. In the summer of 1961, I accepted a tenured full professorship in planning and urban design at Penn, and we moved back to Philadelphia. In those days professors were paid a paltry salary of $25,000 for a nine-month year with a light teaching load, on the assumption that they would have a part-time practice, so I continued my consulting. Fortunately, my wife worked as an editor, which supplemented our income.

Late in 1962, I was contacted by Thomas L. Karsten, whom I had known from my Charles Center days in Baltimore. Karsten represented a group of Baltimore County landed-gentry whose estates were threatened by suburban sprawl. They commissioned me to prepare a plan for the 70-square-mile Green Spring and Worthington valleys area just outside the city to the northwest. It was a big and complex assignment, and I asked Ian L. McHarg, chairman of Penn's landscape architecture and regional planning department and my former Harvard classmate, to join me. I had been a faculty juror for several of his studio classes and I felt his ecologi-

I.1 Clockwise from the upper left, David A. Wallace, architect, urban designer and planner, age 48; Ian L. McHarg, landscape architect and regional planner, age 43; William H. Roberts, landscape architect and planner, age 33; Thomas A. Todd, architect and urban designer, age 38. (WMRT)

cal approach would complement my own planning, urban design, and architectural skills.

Together we formed Wallace-McHarg, Architects, Landscape Architects and Environmental Planners, and hired William H. Roberts as our landscape designer part-time. Roberts was a talented former student of McHarg's, originally from a farm in Wales. Trained in Wales as an architect, he was an associate professor of landscape architecture in McHarg's program. We started work with our office in McHarg's attic near my own house in West Mount Airy, and opened a project office in Towson, Maryland, staffed by William C. McDonnell, who had worked with me at the Planning Council.

The resulting *Plan for the Valleys* became an international landmark for planning and growth management based on ecological principles. The plan was given wide publicity by McHarg as a major chapter in his famous book, *Design with Nature*, and in his missionary-like speeches around the country and abroad. After completion of the plan, McDonnell became the newly formed Valleys Planning Council's executive director to manage its implementation. The valleys to this day remain largely unspoiled in accordance with the plan. Development has been diverted to more appropriate locations on the surrounding slopes and plateau areas, a testament both to the power of the plan and to the vigilance of the property owners in preventing extension of a major interceptor sewer into the valleys and an expressway across them. Lewis Mumford, the famous urbanist and a friend of McHarg's, wrote a laudatory forward to the plan, which McHarg used to publicize our work. This and publication of an article, *Diary of a Plan*, by me and McDonnell in the January 1971 issue of the *Journal of the American Institute of Planners*, gave the firm additional exposure and a national reputation.

No sooner had we started work on the *Plan for the Valleys* in the spring of 1963 than the Greater Baltimore Committee's executive director, William Boucher III, called me to ask for a proposal for a master plan for the Baltimore's Inner Harbor, with the work to be jointly sponsored by the Greater Baltimore Committee and the city. Boucher and I had worked as a team throughout my years in Baltimore. He was responsible for the public acceptance of the plans I generated. This new assignment had been triggered by civic leader Abel Wolman, a member of the Greater Baltimore Committee and a prominent local engineer. Wolman had returned from a vacation to the Stockholm Harbor, which inspired him as a model for what Baltimore's decrepit waterfront might be. He recommended to Mayor Theodore R. McKeldin that the city and the Greater Baltimore Committee bring back "that nice young man who was responsible for Charles Center who had moved to Philadelphia." On the strength of a $50,000 contract, we hired architect/urban designer Thomas A. Todd away from the Philadelphia City Planning Commission as our full-time urban designer. Wallace-McHarg briefly became Wallace-McHarg Associates and in late 1963 was changed to Wallace McHarg Roberts & Todd as McHarg and I recognized Roberts and Todd as full partners. The Inner Harbor Master Plan was published in October 1964 and became an immediate award-winning plan.

We were an interesting foursome, all smart as can be. One of our employees whose name I forget once did a cartoon of the firm entitled "Walrus, McHog, Robin and Toad." In it, I am completely bald, mustached (at the time), portly, phlegmatic, and somewhat authoritarian in my approach to the world, which I try to hide as rationalism. By contrast Ian McHarg was tall, narrow-shouldered, and bombastic. Born a Scot from the poor section of Glasgow, he had risen from private to sergeant in the British army—as he told it, by beating up everyone in his squad—and that was the way he approached life. He ultimately became a paratroop major. Bright, articulate, arrogant, and domineering, McHarg won most

I.2 Walrus McHog Robin & Toad, in needlepoint by Mrs. Washington Sawyer, the mother of a friend and client.

arguments by wearing his opponents down. Not an easy man to be a partner with, but he could charm an audience and write like a dream.

Bill Roberts was the opposite from me in personality. Born and brought up on a Welsh farm, he is as tall as McHarg, but broad-shouldered and athletically shaped. He has the Welsh "gift of gab" and is a wonderful extrovert. He is both an architect and landscape architect whose approach to design is to act as a critic on subordinates' work. His own light sketches have the same delightful ambiguity as his strong environmental design philosophy. Ergo the cartoon robin.

Tom Todd was the best urban designer I have ever seen, did all his own work, but was receptive to suggestions. He and I established a relationship where for many years he and I would jointly conceptualize and he would draw, and then I would sell the result. He tended to be a little toad-like, grumpy, paranoid, hypochondriac, but with a great sense of humor. He is short, bearded, and a painter of great talent.

The *Inner Harbor Plan* and the *Plan for the Valleys* gave WMRT a reputation in widely different but complementary professional fields. Work began to pour in from all over the country and the firm grew. While the city was organizing to carry out the Inner Harbor plan, I continued my Baltimore activity by serving on the Charles Center Architectural Review Board (ARB) that I had helped set up prior to leaving Baltimore. The Architectural Review Board was operated by The Charles Center Management Office (CCMO), a nonprofit organization I had helped establish to manage and promote Charles Center, the city's first 22-acre redevelopment project in the heart of the Central Business District. CCMO was later given the additional assignment of the Inner Harbor and renamed Charles Center-Inner Harbor Management, Inc. (CC-IH) in 1965. WMRT was retained to help prepare the Inner Harbor Project I Urban Redevelopment Plan in 1967, under a contract with the city managed by CC-IH. The contract was open-ended and provided for as-requested professional services, as well as per diem reimbursement for planning and feasibility studies, with fees based on a percentage of construction cost for detailed design work. David C. Hamme, later WRT's managing partner, was hired to run our Baltimore office for the first year of the work.

The firm continued as WMRT until 1979, when McHarg left by request. McHarg took his own few projects with him, and in 1980 we were reorganized as WRT: Wallace Roberts & Todd. McHarg had not contributed materially to the Inner Harbor nor had he been involved with other Baltimore work after the original *Plan for the Valleys,* so the Inner Harbor continued as before, with me as the partner-in-charge.

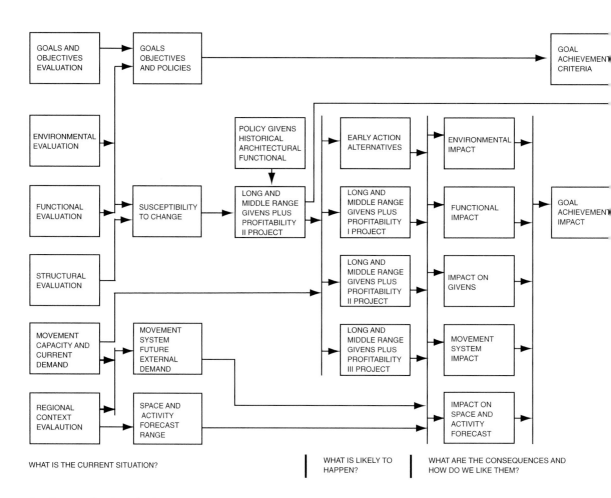

GOALS AND
OBJECTIVES
EVALUATION

GOALS
OBJECTIVES
AND POLICIES

GOAL
ACHIEVEMENT
CRITERIA

ENVIRONMENTAL
EVALUATION

POLICY GIVENS
HISTORICAL
ARCHITECTURAL
FUNCTIONAL

EARLY ACTION
ALTERNATIVES

ENVIRONMENTAL
IMPACT

FUNCTIONAL
EVALUATION

SUSCEPTIBILITY
TO CHANGE

LONG AND
MIDDLE RANGE
GIVENS PLUS
PROFITABILITY
II PROJECT

LONG AND
MIDDLE RANGE
GIVENS PLUS
PROFITABILITY
I PROJECT

FUNCTIONAL
IMPACT

GOAL
ACHIEVEMENT
IMPACT

STRUCTURAL
EVALUATION

LONG AND
MIDDLE RANGE
GIVENS PLUS
PROFITABILITY
II PROJECT

IMPACT ON
GIVENS

MOVEMENT
CAPACITY AND
CURRENT
DEMAND

MOVEMENT
SYSTEM
FUTURE
EXTERNAL
DEMAND

LONG AND
MIDDLE RANGE
GIVENS PLUS
PROFITABILITY
III PROJECT

MOVEMENT
SYSTEM
IMPACT

REGIONAL
CONTEXT
EVALAUTION

SPACE AND
ACTIVITY
FORECAST
RANGE

IMPACT ON
SPACE AND
ACTIVITY
FORECAST

WHAT IS THE CURRENT SITUATION?

WHAT IS LIKELY TO
HAPPEN?

WHAT ARE THE CONSEQUENCES AND
HOW DO WE LIKE THEM?

I.3 For professional planners, this diagram for the Downtown New Orleans Growth Management Program spells out the steps to be taken in the typical planning process. It is in sufficient detail to permit instructions to staff and consultants. For clients, it explains how their money is being spent and what product to expect.

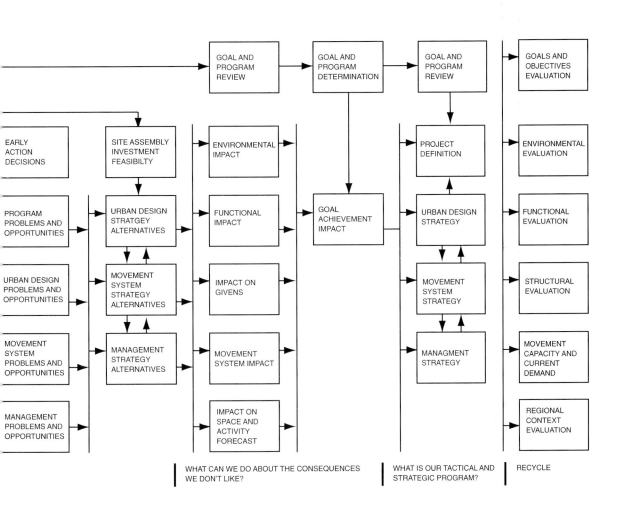

GOAL AND PROGRAM REVIEW

GOAL AND PROGRAM DETERMINATION

GOAL AND PROGRAM REVIEW

GOALS AND OBJECTIVES EVALUATION

EARLY ACTION DECISIONS

SITE ASSEMBLY INVESTMENT FEASIBILTY

ENVIRONMENTAL IMPACT

PROJECT DEFINITION

ENVIRONMENTAL EVALUATION

PROGRAM PROBLEMS AND OPPORTUNITIES

URBAN DESIGN STRATGEY ALTERNATIVES

FUNCTIONAL IMPACT

GOAL ACHIEVEMENT IMPACT

URBAN DESIGN STRATEGY

FUNCTIONAL EVALUATION

URBAN DESIGN PROBLEMS AND OPPORTUNITIES

MOVEMENT SYSTEM STRATEGY ALTERNATIVES

IMPACT ON GIVENS

MOVEMENT SYSTEM STRATEGY

STRUCTURAL EVALUATION

MOVEMENT SYSTEM PROBLEMS AND OPPORTUNITIES

MANAGEMENT STRATEGY ALTERNATIVES

MOVEMENT SYSTEM IMPACT

MANAGMENT STRATEGY

MOVEMENT CAPACITY AND CURRENT DEMAND

MANAGEMENT PROBLEMS AND OPPORTUNITIES

IMPACT ON SPACE AND ACTIVITY FORECAST

REGIONAL CONTEXT EVALUATION

WHAT CAN WE DO ABOUT THE CONSEQUENCES WE DON'T LIKE?

WHAT IS OUR TACTICAL AND STRATEGIC PROGRAM?

RECYCLE

The Inner Harbor became that best of all projects with a life of its own. CC-IH was funded annually by the mayor and city council for its operating money and our contract budget was appropriately replenished. Every three or four years the end of a phase would be reached, and a competition with other firms for the next phase would be held. While the outcome was never a certainty, we always managed to be reselected, in part because of CC-IH's reluctance to subject itself and the process to the uncertainty of breaking in a new firm. Over the 23 years of this arrangement, we were under extensions of the original contract until finally CC-IH was dissolved and its functions taken over by the Baltimore Development Corporation in 1989.

It was an exhilarating experience. We continually lost money on the planning and urban design work because of the low multiplier (1.2) on direct salaries allowed for overhead and profit, but we made modest profits on the landscape architectural design work and broke even overall. We accepted the fee arrangement because of the challenge of the assignments and the enhancement to the firm's reputation. It was a loss leader as well as what is called a bread-and-butter job.

In addition to the Inner Harbor, other city and regional assignments that kept me involved in Baltimore over the years included a plan for the University of Maryland's downtown Baltimore campus; a strategic urban design concept for MetroCenter Baltimore for the city's Department of Planning required to get U.S. DOT to fund the subway; a detailed development plan for the central business district retail area called Lexington Center, to integrate that area with the subway which was then in engineering design; stadium plans for the Orioles and Ravens; a comprehensive growth-management plan for Baltimore County that expanded the *Plan for the Valleys* approach to the whole county; and an update of the *Plan for the Valleys*, to name a few.

Looking back, I remember Baltimore as a city of many unusual and some unique characteristics, memorable buildings, areas and scenes, and of course events and people. My fondest memories of the place are as much about individuals whom I have liked, admired, envied, disliked, or emulated, as about the physical city. It was a great training ground for me and for what has become WRT, the international planning and design firm.

---

1. Alan Ryan, "The Group," *New York Review of Books*, May 31, 2001.
2. David A. Wallace, "Residential Segregation of Negroes in Chicago," Doctoral dissertation, Harvard University, 1953.

1

Getting to Know Baltimore

A man named Hunter Moss was my first contact from Baltimore. He became my Greater Baltimore Committee (GBC) boss and sponsor. Hunter was originally from Philadelphia, had met James Rouse during World War II, and formed a mortgage banking and real estate firm. The Moss Rouse Company lent money to veterans through FHA financing. Hunter had been a Marine captain and looked it. Everything about him was square and regular: face, jaw, shoulders. Hunter was a really nice guy who had parted with Rouse, but they remained friends. Hunter knew everyone in the city and was a major link between the business and political communities.

Before we moved, Hunter strongly urged my wife and me to buy a house rather than rent. It was good advice, but when I toured what a real estate agent felt were eligible areas, I found that we couldn't afford them. I also learned that the city was more segregated than any other I had experienced. Jews were concentrated in Forest Park and Mount Washington; I was advised by the real estate agent—who had asked me what my faith was—that "you wouldn't want to live there with no churches." Today such ethnic bias is illegal, of course. Other ethnic neighborhoods were equally off limits. We were selling a house in Chestnut Hill, Pennsylvania, that I had bought with a no-down-payment Veteran's mortgage a year before, so we had little equity. We finally settled on a modest house in Northwood—a section of Baltimore built by the same people who had developed Roland Park, but to much reduced specifications during and after World War II. Moss underwrote the shortfall in my down payment. A year later we managed to find a house in Roland Park we could afford on Hawthorne Road. We moved to get away from Northwood, where the parking and noise of the nearby Municipal Stadium, and an incessantly barking dog owned by neighboring hillbillies from West Virginia that drove us wild.

Public schools were already a big Baltimore problem; we sent Robert Cunningham (my seven-year-old stepson) to Baltimore Friends. It was a compromise between the Park School, the Jewish choice, or Gilman School, all upper-middle-class Gentile. We couldn't afford a club and didn't want to join one anyway; they were equally segregated. The Elkridge Hunt Club in the suburbs and the Maryland Club downtown were at the top of the heap. But they were for Gentiles only.

We were involved in three all-white social worlds. Hunter Moss and Dora Lewis, his very upper-class wife, were our entree into the top of the WASP pyramid. Walter Sondheim, Jr., the head of the Baltimore Urban Renewal and Housing Authority and vice-president and part-owner of one of the city's large department store chains, became a close friend and introduced us to the Jewish aristocracy. Various others from the Roman Catholic Archdiocese's civic leaders, such as Francis J. Murnaghan, became friends as well as business colleagues. As newcomers we had no certain place, but floated across all three, more as observers than members, with acquaintances in each. The black community had its own social hierarchy. The separate world of my and my wife's professional connections—our colleagues, other planners, architects, engineers, social workers, reporters, columnists, editors—cut diagonally across the groups.

GBC rented the top room in the tower of the Olin-Mathieson office building for me. It was the city's tallest building, at Baltimore and Light streets, and at first I sat there in lonely splendor at the center of the downtown I was to help plan. It was challenging and scary. Later, when I had a secretary and the beginnings of a staff, the Planning Council moved to a lower floor next to GBC's office. And so I began.

Understanding the city and its downtown was the first order of business. I believe cities are like people, with personality, character, and soul. How one feels about a place is important to how its problems are approached. First impressions are indelible. I immediately fell in love with Baltimore.

The first view of downtown Baltimore's skyline from the Metroliner, as the train approaches Penn Station from the north before entering the tunnel, always excites me with its elegant and many-faceted towers glittering in the sun. My pulse quickens and I feel like a Dick Whittington (albeit minus the cat) approaching London. I can't count the times I've paused over the years in gathering my papers and briefcase to get off the train from Philadelphia to marvel at this city that I have come to love, with its distinctive broad tapestry of row houses and white steps flowing across the land, interrupted by the high mass of Johns Hopkins Hospital, intermittent residential towers, church spires, and the nation's first monument to George Washington dotting the cityscape until the climax is reached in the distant downtown.

In my mind's eye, I visualize the changes from my introduction to the city in the fall of 1956 to today. The Olin-Mathieson Tower, then Maryland National Bank, now NationsBank, was the only really tall building. Today, downtown is both dramatically different and yet recognizably the same over 45 years. The silver trim on Deutsche Banc/Alex Brown's 35-story tower and elongated Mansard roof, completed in 1990 as the bottom fell out of the office market, outshines the newly gold-plated NationsBank tower, similarly shaped but much more elegant. Ten million square feet of office space have been added, doubling the central business district's inventory north of the Inner Harbor. What I can't see, but I know they are there, includes a restored City Hall, a subway, and a surface light-rail transit system, and more. Then comes the tunnel and the announcer says: "The only stop in Baltimore."

I step off the Metroliner and climb the almost always motionless escalator to Penn Station, which looks much the same, perhaps somewhat cleaner. That there is an escalator at all is owing to Mayor Thomas J. D'Alesandro, Jr., who held up legislation for the Pennsylvania Railroad when he was in Congress in the early 1950s until they agreed to install one. Or so he said. I had learned already that a politician's ability to reinvent history and put a spin on the facts was infinite.

The Maryland Transportation Authority operates a light rail transit line mostly using existing tracks. It is called an LRT and connects Penn Station to the old B&O Mount Royal Station next to Bolton Hill, where it then joins the LRT that runs from the edge of the Green Spring Valley north of the suburban beltway south through downtown on Howard Street, then all the way to the Baltimore/Washington International Airport and Glen Burnie. It reminds me of a slicked-up version of the now-abandoned trolleys I grew up using in Philadelphia. Ticketing is on the honor system and a police officer is on board for security. There are five other passengers and I doubt that the LRT pays its own way, but the system increases mobility for the poor, the young, the handicapped—and me.

As we roll south past Mount Royal-Fremont and historic Bolton Hill toward downtown, my chain of memories starts with meeting Gerald Johnson in Bolton Hill for the first time. Like many of Baltimore's leading citizens, Johnson, a noted author and journalist, was a Southern transplant. Unlike most, he was a liberal and was reported to have resigned from *The Baltimore Sun* when that paper came out against President Franklin D. Roosevelt. By the time I met him, his reputation as a local commentator rivaled that of his better-known friend and compatriot, H. L. Mencken, who had recruited him to *The Sun* from Winston Salem, North Carolina. A small, intense man with a white moustache, he lived with his wife in a first-floor apartment in a handsome Victorian townhouse on Park Avenue overlooking the city's center to the south.

My interview with Johnson was to be one of several hundred my staff and I were conducting in preparation for our downtown planning for the GBC, which was under contract to the Committee for Downtown. The purpose was to get informed thoughts on Baltimore issues and the potential future of the city from people who could later influence public opinion. While it was often difficult to get a subject to expand on open-ended questions, I needn't have worried about Johnson, who knew exactly what to say. Over tea and cookies, Johnson elaborated on what he felt was good and bad about his adopted city, and sketched out a thesis that he felt would help explain its historic changes in fortune. He was a great student of Southern history and our conversation continued for more than two hours. It was immensely informative, and he provided introductions to many other people, whom I subsequently interviewed.

Eight years later, after the renaissance was well under way, Johnson summarized his thesis in an article on Baltimore's past and future in *The New Republic*. In the article, "Baltimore Might Make It," Johnson calls the city's municipal history a "fascinating demonstration in miniature of (historian Arnold) Toynbee's challenge-and-response theory of the life of a civilization. Three times the very existence of Baltimore has been sternly challenged. Twice the city overcompensated and flourished; but the third challenge was too much, and it slowly sank from second to sixth city and twelfth metropolitan district."[1]

Johnson cites Baltimore's first four challenges: the struggle for independence; the canal era; the Civil War; and the long period of urban decay that followed until the 1950s. As Johnson tells it, the struggle for independence didn't end until 1812 when Baltimore beat off the last British attack, built a monument to that victory that still stands downtown in the middle of Calvert Street, and overcompensated in response to the block-ade by developing the famous Baltimore clipper, on which many a local fortune was founded in trade with the Orient. Thirty years later, New York's Erie Canal opened up commerce to the west by breaching the Appalachians. Responding to the second challenge, Baltimore's leaders again overcompensated by creating the Baltimore & Ohio Railroad as a municipal venture, and by pushing this just-invented form of transportation across the mountains to compete successfully with New York, Philadelphia, and other seaboard cities.

The third challenge resulted from the Civil War and Baltimore failed the test. Johnson allows the city's failure was predetermined by circumstances mostly beyond its control. Its border location, Southern sympathies, and federal expropriation of the B&O for four years for war purposes condemned the city to losing its traditional role as wholesaler to the South, in favor of Norfolk and Atlanta. Adding insult to injury, Philadelphia and New York took advantage of Baltimore's absence, capturing most of the new markets to the West. Johnson cites the consequent urban decay, as starting after the Civil War, and continuing for almost 100 years, through the turn of the century, the downtown fire of 1904, World War I, the Great Depression, and World War II, culminating in the early 1950s. While new local fortunes were made in industry, munitions, and shipbuilding, Baltimore declined.

Johnson continues his thesis that by the end of World War II, Baltimore had become a branch town and what the French call a "rentier" community, where the moneyed aristocracy clip coupons and invest elsewhere. Evidence of urban decay was everywhere, the city's physical plant had badly deteriorated, and the community was "living on its capital," by letting things slide. Johnson noted that major Baltimore corporate decisions were being made in places like Pittsburgh, where a single bank had assets greater than all of Baltimore's banks put together. The entrepreneurial energies of titans such as the 19th century Howards, Garretts, Pratts, and Abells were not to be seen. In my interview with him, Johnson quoted then-Mayor D'Alesandro, Jr., who liked to say: "Pittsburgh has its Mellons and Baltimore has its watermelons." In his article Johnson adds, "In any sizable undertaking, Baltimore enterprise seemed to be a consistent flop."

My first impressions were not deceptive. Facts and figures that my staff and I developed confirmed Johnson's gloomy view. By the early 1950s, downtown employment had been stagnant for 20 years. Real estate assessments in the central business district declined 10 percent between 1952 and 1957, department store sales spiraled downward 12 percent in the same period, and the overall building vacancy rate was more than 25 percent in many areas.[2] New suburban malls lured retail customers away. Finally, the closing of O'Neill's Department Store at Charles and Lexington streets, which was owned by the Baltimore Archdiocese and located in the heart of the central business district, served as a wake-up call.

It took the bleak state of downtown to convince Baltimore business leaders such as J. Jefferson Miller, executive vice-president of the Hecht chain of department stores, that their investments were seriously jeopardized and that their futures depended on action. Miller was a wonderful man who mixed conviviality with sardonic humor. Short, compact, and energetic, he was rich, a partner in the Hecht Company, of which he managed a branch at Baltimore and Charles streets. Miller first formed a Committee for Downtown, then became a messenger of doom in raising money for an action program. When the leaders and the city finally responded, they overcompensated, finally confirming Johnson's thesis. Spearheaded by people bursting on the national scene like James W. Rouse, founder of the Rouse Company, the new leaders—like Miller and Rouse—challenged the older defeatist group who retired to the sidelines.

As Hunter Moss told it, he and Rouse had just attended another fractious lunch meeting of the Citizens Planning and Housing Association, a forum headed by Francis Morton and dominated by do-gooders whose idea of a successful meeting was to have lots of controversy. Walking up the street, Rouse turned to Moss and said, "What are you and I doing here? These are well-intended people, but we need to get the movers and shakers together as they did in Pittsburgh if we want to get anything done."

And that was how the Greater Baltimore Committee was formed, with 100 CEOs as members to focus on specific, doable projects to supplement the usual Chamber of Commerce's broad-brush approach. After a few false starts, politicians began to talk to and trust GBC's businessmen and educators and vice versa. All began to appreciate Baltimore's desperate plight, exemplified by its downtown. GBC and the Committee for Downtown joined together, realizing they needed a plan of action and their own planner to prepare it, and help them carry it out, rather than relying on the city.

In my revisit to downtown, as the LRT carries me south from Bolton Hill and the B&O Station down Howard Street, past Antique Row, I remember how my love affair with Baltimore began with a raw oysters and crab cakes lunch at Miller Brothers Seafood Restaurant on September 25, 1956. I had been invited by Hunter Moss, who had gotten my name from the Urban Land Institute, to meet him, the Greater Baltimore Committee's Robert Levi, the Committee for Downtown's Jeff Miller, and Rouse to see if I was the man they wanted to help Baltimore revive.

They decided I was. After four years as director of planning and development for Philadelphia's Redevelopment Authority, the opportunity to work for the private sector was a breath of fresh air. I had been managing multiple redevelopment projects while heading a task force that developed an overall strategy and tactics up to then missing from Philadelphia's redevelopment program. This new approach introduced hard economic and social realities, implemented stalled projects, initiated new ones, and was based on my belief in a strong downtown as a necessary anchor to overall city revitalization, a belief very appropriate to my prospective Baltimore assignment. The new approach, published as the "Central Urban Renewal Area Report," (CURA), was the methodology that other cities looked to as a model, including Baltimore.

In between the oysters and crab cakes, I outlined my credentials. I told them that until I started work in Philadelphia in 1953, Edmund N. Bacon, that city's famous director of city planning, had been acting *de facto* as the planner for the Redevelopment Authority, as well as carrying out his own job. I had been recruited from the University of Chicago by Professor Martin Meyerson of the University of Pennsylvania, who was acting as a consultant to Dorothy Montgomery, a new member of the authority board. As I was being interviewed by Montgomery, other members of the authority and Bacon—but had not yet been hired—Bacon proposed that I become head of comprehensive planning for his City Planning Commission. I rejected his offer with the realization I had probably made an enemy. Instead, we became friendly, but instinctive, rivals. We thought quite differently, Bacon arriving at conclusions intuitively, while I am a believer in the rational planning process. He saw me as usurping much of his turf. In the ensuing competition, I often won out partly because of the strength of my ideas and arguments, but also because Mayor Joseph S. Clark's redevelopment board appointees backed me as part of Clark's "new broom" approach to government.

Dorothy Montgomery acted both as my political and intellectual sponsor. She was head of the watchdog Philadelphia Housing Association and a strong supporter, close friend, and appointee of Mayor Clark. Her views were reinforced by a heavyweight advisory committee consisting of G. Holmes Perkins, dean of Penn's Graduate School of Fine Arts, Penn planning professors Martin Meyerson, Robert B. Mitchell and William L. C. Wheaton, Aaron Levine, head of the Citizen's Council on City Planning for which my wife worked; and the city's development coordinator, William L. Rafsky, who was also a natural enemy of Bacon. Together, the committee hammered out policy and programs in which Bacon's narrow physical design focus was an important element, but only one of many.

However, by late 1956, Clark had left for the U.S. Senate and his successor, Richardson Dilworth, had died. Clark's appointee as authority board chairman, former U.S. Senator Francis J. Myers had also died and Montgomery's influence had eroded. Philadelphia City Council President James H. J. Tate, an old-school politician, had become mayor. Tate appointed criminal lawyer and political lightweight Michael von Moschisker to replace Myers, and Tate expected to gain control of the authority. Von Moschisker knew I was thinking of leaving and offered me a part-time consulting contract with the authority to do what I had been doing as an employee. My old mentor from Harvard, Dean Perkins, proposed I join the Penn faculty. At the time, it sounded like a pretty good combination.

It was at this point that Moss had called to invite me to a first interview in Baltimore, where he showed me around the city and outlined what they wanted. When I asked why the local city planners could not do the plan, he explained that the commission did not have the staff and its director, Arthur J. McVoy, was not in the mayor's favor. This introductory trip was followed by the lunch meeting and the news that they wanted me to take the job.

Although Moss's offer was very appealing, at first I turned it down. The possibility of being both a consultant and teaching at Penn was very alluring. But after sobering discussions with several of the authority's other consultants, and with my wife, Joan Dulles, who knew Philadelphia's politics, I realized I would need a heavyweight political sponsor to replace Dorothy Montgomery. Without one my contract with the authority would always be in jeopardy and my recommendations ignored. Joan really made the decision, so I called Moss back and accepted.

When I announced my resignation, Von Moschisker asked me to lunch in the Palm Room at the Bellevieu Stratford Hotel, the political restaurant of choice. He offered me the executive director's job if I would stay, and he was taken aback when I told him the job was not his to give. I pointed out that Francis J. Lammer—the incumbent and my boss whom I respected—had so ingratiated himself with Mayor Tate when Tate was president of city council that Tate would not replace him. Lammer had, among other things, gotten Tate an honorary doctorate at St. Joseph's College where Lammer was chairman of the alumni association.

So there went any hope I might have had for a political sponsor. That wasn't my style, anyway. I also realized that Bacon, who as director of city planning, was a mayoral appointee and was skillful at ingratiating himself with whoever was mayor, would constantly have the upper hand. In recent years, Bacon, with tongue in cheek, likes to take credit for initiating Baltimore's renaissance by saying he drove me out of town. But by then I was on my way.

The Baltimore challenge was very attractive. I was to be in complete charge, reporting to Moss and the Planning Council of the GBC. The fact that the Planning Council was a creature beholden to the GBC gave me some pause, and I only later learned that Moss and Charles Buck, chairman of the GBC, had a battle about the council's independence, which Moss had lost. As it turned out, this dependant relationship was both a help and a hindrance.

Looking back, I can't believe I accepted a starting salary of $15,000. Actually it represented a raise of $3,000 from my Philadelphia Redevelopment Authority income, where I had been held below that of Lammer as executive director, a standard administrative trick to keep salaries low. The same kind of organizational ceiling also existed in Baltimore, where it was explained I could not make more than Bill Boucher, GBC's executive director. Obviously, had the council been independent, the ceiling would not have existed.

As to the assignment for the plan itself, the Planning Council members and the GBC had been very impressed by architect Victor Gruen's recently published visionary Plan for Downtown Fort Worth, Texas. However, that plan had been financed by a local utility company and had been prepared without any community involvement. As a consequence it was never implemented, and served primarily as an advertising vehicle for Gruen and its sponsor, the local gas company. The GBC decided it needed its own in-house planner. A number of Baltimore leaders had Pittsburgh connections. They saw an organizational model in the Pittsburgh Regional Plan Association that had produced the Pittsburgh Regional Plan. The GBC fashioned its Planning Council after the

1.1 The proposed Civic Center (sports arena) was to be located in the Inner Harbor southeast of Pratt and Light Street. The plan was done in 1957 for the Greater Baltimore Committee by Pietro Belluschi, Dean of the School of Architecture at M.I.T., shortly after I arrived in Baltimore. It was rejected by the Park Board and the Center was finally placed next to Charles Center. Some of Belluschi's other ideas are interesting.

Pittsburgh example with a small board of top people, such as executives from department stores, real estate, banking, the head of the Western Maryland Railroad, and chaired by Moss, Rouse's former partner.

My task was to prepare a plan for the Central Business District (CBD) as exciting as Gruen's, but with the built-in approval of key representatives of the city administration and the business community to "insure" its acceptance and implementation. When I asked why Baltimore's leaders didn't rely on the city planning commission to prepare a plan, they said that they wanted the planning one step removed from the political process. I later realized that this attitude stemmed from GBC's leaders' desire to be involved in preparing plans as "stakeholders," because they had more at stake than the members of the average citizen's group.

I moved with my wife and stepson to Baltimore and began work in early January of 1957. While my initial assignment was to prepare a plan for the CBD, I had no sooner arrived than a crisis about the location of a proposed sports arena—the Civic Center—came to a boil. There wasn't enough money in the city's bond issue to build it if a downtown site had to be acquired, so Mayor D'Alesandro proposed to put it in semi-suburban Druid Hill Park.

The GBC was dismayed. Not only was the proposal anti-downtown, it was also a direct challenge to the GBC's hopes to work with the city. In response, feeling it needed a heavyweight consultant, the GBC brought in Pietro Belluschi, M.I.T.'s architecture dean, to prepare a concept for the facility to be on a city-owned pier in the Inner Harbor, a-la-Sidney, Australia's, opera house. It was an interesting design, but an inappropriate location. Having just arrived, I kept my opinion to myself. Fortunately, the Baltimore Park Commission had jurisdiction over Druid Hill Park and refused to let the mayor have his way. Neither scheme was carried out, and we were later able to place the arena downtown next to our first major project, Charles Center.

After this debacle, the city administration understandably took a somewhat skeptical view toward the GBC's "elitist" muddling in city business, but nevertheless began to cooperate. Although he had not gotten the assignment to undertake the CBD plan, McVoy had his staff prepare a land-use concept for downtown that was both thoughtful and a useful guide to us. Unfortunately, McVoy still was not in the mayor's favor and was ignored, which was too bad because he was talented. He had lectured at M.I.T. and was the author of Baltimore's regional expressway layout, initially developed in a graduate studio at M.I.T. However, McVoy died shortly after I arrived. Civil engineer Philip Darling replaced him, and we worked closely with Darling.

As we proceeded, Moss introduced me around in the business, civic and city worlds and was very much a hands-on chairman. Together with the first-rate staff I recruited, we became a formidable team. George Kostritsky, later the "K" of RTKL, Inc., was my chief of design. He was a brilliant designer and creative thinker who had been on Ed Bacon's downtown Philadelphia planning team, where he had conceived of connecting the various commuter lines through Market Street East. Architect John Adelberg, who became a partner at Sasaki Associates in Watertown, Massachusetts, had just graduated from Harvard's Graduate School of Design along with planner Jeremiah D. O'Leary, who subsequently formed the well-regarded firm of Marcou-O'Leary. Landscape architect/planner William H. Potts also had been trained at Harvard and had

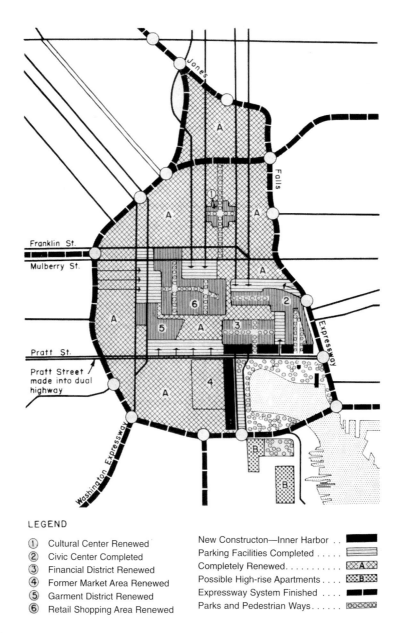

LEGEND

① Cultural Center Renewed
② Civic Center Completed
③ Financial District Renewed
④ Former Market Area Renewed
⑤ Garment District Renewed
⑥ Retail Shopping Area Renewed

New Constructon—Inner Harbor ..
Parking Facilities Completed .....
Completely Renewed...........
Possible High-rise Apartments ....
Expressway System Finished ....
Parks and Pedestrian Ways......

1.2 This concept plan for what was later called MetroCenter was presented to the Planning Council by Arthur McVoy, director of city planning early in 1957. McVoy unfortunately did not have Mayor Thomas D'Alesandro's confidence or Baltimore's CBD planning would have been done by the City Planning Commission. The plan contains some good ideas. McVoy died shortly after.

worked with me at the redevelopment authority in Philadelphia. Economist Harry B. Cooper was recruited from the New York Planning Commission, and together with internist Hiroshi Matsumoto from Japan, rounded out the professional staff. Millicent P. Gordon, who later married Potts, and Ruvelle "Mickey" Falcone were our support staff.

The Civic Center fracas led to one good thing: designation of the entire CBD, the Inner Harbor, and the Mount Vernon community to the north as a single urban renewal area. This designation was a necessary first step toward any redevelopment projects. I suggested this change to Bill Boucher, who had the ear of the mayor. Since Mayor D'Alesandro had just kicked the GBC where it hurt, he might be willing to make a concession. The urban renewal area was so large that individual property owners would not feel threatened by such general designation. This was consistent with the comprehensive approach to urban renewal that I had developed in Philadelphia. Procedurally, it meant that the Baltimore Urban Renewal and Housing Authority (BURHA) had the right to undertake initial investigative studies anywhere in the urban renewal area in the search for eligible projects. Later when we had a specific project in mind, this first all-important step could become controversial and potentially hold us up. D'Alesandro seized on the idea to placate the GBC because it cost him nothing; he rushed it through the city council without debate. This action was later more than justified by accelerating the first project approvals for Charles Center and the Inner Harbor.

As we proceeded with our surveying, fact-finding, and interviewing, Harry Cooper, Jerry O'Leary, and I interviewed more than 250 business and civic leaders—we realized that the self-fulfilling prophecy was at work in the community. The prevailing opinion was that downtown was "going to hell in a hand basket." Private decisions to abandon the city, such as the closing of O'Neills Department Store, and public proposals such as the mayor's plans for the Civic Center, were matched by the state pulling out of downtown to concentrate its offices in the Mount Royal-Fremont area to the north next to Bolton Hill, and the federal government moving the national Social Security headquarters from the Candler Building at the northeast corner of the Inner Harbor to Woodlawn at the beltway in the western suburbs. These and many more moves were ensuring the prophecy would come true. We needed an early action program to counter the trend and to build enthusiasm and opportunity for further investment or a CBD plan would have no market left to support any action proposals.

---

1 Gerald Johnson, "Baltimore Might Make It," in *The New Republic*, February, 1965.

2 Hunter Moss, "The Downtown Problem," in *Baltimore's Charles Center: A Case Study of Downtown Renewal*, ed. Martin Millspaugh, Technical Bulletin 51, The Urban Land Institute, p. 13, 1964.

2

Charles Center and the Downtown Program for Action

In response to the need for action, my staff and I presented Planning Council members the proposal that we put preparation of the overall CBD plan on temporary hold. Rather we would search for an urban renewal project big enough to have a major impact, yet small enough to be "doable" in a relatively short time, say 10 years. We reported that our hundreds of business interviews showed that between 200,000 and 300,000 square feet of private office market demand was being generated each year; office development would be the bellwether for renewal. There was also a growing need for a federal office building to consolidate scattered government agencies. Unless appropriate sites were made available, this demand was going to be satisfied in the suburbs.

The council itself was a great sounding board for ideas. Moss, the chairman, was the city's top real estate appraiser and he knew downtown properties intimately. He was a prominent member of the Urban Land Institute in Washington, D.C., through which he was familiar with what other cities were doing around the country. He and I worked as partners and I talked with him daily. Vice-chairman John E. Motz was president of the Mercantile Safe Deposit and Trust Company, the bank that had control over major properties in the area, which were owned by large trusts for which the bank was trustee. His chairman, Samuel Butler, really ran the bank, but Motz gave us entrée to the local aristocracy who dominated Baltimore's business world. That aristocracy ruled through trusts that

2.1 Archibald Rogers, head of Rogers Taliaferro & Lamb and GBC Planning Council member (PC); William G. Ewald, executive director, Committee for Downtown; David A. Wallace, PC director; John McC. Mowbray, Roland Park Company and PC member; Hunter Moss; PC chairman; Richard Turk, PC member; Charles H. Buck, GBC chairman; all grouped around Mayor Thomas D'Alesandro, Jr., who is witnessing the signature of J. Jefferson Miller, Committee for Downtown, chairman.

owned major real estate holdings downtown. Robert Levi and Jeff Miller were chief executive officers of the Hecht Company Department Stores. They knew the retail situation and were part of the community's Jewish elite. Levi had met Rhyda Hecht, his wife, when he was a Maine guide, and was the real brains in the company. Miller was independently wealthy and had run the Hecht Company's Baltimore Street store for years. He had an instinctive sense of what was politically feasible as well as good business. Archibald C. Rogers, who had preceded William Boucher as GBC's first executive director, came from an old Maryland family and was head of the city's largest architectural firm, then Rogers Taliaferro & Lamb, one of the few local professional outfits with a national reputation. These were the members who acted as an executive committee on whom I particularly relied to be available for advice. Our monthly meetings were workshops on our activities and progress.

The other council members were less active but still involved and important links to the community. They included: Charles H. Buck, chairman of GBC and head of the Maryland Title Guarantee Company; W. Arthur Grotz, president of the Western Maryland Railway Company; Dr. Otto Kraushaar, president of Goucher College; John McC. Mowbray, a Realtor and president of the Roland Park Company; Richard H. Turk, Sr., chairman of the board of the Pemco Corporation; and E.C. Wareheim, chairman of the Commercial Credit Corporation. The Commercial Credit Corporation, then still locally owned, was the only organization that had constructed its headquarters office building downtown since 1929—solid evidence that it could be done.

Jim Rouse was not a member of the council, but I frequently sought his advice. With his national reputation, Jim Rouse was the most influential individual in the city's business community. He and Moss had started the Moss-Rouse Company as mortgage bankers to take advantage of the Federal Housing Agency's new program after World War II. They parted company amicably over their different objectives. Moss wanted to stay an appraiser and mortgage banker, but Rouse was much more entrepreneurial. Rouse was not only the head of the Rouse Company as a mortgage banker, but also became a "world-class" developer of shopping centers. He was a poor boy from the Eastern Shore with a strong religious bent who had worked his way through law school at the University of Maryland parking cars in downtown garages.

The other close advisor, but not a member of the Planning Council, was Walter Sondheim, Jr., chairman of the Baltimore Urban Renewal and Housing Agency (BURHA), the organization that we hoped would be implementers of our product. Sondheim, a vice-president and major stockholder of the Hochschild-Kohn Department Store chain, was brought in on the council's deliberations as an "honorary" member to avoid any conflict of interest. Sondheim and I, and our families, became close personal friends. Sondheim was not only a member of the city's Jewish aristocracy but also the businessman most trusted by the politicians. He had been president of the school board during desegregation after the U.S. Supreme Court's *Brown v. Board of Education* decision in 1954 and was a real *deus ex machina* in civic affairs. All of the participants in the planning of Charles Center were significant "stakeholders" in downtown affairs, with Sondheim the most likely to look out for the unrepresented owners and operators, the little guys. He was a political conservative who believed in social activism with a wonderful sense of humor expressed by a delightful giggle. As I write he just had his 94th birthday, and I call him every month or so to keep in touch.

It was with input from these members among many others—including such key city officials as Philip Darling, director of planning; Frank Kuchta, director of public works; Oliver Winston, director of BURHA; and Eugene Feinblatt, that agency's counsel—that Charles Center emerged as the first tactical action in the long-range strategy of the CBD's revitalization. As we proceeded, we briefed the editorial boards of the three daily newspapers, *The Sun*, the *Evening Sun*, and the *News American*, off the record. The editors seemed impressed, but gave no guarantee not to print the story if a reporter came up with a complete account. None did and the secret was kept until we were ready.

The 22-acre, mostly clearance Charles Center project became what architectural critic Jane Jacobs called "A New Heart for Downtown."[1] It was carefully located in an area of mostly small, deteriorated old buildings between the CBD's office and governmental center on the east and the still-viable, but increasingly troubled, retail center on the west. The properties between them were characterized by urban obsolescence and

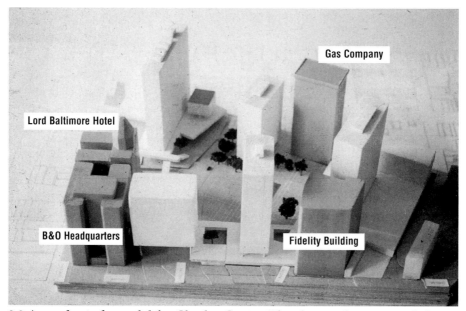

2.2 An early study model for Charles Center. The site was later expanded to the south (left) to Lombard Street and on the north (right) to Saratoga Street.

2.3 Walter Sondheim, Jr., chairman of the Baltimore Urban Renewal and Housing Agency, and Charles H. Buck, GBC chairman look on as Hunter Moss, chairman of GBC's Planning Council, points out details in the Charles Center model to Mayor D'Alesandro during the presentation of Charles Center to the public at City Hall on March 27, 1958.

deterioration and were eligible for public renewal action to "eliminate blight" through clearance, and thus allow private construction to strengthen the overall CBD. This action was considered a catalyst for additional development in the CBD and for ultimately setting the stage for the Inner Harbor to the south.

FOCUSING ON THE SITE

Our first analysis focused on the problem area around the vacant O'Neill's Department Store. Its boundaries ranged from Baltimore Street on the south and Clay Street on the north, from Charles Street on the east to Cathedral Street on the west. At the center was Lexington Street, which had acted as a retail bridge between the main shopping center two blocks west, and the business center's ancillary retail along Charles Street for which O'Neill's had been the anchor. This complex of stores and a movie theater had begun to unravel with vacancies appearing as leases ran out and parking lots replacing demolished structures as the "highest-and-best-use."

Jim Rouse gave us an early critique and agreed with our analysis, but said that we were concentrating on too small an area for it to be viable. He felt clearance would not get rid of enough of the obsolete property nor would it make sufficient room for a mixed-use project, which he said was essential. He urged us to expand north to Saratoga, which coincidentally happened to be across the street from the Rouse Company's office. He also proposed that we extend south to include the four blocks from Baltimore Street to Lombard Street, which included the headquarters of *The Sun* and the *Evening Sun* at the southwest corner of Charles and Baltimore streets. This turned out to be a bold move that helped spur the paper's owner, the A.S. Abell Company, to relocate its publishing facility to North Calvert Street. Much of the study area had been destroyed in the great fire of 1904 but most of the buildings had been replaced *in situ*, with water towers the only real improvement.

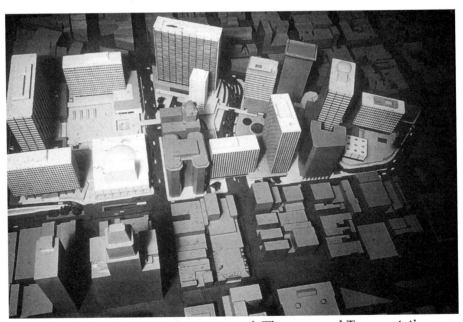

2.4 The Charles Center model as presented. The proposed Transportation Terminal under the south plaza was eliminated, the unified parking levels throughout were parcellized, and the two office buildings at the right (north) end of the project were changed to residential. Otherwise the model was followed very closely in the actual construction.

As the site grew larger on paper, we calculated the economics of acquisition, relocation, clearance, and resale, and planned the new uses and a detailed illustrative site plan began to emerge that was more than just conceptual. It was worked out with great attention to impact, economics and urban design principles. When given a three-dimensional form by our own designers, ably assisted in the final push by Charles Lamb, an Archibald Rogers partner, it created a memorable image that became important in the "selling" of the project to the city and in convincing the electorate to pass a bond issue for public costs. The promotion of the bond issue was effectively done by Bill Boucher using our site plan and other attractive graphics along with compelling economic arguments.

In fact the image was so memorable that after the project had been approved by the Baltimore City Council in March 1959, and economic consultants Larry Smith and Company—who were brought in to test the project's feasibility—had given it the go-ahead, Richard L. Steiner, the renewal agency's new executive director, realized that the authorization for acquisition and clearance was closely geared to the specific reuse plan we had developed. He had not been involved in its development and expected that council approval was a "ticket to anywhere," but found he must rely on our concept as the agency proceeded with acquisition, relocation, new streets and infrastructure, and marketing the product. The Charles Center's image was what the electorate had voted for and wanted with minimum changes.

It also helped the continuity of positive thinking and approvals that I and my staff and the Planning Council were placed under contract to assist BURHA, still chaired by Sondheim in the next phases: specific feasibility studies, preparation of the urban renewal and relocation plans, and parcelization and marketing the land. As a consequence, we made sure the rationale for the elements of the plan were properly considered in the evolving redevelopment process.

CHANGES DURING IMPLEMENTATION OF THE PLAN

Charles Center was built largely as conceived, but with three notable exceptions. The proposed transportation terminal under the southern superblock was eliminated, the northern five acres were converted from office to high-rise residential use, and separate underground parking was designed to serve each parcel instead of the unified underground garage we had designed. The reasons were edifying.

Our inclusion of a "transportation terminal" was due to the involvement of my Northwood neighbor, Henry Barnes, author of Baltimore's famous "Barnes dance," a description of pedestrians crossing streets in step to his orchestrated traffic light system. I got a lift to work at least once a week with Barnes, Baltimore's director of traffic, and later commissioner of traffic in New York. Barnes had been a policeman turned traffic director in Flint, Michigan, where he had invented a centralized computer control system for regulating continuous traffic flow. He had his mind set on a transportation terminal under Charles Center's southern superblock to function like Manhattan's West Side Bus Terminal, where New Jersey's buses must unload to transfer people to the city's systems. He couldn't be convinced that it wouldn't work in Baltimore where almost every passenger would have to get off somewhere else downtown before the buses arrived at the terminal. We included the terminal even though we knew it would never work. It was that or give up my rides and lose Barnes's support. The terminal did not survive feasibility analysis, and it was replaced with underground garages on each parcel.

The second major change was to convert the north end of the site from proposed office to residential use, thus making the project truly mixed-use. This happened well after the first office development had been completed. In 1959, shortly after the redevelopment plan was under way, we had undertaken a study of the feasibility of extending Charles Center's boundaries to the north by adding a residential section. We were convinced that with the new office space, there was a potential for high-rise upper-income apartments, of which there were none in the downtown area. We hired local economist Morton Hoffman, who showed that indeed there was such a market, but Jeff Miller co-opted the idea for the north end of the Charles Center project rather than expand the project's area. He said he wanted Charles Center to be completed in his lifetime and couldn't wait around for the market to absorb all of the office development. It was a good lesson that indicated to us one of the advantages of mixing uses to accelerate the rate of overall market absorption. Miller got his wish and Charles Center's build-out was advanced by at least five years.

The third major change was to abandon the single large underground garage beneath each superblock that would have had to be publicly financed. Instead, parking would be provided under each parcel. By this device, each separate garage was to be financed by its surface developments and only the parking under the public parks required public financing. Unfortunately, it also meant many more entry and exit points to the garages, which conflict with pedestrian flow and look unsightly.

CHARLES CENTER MANAGEMENT IS CREATED

Although BURHA executive director Dick Steiner was a better manager than Oliver Winston, whom he replaced, I was convinced that if left to BURHA, Charles Center's development would be poorly managed. In Philadelphia, where I had been responsible for 30 redevelopment projects at once, it had become evident that the success of a project of the importance and scale of Charles Center needed to be sponsored by an advocacy group whose sole responsibility was to promote the market for developers, spoonfeed the city agencies, and manage the project's implementation. It could not be just one more assignment. As a consequence, I recommended forming the Charles Center Management Office (CC-MO), of which Miller became general manager for $1 a year. Miller gave the project great credibility, and as a successful businessman, was a heavy hitter with both the city council and potential developers. He was rich so he could afford to give his services for a dollar a year, which he proudly framed, and frequently showed visitors. CC-MO and its successors created an important innovation copied by many cities across the country. Dennis Durden became his executive assistant. Dennis had headed the Charles Center feasibility analysis for the Larry Smith Company, which was under contract to BURHA and Dick Steiner. Martin Millspaugh took over when Durden left. In a letter to me, Millspaugh describes his role as follows:

> The Charles Center Management Office was never incorporated. It was just Jeff (Miller), as general manager of the Charles Center Project under a contract with the city for $1 a year plus expenses. As deputy general manager, I had a subcontract with Jeff, which was also approved by BURHA.
>
> In 1965, when the mayor asked me and Jeff to take on the management of the Inner Harbor in addition to Charles Center, we realized we would have to have a corporation for liability protection and to provide pension and health benefits for the staff.
>
> Jeff did not want to continue as the one in charge, and he told me I would have to be No. 1, while he would help out in an advisory role, providing his contacts and influence in the community. The custom at that time (mid-'60s) was for the president of a company to also be the CEO, while the chairman conducted board meetings and acted as oversight and advisor. So we made

me president and Jeff took the title of non-executive chairman.

Under our contract the overall policy decisions were dictated by the city; so we had only a token board of directors, made up of me and Jeff and the immediate past president of the GBC—Bob (Robert) Hobbs in the beginning. We met for lunch once a year and decided housekeeping questions like what holidays the company would take.

That—plus Al Copp, whom I recruited from my former staff at URA in Washington—was the CC-IH leadership from 1965 to 1970. During that time we closed the deals for nine major buildings, from the Harbor Apartments to USF&G (United States Fidelity and Guarantee), IBM, and the Federal Reserve, while also acquiring the bulk of the property, relocating 300 businesses and supervising the design of the Shoreline construction and the infrastructure of streets and utilities. Renewal plans were approved and funded for Inner Harbor Project 1, Inner Harbor West, and the Harbor Campus. When Walter retired from Hochschild-Kohn in 1970, the mayor asked him to take on the job of ombudsman for the overall MetroCenter area. Both we and he saw that this could be competitive with CC-IH; so we asked Walter to join CC-IH in the new position of non-executive Vice Chairman. When Jeff died in 1972, Walter took over the advisory role of chairman, in addition to his duties as ombudsman. I left in 1985, when the original project was substantially completed.

That's a long way of explaining why I now simply say that I was chief executive of CC-IH during my tenure from 1965 to 1985.[2]

The Charles Center Management Office later became Charles Center-Inner Harbor Management, Inc., (CC-IH) when the Inner Harbor was added. Miller became chairman of CC-IH until he died. The job of chairman was then taken over by Walter Sondheim, who was no longer with Hochschild-Kohn and was retired as chairman of BURHA when it was converted to a city department with a commissioner. The president and CEO of CC-IH was former *Evening Sun*-reporter-turned-renewal-specialist Martin Millspaugh, until he resigned to join Rouse's new Enterprise Development Company, which was formed when Rouse retired as head of the Rouse Company. Millspaugh's deputy, Albert Copp, took over until 1990 when CC-IH disappeared into the citywide Baltimore Development Corporation, with M. Jay Brodie as its head.

Organizations like CC-IH sprouted up across the country in response to similar situations. They have often been criticized as the "privatization of public planning" by local activists. Critics claim, with justification in some cases, that this is elitist and anti-democratic, as the planning is done behind closed doors by and for business or civic leaders who have no responsibility to an electorate. While this is sometimes a valid criticism, I defend the quasi-private planning process as a means of allowing development concepts that must ultimately be publicly approved to be developed to sufficient maturity in private before meriting public discussion, enriching the ultimate public dialogue. As will be seen later in the discussion of the Jones Falls Valley Plan, this process has its flaws. Nevertheless, in contrast to the almost completely private planning for Charles Center, CC-IH was directly under contract by the city, and supervised by a city department head who was politically answerable to the mayor and council.

CC-IH is easily defended, as is the preparation of large-scale plans by organizations such as GBC and the Valleys Planning Council. Where government cannot or will not make plans for special areas, citizens may legitimately step in to provide them, assuming that they will be ultimately reviewed through the democratic process. As to my own participation in privatization of public planning, I brought to my work a strong public ethic from my years at the Philadelphia Redevelopment Authority and before that at the Chicago Housing Authority, so I more often than not shared the point of view of the public officials and the citizens with whom I interacted. Even so, good plans sometimes fail in the public arena simply because noses get out of joint when citizen groups are not sufficiently consulted.

MEETING CHARLES CENTER'S GOALS

Charles Center by and large achieved its purposes. The stated goals included eliminating the deteriorated and obsolete buildings at the center of the CBD that acted as a spreading dry rot. In addition to getting rid of what was bad, our goals were to create a focus of activity for a downtown that didn't then have one, to increase tax ratables and employment opportunities, to stimulate development of a highly concentrated business district, with heavily leveraged public renewal, for example, private investment in a ratio of five or six times every public dollar spent. Finally, the intent was to give the region a strong employment anchor and make Baltimore competitive with its own suburbs and with communities to the north and south. Alternatives to this strategy were briefly considered, but were not taken seriously because they were judged to be unrealistic and much less in the interest of our clients.

The Charles Center Plan was presented to the mayor and the city on March 27, 1958, fifteen months after I had started from scratch with no staff in January 1957, and almost exactly a year after the contract between

2.5 At top, the Charles Center model dubbed in to an aerial photo of the 1957 site by photographer Marion Warren. Below, an aerial photo from 1967 showing completion of residential towers in the foreground.

the Committee for Downtown and the Planning Council had been signed. Two-and-a-half months later, on June 14, 1958, a bond issue was authorized by the Maryland General Assembly, approved by city voters on November 4, 1958. The Charles Center Plan was then converted to an urban renewal plan and submitted to and approved by City Council on March 25, 1959. The Charles Center Management Office opened June 1 of that year, not quite two-and-a-half years after I had arrived in 1957.

That sounds like a long time in retrospect, but is an extremely fast schedule for urban redevelopment, particularly one which survived a court challenge of the validity of the public taking of private property to be resold to another private party. One of the major owners of a large office/industrial building in the middle of the Charles Center site sued the city and everyone else involved, claiming that his particular building was not deteriorated and therefore should be exempt from the taking. It so happened that I had inspected his property myself and was able to testify in court that the building had open elevators, no central air conditioning, did not meet building code requirements in a number of ways, and was clearly obsolescent albeit not deteriorated. Regardless, an overall area can be declared blighted allowing condemnation of standard structures whose elimination is necessary for the implementation of an overall plan as had been established by the U.S. Supreme Court, and the local court upheld the Charles Center ordinance.[3]

By April 1964, the Charles Center project was budgeted at a gross project cost of $41.2 million, with proceeds from land disposition of $10.6 million, and a net project cost of $30.6 million. The city's share was 1/4, or $7.6 million, and the federal contribution was $24.2 million. Charles Center was half completed.

In 1965, the same year Gerald Johnson ventured that "Baltimore Might Make It," the Urban Land Institute held a two-day seminar on Charles Center, resulting in a publication which characterized Charles Center as "famous for the ingenuity and sophistication of its plan, and the clarity of its message in urban design."[4] The project not only had succeeded, but also had triggered new office development and renovation of existing structures to the east, created the market for high-rise, upper-income housing at its north end, and set the investment stage for what was to become the new Inner Harbor to the south.

SELECTING DEVELOPERS

Getting good developers was no mean trick. The detailed economic background material from our interview notebooks demonstrated the character and depth of the market, and was the basis for preparation of Charles Center's initial land offering for developers. CC-MO issued a Request for Proposals (RFP) in which we had included site-specific design guidelines and restrictions that ensured the first building would properly fit the context and subsequent development. The first site for private development had been widely advertised through all the networks available to ensure we would receive viable and responsive proposals. Five were received and evaluated, of which two went to the finals: Metropolitan Structures, Inc., of Chicago and Jacob Blaustein of Baltimore.

The selection process started with a Planning Council staff review and evaluation using objective criteria, followed by presentation to and required concurrence by the architectural review board set up to advise BURHA on selection, with CC-MO finally recommending a winner to the BURHA board, and ultimately the city council. The architectural review board had been created at my suggestion to assist and advise CC-MO and BURHA in selecting developer teams. The board was chaired by G. Holmes Perkins, who had been my mentor at Harvard and was Penn's dean of the Graduate School of Fine Arts, with Dean Emeritus William Hudnut of Harvard's Graduate School of Design, and world-famous architect Pietro Belluschi of M.I.T. as the other members. Belluschi had shortly before designed an award-winning church in Baltimore and was the author of the GBC's Civic Center proposal. Miller represented the city and I acted as secretary and chief presenter.

Blaustein would have probably won hands down except for his architectural submission prepared by world-famous architect Marcel Breuer. Blaustein was a native son who started out peddling kerosene from a pushcart on the streets of Baltimore and had made it to the top of a petroleum empire. He clearly had the resources, but Breuer's design thumbed its nose, so to speak, at the design guidelines, which we had prepared and which had been endorsed by the Charles Center architectural review board. For example, his truck service opened in an unsightly way directly onto Charles Street, his first floor had no retail use contrary to our specification, and the whole scheme was in Breuer's so-called "brutalist" style, very context-unfriendly. A bad building by a good architect? The entire concept would have had to be revised to conform to the RFP.

The architectural review board was unanimously in favor of the Metropolitan Structures, Inc., submission over Blaustein's, and Miller sadly concurred, to his credit. He and Sondheim, acting as chairman of BURHA, made the final decision. They moved in the same social circles as Blaustein, and they each told me they took the heat for five years before the enraged Blaustein would talk to them. The winning design conformed in every respect to the requirements of the RFP, and it was hard to argue against its equally world-famous architect, Mies van der Rohe.

Metropolitan Structures's head was Herbert Greenwald of Chicago, whom I knew well and whom I had urged to respond to the RFP. He had been responsible for the well-regarded Gratiot luxury housing redevelopment complex in Detroit, designed by Mies. Greenwald was so enchanted with Mies's architecture that he declared his intent to use no other

2.6 The Architectural Review Board. Seated left to right are G. Holmes Perkins, Dean of the University of Pennsylvania's Graduate School of Fine Arts, Pietro Belluschi, Dean of M.I.T.'s School of Architecture, and Robert L. Geddes, Dean of Princeton University's School of Architecture and partner with Geddes Brecher Qualls & Cunningham, Architects. They made up the Architectural Review Board in Baltimore. Standing left to right are, Robert Embry, commissioner of Baltimore's Department of Housing and Community Development; Norman Waltjin, vice-president, Albert M. Copp, executive vice-president, and Martin Millspaugh, president and CEO, all of Charles Center-Inner Harbor Management, Inc.

designer. Unfortunately Greenwald was killed in a plane crash in Jamaica Bay, New York, shortly after starting the project in Baltimore. His place was ably taken by his attorney, Bernard Weissbourd, who later also developed the Baltimore Hilton Hotel in Charles Center, which occupies the site of the Miller Brothers Seafood Restaurant (no relation to Jeff Miller) where I first lunched. The Hilton's first-floor restaurant was called Miller Brothers, named for the old facility, but is now a Shula's (one of the chain run by former Miami Dolphins coach Don Shula) and the hotel is a Wyndham.

In fact, we were all pretty enchanted with Mies as an architect and with the building he designed. One Charles Center has been faulted for being a copy of Mies and Philip Johnson's Seagram Building on Park Avenue in Manhattan, to which my response has been, "If somebody else has a Rolls Royce, why can't I?" I was particularly pleased that Mies thought my sketch in the original Charles Center brochure of a ceremonial stair from the building to the park "a nice conceit" and followed it in his design more or less exactly. Unfortunately, when Al Copp took over as head of CC-IH, the stair was demolished because it was in need of repair and not much used. Too bad.

Jacob Blaustein was a sore loser, but took our office market forecast literally. He assembled a site at Fayette Street across the street from Charles Center and developed the property with a building designed by architect Vincent Kling from Philadelphia in competition with Mies's One Charles Center. The two buildings struggled for tenants, but both succeeded, demonstrating that downtown really had the potential we forecast and was on its way up. Thomas L. Karsten, who was one of my clients for the Green Spring and Worthington Valleys plan, ran the project for Blaustein.

---

1   Jane Jacobs, *Architectural Forum*, June, 1958, pp. 88-92.
2   Letter to Author dated December 4, 2002.
3   J. Jefferson Miller, "Land Acquisition," *Baltimore's Charles Center*, p. 42.
4   Martin Millspaugh, "Editor's Introduction, *Baltimore's Charles Center*, op. cit., p.9.

CHAPTER

3

Charles Center Today

As of March 1999, the 40-year-old urban redevelopment controls under which Charles Center was designed and built expired. The city's zoning code allows a floor area ratio (FAR) of 14, or 14 square feet of development for every square foot of site. This is virtually no limit and with this in mind, I decided to take a new look at what might happen.

At the beginning of a walking trip through the central business district, I stepped from the LRT at the Lexington Street Station on Howard Street and walked east on Lexington, through the old retail center, to Charles Center's western edge at Liberty Street. Lane Bryant is the only chain store I saw except for the ubiquitous Rite-Aid in the first floor of the huge old Hecht-May six-story department store building. However, all the storefronts are occupied; there are no vacancies.

Crossing Liberty Street, I entered the Charles Center site and immediately saw where Mies's ceremonial stair that I had conceived as part of the original Charles Center brochure had been the victim of demolition. Further, the elevated walkway, which served to connect the Center's three pedestrian levels from the north at Saratoga and Charles, to the intermediate level at Fayette, to the lowest at Baltimore Street, has been completely demolished along with Hamburgers Men's Store, which was served by the walkway as it bridged Fayette Street. Peter J. Angelos, owner of the Baltimore Orioles, has bought Metropolitan Structure's One Charles Center into which he has moved his law firm. He is reported to have wanted to open up the Fayette Street vista to allow a better view of his building. Across Fayette Street to the south of One Charles Center, he has replaced Hamburgers with a small downtown branch of Johns Hopkins University. Angelos has become very rich winning asbestos-

3.1 Architect Mies van der Rohe's One Charles Center, the first building in Charles Center set the standard for high design. Unfortunately the stairs and landing have been demolished and the current owner, lawyer Peter G. Angelos (who also owns the Baltimore Orioles) has plans to expand the first floor.

related liability lawsuits, and will become even richer when the tobacco settlement money is distributed. He is alleged to have been one of the top five contributors in the U.S. to the Gore/Lieberman presidential campaign, and I am surprised if he doesn't get his way in whatever he wants.

Nevertheless, from an economic and fiscal point of view Charles Center has been an outstanding success. It served as the catalyst for turning the CBD from an urban disaster into a national model of revitalization. Still though, looking at it now from an objective design and quality-of-life's 42-year perspective, it has some intrinsic faults. It has stood the test of time quite well even though most of its buildings are architecturally out of style. Newer development has attracted many of its tenants, and the nearby Inner Harbor is a seductive competitor, but this is a normal part of the process of growth and change. Charles Center's office buildings are mostly full, the two hotels busy, and the residential towers are successful, filling a niche rental market for newly transferred corporate mid-level managers.

However, although Charles Center has never been as memorable from an urban design or architectural viewpoint as say Rockefeller Center in Manhattan, it is more interesting and effective as an urban place than Penn Center in Philadelphia, or most other major renewal projects of its era. That portion of Charles Center north of Baltimore Street suffers from its irregular shape, poor design coherence, and has a lack of enclosure around its somewhat barren central park.

Mies's One Charles Center stands out as a first-rate piece of architecture, and the original Mies-designed balcony fascia and railing surrounding the central open space was intended to, but could not quite, pull the other mediocre buildings together as an urban group. Now the balcony is gone, and the variety of facades have little coherence. When George Kostritsky, by then a partner at RTKL, began to design the Center Plaza central park, I urged him to fill it with trees to make the open space more humane, but George no longer worked for me, and I didn't have much influence over him.

Today, Center Plaza is an empty oval park surrounded by a nice ring of trees. Elderly men lounge in the tree's shade, reading or playing chess. Beyond the trees, what were to have been lively retail shops under the office towers are mostly blank and empty. Angelos originally proposed to use the open park for surface parking, saying he needs it to be able to rent his space. Now he says that he wants to build the first floor out to the limit of the building line, filling in the space between the columns.

The five original buildings on the Charles Center site that were not demolished—the former B&O Railroad headquarters, the Lord Baltimore Hotel (now a Sheraton), the Fidelity and Deposit Building, the Baltimore Gas and Electric Company headquarters, and a large parking deck (now removed from the project's northwestern corner)—all were remodeled as planned, but their locations made it difficult to fit buildings between them. This became particularly apparent when the residential towers replaced the office space designed for the original plan. Charles Plaza, the small park that opens onto Saratoga and Charles streets, also designed by Kostritsky, has a nice residential scale with the small shopping center at the base of the towers, but the pedestrian walkway and escalator connection through to Center Plaza to the south was very circuitous and hard to find. It is now closed.

As I walked through, I saw that the Fidelity and Deposit Building at Charles and Lexington streets is vacant and remember that the Downtown Partnership has proposed it for renovation as residential

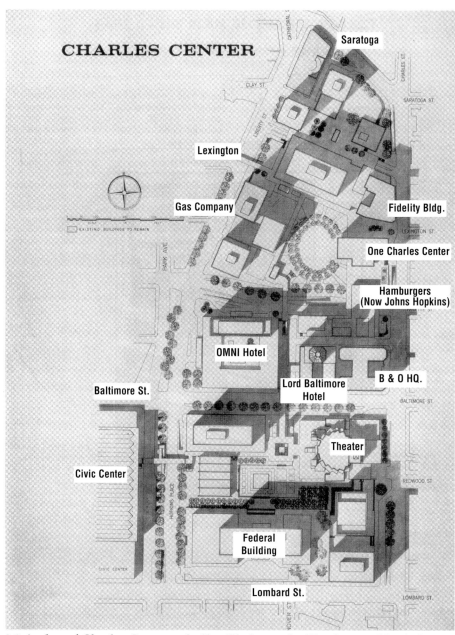

3.2 A plan of Charles Center as built still shows the Hamburger Men's Store spanning Fayette Street just north of the B&O Headquarters at Baltimore and Charles streets. Angelos removed it and built a downtown branch of Johns Hopkins University next to the B&O.

apartments. The southern superblock, Baltimore Street to Lombard, Light to Charles, has fared better. It is a more memorable environment, with good visual and pedestrian connections to the adjacent areas. It has recently undergone complete renovation. The interesting, if not outstanding, buildings relate well to each other and create an ordered and substantial urban design quality to the scene.

Architect John Johansen's Morris Mechanic Theater didn't ever work all that well as a theater but is a fine piece of freestanding urban sculpture. The theater's design came about because I had explained to Mechanic that his first choice, Frank Lloyd Wright, was dead, and his second, LeCorbusier, was in France and probably not available. His third choice, Phillip Johnson, came down from New York for a lunch interview with me and Mechanic at the old Southern Hotel (now demolished), and turned the assignment down when Mechanic told him he didn't want to spend more than $100 a square foot. It wasn't that Mechanic couldn't afford more, he just didn't want to spend it. Mechanic had owned a substantial amount of the Lexington Street retail property including the movie theater that was acquired and demolished for the project, and he saved a lot of capital gains taxes by reinvesting in Charles Center within five years.

Johnson recommended Johansen as an architect who might work within Mechanic's budget. The multi-use complex's layer-cake of public parking underground, retail on the first and theater on the second level with different ownerships on each was an innovative legal as well as architectural creation. Unfortunately, the first-floor retail under the theater has never been very successful and is only partly occupied.

The recent plan for Charles Center by the Downtown Partnership is somewhat ambiguous about the theater. The plan's cover illustration features the theater as the centerpiece, but the recommendation in the long term, is to replace it with a premier Class A office building. Based on the CBD's allowable FAR 14, the site could support close to one million square feet, right on the Baltimore and Charles streets subway station. That would be five years of office market absorption based on Hammer Siler George's economic projections for the plan.

The other buildings surrounding Hopkins Plaza, the central square, give a nice sense of enclosure, with vistas and walkways that lead engagingly outward. Originally designed by George Kostritsky, the park's trees, fountain, and changes in levels created a very pleasant place, albeit always seemingly in need of maintenance. It has now been dramatically

3.3 The visual centerpiece of Hopkins Plaza at the south end of Charles Center is architect John Johansen's theater, which has closed and the site is being considered for another office building. The 40-year controls under the urban renewal plan have now expired and a floor-area ratio of 14 in the zoning would allow more than a million square feet of development on the site.

refurbished with the skywalk across Baltimore Street from the north eliminated, which opens up the views to the street. The four big office buildings around the plaza have many visitors and should deliver people to the park at lunchtime, but they all offer lunchrooms with subsidized prices.

The largest of the four, the George H. Fallon Federal Office Building, anchors Charles Center's south end with 460,000 square feet of space. Getting it built there instead of in the suburbs is an interesting story. The federal government never likes to play by local rules. Their bureaucrats start any discussion reminding you that they do not have to conform to any local regulations, building codes, zoning, whatever. Until you agree, they are adamant, and only when you agree in principle are they then willing to listen to what you have in mind. That the Fallon Building is in Charles Center, or in fact in Baltimore at all, is thanks to then-Congressman George Fallon.

Congress had authorized the consolidation of federal employment in one location in a number of cities—San Francisco, Denver, Columbus, Ohio, to name three with whom I was in touch—and Gerald Floete, the director of the General Services Administration, playing local politics, was doing all the site selection himself. When he threatened to put Baltimore's federal building in the western suburbs as had been done with the Social Securities Administration, Jeff Miller enlisted Fallon's aid. He, Boucher, Fallon, and I went to see Floete, made our pitch for Charles Center, and as we were leaving, Fallon said "See you on the Hill, Gerald." Fallon was chairman of the Public Facilities Subcommittee of the House Committee on Appropriations, and suddenly Floete was on our side.

But it's never over til it's over. We still had to convince the regional GSA administrator that his offer of $3 per square foot for the land was ridiculous, and to persuade his architects of the reasonableness of our design concepts, not an easy thing to do since architects are taught at school that a program is to question and a design concept by someone else is to disregard if at all possible. GSA ultimately paid $12 per square foot, and while the Fallon Building will win no awards, it performs its urban design function very nicely and in accord with the original site plan. It has been recently remodeled extensively by the GSA.

As Charles Center proceeded, we invented the concept of urban design guidelines to go with the various Requests for Proposals as conditions of sale after architectural review board approval. These became expressions, site by site, of how each separate building was to fit into the place as a whole and connect to its surroundings. The use of guidelines in developer selection and performance was watched with interest by the federal government and became a model for projects funded through urban renewal. I learned from the experience, however, that no number of guidelines can substitute for skilled architects in producing good designs and memorable places.

Most recently the Downtown Partnership, Inc., has retained economic consultants Hammer Siler George of Washington, D.C. and the Design Collective, Inc., of Baltimore to study how Charles Center can be updated with a particular emphasis on revitalizing the open spaces that were such crucial elements of the original plan, and mitigating the Center's somewhat introverted layout.

As I walked through Charles Center, I chanced to meet M. Jay Brodie, head of the Baltimore Development Corporation, on his way between meetings. Formerly commissioner of the city's Department of Housing and Community Development, Brodie was one of the clients for whom my firm, then Wallace McHarg Roberts & Todd, planned the Inner Harbor. He tells me that the future of the Morris Mechanic Theater is indeed in doubt. At 1,500 seats it is too small for New York Broadway play tryouts, and its main tenant, the Performing Arts Center, will soon move to the renovated Hippodrome Theater on Eutaw Street.

4

CBD Plans and
the Retail District

I was widely criticized in traditional planning circles for immediately focusing on Charles Center, an individual project, rather than first preparing the master plan for the entire CBD. I think most critics would agree that what we did turned out to be the right thing, but it was not without its unintended consequences, one of which was that, although the CBD Plan had a number of action programs, these were not aggressively pursued. The city had the feeling it had enough on its hands with Charles Center. After adoption of the project's redevelopment plan, Baltimore rested on its oars awhile, astonished at its own temerity.

THE 1959 CBD PLAN

The CBD Plan, which had been the Planning Council's original assignment, was prepared and presented to the Committee for Downtown, the GBC, and the city on April 23, 1959, almost a year after the Charles Center Plan was unveiled. Unlike the typical downtown plan of that era—compilations of local architects "wouldn't it be nice if" dreams—the plan contained no overall illustrative site plan or "vision." Except for Charles Center and proposals for the shopping center, much of it was what would be called a policy plan. The plan included the usual required elements—land use, transportation, and so on, but it consisted of essentially a proposed sequence of action programs beginning with the Charles Center project as the first. For example, the Civic Center was still floating around looking for a location, so we placed it next to Charles Center to the west and immediately south of the retail center. Six additional focused projects were proposed that included the redevelopment and expansion of the University of Maryland's downtown campus to anchor the southwest corner of the CBD.

It turned out that what Charles Center didn't and couldn't do was help stimulate the main retail center, although not for want of our intention. By the time the CBD Plan was presented to the city, Charles Center had become officially adopted by the BURHA and was well under way, thanks in no small part to Sondheim. He persuaded us that the city should be allowed to "digest" Charles Center before it would be ready for another major project downtown. Money was always in short supply and he noted that there were many neighborhood programs that good planning and public policy demanded funding. He was right, but in hindsight I wish we had argued him into a more aggressive position.

Nevertheless, Sondheim, in his capacity as vice-president and a major stockholder in Hochschild-Kohn's department store chain, knew all too well how badly off downtown retail was. He, along with Robert Levi and other retail leaders, urged us to develop what turned out to be a dramatic, but futile, attempt to revitalize the retail center. The nucleus of the center's area consisted of five department stores and assorted specialty shops focused at Howard and Lexington streets. Retail sales had declined 3 percent each year for the preceding 10 years. During the 1950s, as white customers from the suburbs switched to the new malls, minority shoppers from the neighborhoods to the west began to predominate at Howard and Lexington, further discouraging white patronage. Also management attitudes were slow to change: When I arrived in Baltimore, a black customer was required to buy a hat before being allowed to try it on. O'Neill's closing, triggered by a breakdown in rent negotiations with the owner, was a harbinger of disaster to come. Even dramatic action would not have countered the flight of white and later middle-class black customers to the suburban branches of these same stores.

The concept we developed for the Central Retail Area in the CBD Plan envisioned the kind of mall that was getting to be all the fashion in the suburbs. Little new retail space was to be added. Instead, the five major department stores were to be linked with a cruciform two-level air-conditioned glass enclosure intersecting at Howard and Lexington streets, and extending two short blocks over Lexington Street to the edge of Charles Center. Lexington would be closed completely and Howard would stay open for buses but would be bridged at the second level to connect Hecht's, Hochschild-Kohn's, and Hutzler's on the west to

The Lexington Street intersection is viewed looking south on Howard Street.

4.1 A two-story retail mall was proposed to tie the five department stores and smaller shops into a shopping complex to compete with suburban development. A five-member team of retail specialists reported that if the city's expressway and subway plans were in place, our concept was much too timid. Absent these, it was not feasible.

Stewart's and Brager-Gutman's on the east. We tried, but could not get Henry Barnes to allow the closing of Howard Street.

The concept was visually quite dramatic although in fact did little to deal with the market area's basic obsolescence. Despite the drama, it was greeted with skepticism. Mayor Thomas D'Alesandro and the city administration were unsympathetic, feeling that the department stores had caused their own problem by building in the suburbs, which was hard to argue against because it was true, albeit irrelevant. The smaller storeowners, particularly those who would not be directly connected to the mall, felt they would be left out and saw only trouble at their expense. The department store owners also knew that such a major investment in renewal would not be made by the city, and would require at least a doubling of sales to be privately feasible, an unlikely future in the face of the trends. Without city support and involvement, not much was going to happen.

Even so, the stores got together and appointed a blue-ribbon panel of retail experts to review the plan and report back to them. Larry Smith, the dean of retail economists and the principal feasibility consultant on Charles Center was named chairman, with Colonel Richard Tatlow, William Snaith of Raymond Loewe, and architect Victor Gruen as members.

The panel and I met one day in a suite at the Hotel Roosevelt in New York City. It was one of the more humbling professional experiences of my career. Building the case for the plan, I spelled out to them the regional network of expressways then building, and the spur proposed to connect it to the retail area, from the west. Regional mass rapid transit in the form of the subway system now in place in Eutaw Street one block west of Howard was in the earliest planning stage, but I made it sound as real as I could. Nice try, they said.

The gist of their conclusions was that, in the absence of both expressways and mass rapid transit to deliver customers from the suburbs, our retail concept was wildly optimistic and infeasible. Interestingly, they also concluded that if those infrastructure elements, which I had outlined, were actually in place, the concept was much too timid. Larry Smith, an advocate of "Reilly's Law" theory (or gravity principle) of retail location, particularly felt that Baltimore's suburban malls, still not fully built-out at that stage in the region's development, would have been vulnerable to a doubling and modernization of downtown retail—but such was not to be. I went back to Baltimore sadder and wiser.

Stewart's, the only store not then locally owned, closed shortly thereafter. Several years later, the city was persuaded to give the retail area some help, and closed Lexington Street, converting it to a pedestrian open-air mall. One by one, the department stores sold to large chains. They were valued mainly for their branch locations, and by 1976 only Hutzler's was locally owned. Today, none are in retail use above the first floor, with Hochschild-Kohn's and Hutzler's converted to state office use.

While Charles Center had some positive impact on the retail center, there were a substantial number of smaller stores in the CBD outside the retail core that were in fact helped by the CBD Plan's proposed office development, government center, and traffic proposals. For example, North Charles Street had always been an upscale specialty street oriented to the northern suburbs until Henry Barnes made it one-way northbound and it lost a lot of its clientele. Then its anchor, O'Neill's was closed.

THE 1969 METROCENTER PLAN

The retail center continued sliding downhill until 1969, when the city mounted a second planning effort, supported by the GBC and other "stakeholders." It was really only a gesture toward trying to solve the retail riddle. The U.S. Department of Transportation's Urban Mass Transit Administration was being petitioned for money for the subway, which was to run under Eutaw Street at the retail center's western edge. The city was told that it needed an overall master plan to qualify for the funds.

In response, the then-city planning director Larry Reich (who had come to Baltimore from Philadelphia's City Planning Commission) applied the word "MetroCenter" to describe all of downtown including the Mount Vernon neighborhood within an inner beltway, and divided it into three urban design assignments. Architects William Conklin and James Rossant of New York City got the northern Mount Vernon/Penn Station section. George Kostritsky and RTKL got the retail district, which was called CBD West.

By 1969, I had returned to Philadelphia, and was teaching planning and urban design at Penn's Graduate School of Fine Arts. My firm, WMRT, had become famous for the Inner Harbor and the Valleys master plans. Reich assigned us the financial and government districts—CBD East. Kostritsky's product for the shopping center was a so-called "megastructure," a not very creative variation of the Planning Council's 1959 concept that he superimposed on Howard Street without much attention to its feasibility. Conklin and Rossant's CBD North was an equally facile "wouldn't it be nice if" design exercise with little basis in reality.

WMRT's CBD East, in contrast, was based on the new urban design method I had developed while preparing an innovative plan for Lower Manhattan in 1965. The method involved an analysis of an area's susceptibility-to-change, evaluating the sequential probability of growth, and then introducing an overall urban design framework to guide development. Like time-lapse photography, the result for CBD East was an evolving urban design concept that wove the study area together with the plans for the Inner Harbor and other adjacent neighborhoods. Disregarding what the other firms had done, we also applied it to the rest of the MetroCenter area. This method, an urban counterpart to the growth

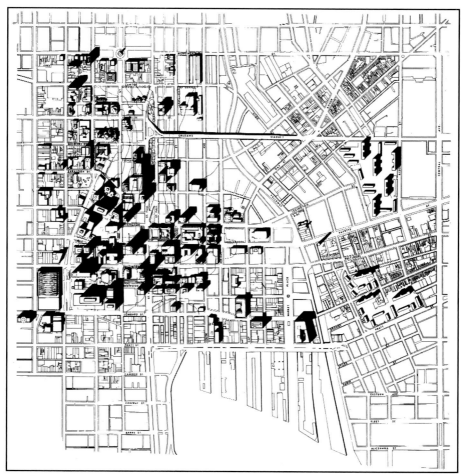

4.2 CBD East was part of a planning effort called MetroCenter, done to satisfy U.S. DOT's requirement for funding for the subway. WMRT's assignment was used to apply the urban design modeling method originated in our Lower Manhattan Plan in 1966. Existing urban form consists of long-range givens used as a framework upon which to impose the "probability of change"in three levels of specificity, the last level including design ideas.

management method we had developed for the Valleys, became a trademark of my firm's downtown plans in many cities across the country.

However, while our effort in Baltimore was not treated by the planning department as a plan, our resulting image was simply pasted together with that of the other two firms as a pastiche of ideas. Reich and the Baltimore Regional Planning Council then commissioned WMRT to

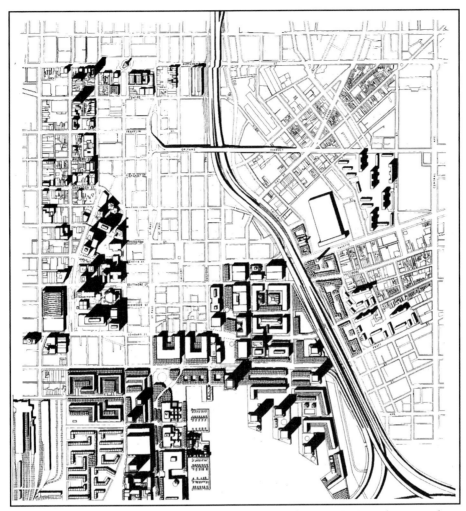

4.3 Existing Givens and New Proposals Surrounding CBD East shows early concepts for the Inner Harbor.

combine the products, which he then published. Called "MetroCenter/ Baltimore," the document included a one-page map entitled "Baltimore's Comprehensive Plan" to satisfy UMTA.

In an unfortunate but prophetic choice of pictures, the report's front cover shows a shopping center crowd of seemingly all-white customers; the inside back cover shows what appear to be all blacks, and can be folded to cover the front. The effort was a cosmetic planning exercise that served its narrow purpose to get federal money. For the thoughtful reader, the separate Technical Report that I produced supported the flashy

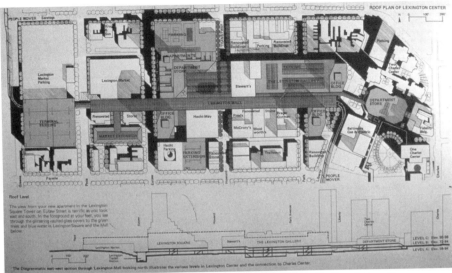

4.4 Lexington Center was a final effort to save the retail district as the region's major facility. The north end of Charles Center was to be developed by a new department store and massive parking was to surround the central mall. Even though the expressway network and subway system were nearly completed, we had missed the bus of history, and the plan was doomed.

brochure and presented for the first time in print the philosophy for the overall regional, citywide, downtown, and Inner Harbor renaissance strategy. U.S. DOT and the city of Baltimore were delighted, the subway was funded, but no other retail action resulted.

THE 1976 LEXINGTON CENTER PLAN

Six years later, the GBC's Bill Boucher promoted another study of the still alive, but greatly reduced, central retail district. His argument was that the expressway and mass transit systems, missing in 1959, but now well under way, would recapture the suburban customers. Boucher saw this as an opportunity, as he put it, "to reassemble the winning team that was responsible for Charles Center and the Inner Harbor." But it was too late.

In the plan called Lexington Center, we took Larry Smith's earlier advice to heart, still persuaded that the shopping district could be revitalized as an expanded regional retail center. The existing department store buildings were to be renovated as retail uses and 590,000 square feet of new department store, specialty, and entertainment space was to be added, mixed with 750,000 square feet of office space, 300 apartments and

Downtown People Mover For Baltimore

Application For Downtown People Mover Demostration
Prepared By DPM Task Force

People Mover Track
People Mover Station
Rapid Transit Phase I
Rapid Transit Station
Bus Transitway
Pedestrian Mall

Horizontal Alignment

4.5 People Movers were on the national agenda with Detroit and Miami as examples.

... and the same view in 1985 toward the Howard Street Station of the People Mover.

4.6 Tom Todd's sketch shows how it might have looked as it went through Lexington at the Howard Street Station.

4,250 additional parking spaces. Three blocks of both sides of Lexington Street were to be cleared to make room for the complex. It stretched from the still very viable Lexington Market on the west (a centuries-old farmers market), to a new department store anchor on the east in Charles Center on what is now the site of the Park Charles apartments. A Disney-type automated people-mover, by then on the federal agenda as an approved form of transportation, was to extend from Bolton Hill northwest of downtown through Lexington Center, then south to the Convention Center in the Inner Harbor, east along Pratt Street, and turn north up South and Guilford streets past City Hall to a connection with a Northern Central LRT station at Jones Falls.

Shortly after we had gotten started with the Lexington Center planning process, Robert C. Embry, Jay Brodie's predecessor as commissioner of the city's Department of Housing and Community Development and a former city councilman, strangely commissioned Arthur Cotton Moore, an architect from Washington, D.C., to prepare a master plan for the same area, not in coordination with our work, but in competition. The only explanation I ever got was that Embry and Boucher did not get along. And that he viewed WMRT as "not his guys."

The two plans ended up very much alike, but with a lot of hard feelings all round. In the middle of the process, CC-IH and the city secretly negotiated with Hutzler's Department Store for a branch store to be placed on the second level of what is now the NationsBank Center at the Pratt Street Boulevard and Charles Street. The store was linked by bridges to the Convention Center across Pratt and to Charles Center across Lombard to the north by an elevated pedestrian walkway. In this isolated location it survived for a few years, to be replaced by small shops and office-support facilities.

In 1976, Mayor William Donald Schaefer was in charge of Baltimore, and he was no more a friend of the retailers than D'Alesandro had been. Schaefer took pretty much the same attitude toward both versions of the plan as D'Alesandro had 17 years before. The only outcome of the Lexington Center effort was the creation of a quasi-public organization called the Market Center Development Corporation, Inc., (MCDC) to do something. MCDC, under Richard Stein and Robert Tennenbaum, managed the expansion of the Lexington Market across Lexington as the plan proposed, and was able to convert Hochschild-Kohn's into a State of Maryland office use. MCDC also was instrumental in selecting developer David Murdock from Arizona, another of Embry's "famous" guys who promised housing in the retail center—but Murdock failed to deliver, although he succeeded in developing the ugly Harbor Court Hotel on Light Street in the Inner Harbor.

I believe that the Lexington Center Plan, had it been vigorously pursued by the city and the business community, could have succeeded in reversing the downward spiral of the retail area and been of sufficient strength to integrate that area with the rest of the CBD and the Inner Harbor. But now we'll never know.

THE 1991 CBD RENAISSANCE AND THE 1998 WEST SIDE PLANS

Thirteen years later another plan for the CBD and the retail district was proposed. Baltimore's demographics had changed sufficiently for a racially combined coalition to elect an African-American lawyer and former Rhodes Scholar, Kurt L. Schmoke, as mayor. Schmoke announced his main emphasis would be education, with the Inner Harbor and downtown taking a back seat. To mollify the business community, Schmoke shrewdly endorsed a massive, two-year downtown visioning process, the fashion at the time. It involved some 300 stakeholder participants with a large Strategy Management Committee headed by, who else but my old friend, the ubiquitous Walter Sondheim.

The result was entitled *The Renaissance Continues: A 20-Year Strategy for Downtown Baltimore*. It was a non-design, policy statement and goals plan, in spite of the participation of many local designers. Published in 1991, its visions for all of MetroCenter, including the shopping district, were nothing more than colored patterns on a map, neither cost nor project specific, ideal for a mayor who didn't want to be pinned down. And the national economy went into a tailspin, undermining the plan's optimistic forecasts.

Although still working on various Baltimore projects, WRT was not involved in *The Renaissance Continues*, nor were we the authors of the most recent master plan for the West Side, the portion of the CBD that includes the retail district. In the competition for the West Side job, WRT was chosen by the selection committee, but the committee was overruled by representatives of the Weinberg Foundation, co-sponsors of the work. We were replaced by The Design Collective of Baltimore, who had worked for the Weinbergs on retail before. The resulting West Side plan was presented to the city and an enthusiastic Mayor Schmoke on June 25, 1998. My firm and I were responsible for the adjacent master plan for the

University of Maryland at Baltimore, which forms the southern portion of the West Side area and responded to the West Side Plan.

The Design Collaborative did a good job. The West Side Plan was a very ambitious proposal to finally do what previous efforts had not, namely eliminate the old regional shopping center, knit the booming University District together with Charles Center, the financial and government districts, and the Inner Harbor, wrapping them all into a unified CBD. The remnants of the old regional shopping center are to be wiped out entirely, to be replaced by new neighborhood-serving retail on the first floors of apartments and office buildings.

The driving force behind the West Side Plan is the Weinberg Foundation. Harry Weinberg was an owner of many commercial properties in the retail area, which he willed to the Harry & Jeannette Weinberg Foundation. The foundation joined with the University of Maryland at Baltimore, the University Hospital, and Peter Angelos, the lawyer-owner of the Baltimore Orioles. They propose to recreate the West Side into a "diverse, vital, desirable urban neighborhood" with housing, offices, shops, and entertainment. In other words, it's finally goodbye to any further dream of a regional shopping center as part of the downtown mix. In the meanwhile, downtown retail has shifted to the Inner Harbor, which already has more than one million square feet of retail and is still growing.

The West Side Plan proposes 1,899 residential units, with many of them over new retail on the first floor on Lexington Mall, which would be reopened to traffic. Total retail would be 306,000 square feet with 270,000 square feet of office space, 150 hotel rooms, and 3,000 parking spaces. Market demand for these additions has been estimated as strong by the late Morton Hoffman, who did the economic surveys for Charles Center and the Inner Harbor. While the plan document does not include an estimate of costs or a budget, David Stein of the foundation forecasts new investment at $350 million.

Public costs for the project were estimated at $28 million. Eight to ten city blocks were to be acquired and cleared by the city's urban renewal agency under direction of the Baltimore Development Corporation. Since the intensity of new uses would not be sufficient to offset costs, in most cases a substantial write-down would be necessary along with tax abatement to allow some affordable housing. Major infrastructure upgrading was included in the estimate of total public costs.

The design concept by The Design Collective, Inc., has attractive features, including a residential commons on the east side of Howard Street, a public park at the north end of the present Baltimore Arena site on Baltimore Street, and another opposite the restored Hippodrome Theater on Eutaw Street. The Civic Center site was to be redeveloped with mixed housing and office development, with the Baltimore Arena to be moved to an undesignated location.

In one sense the plan is already under way. As a first action, the former Hecht-May Department Store has now been converted into loft apartments by Southern Management, Inc., of Washington, D.C. The Weinberg Foundation is to renovate the six-story Stewart Department Store building. The store is diagonally across Howard and Lexington from Hecht-May; it is to become office use above reconfigured retail on the first floor. The Hippodrome is being revamped for the Performing Arts Center with a grant from the state legislature assisted by the Maryland Sports Authority, developers of Oriole Park at Camden Yards and M&T Bank Stadium, where the NFL Baltimore Ravens play, for which my firm has been planners, urban designers, and landscape architects.

TODAY'S PROSPECTS FOR THE RETAIL CENTER

As I walked east on Lexington Mall through the old retail center to Charles Center's western edge at Liberty Street, all shops appeared to be catering to the low end of the market, with a couple of accessory/wig outlets in evidence. I didn't see a single white person in the crowds on the Lexington Mall. While there appear to be no first-floor vacancies, the upper floors are probably as vacant as they were in our last survey in 1976. All of these narrow three- to five-story buildings on both sides of Lexington Mall would be demolished, by the plan, replaced by larger first-floor shops, above which are to be five- and six-story apartments catering to downtown professionals.

So what went wrong with the previous plans, and what chance does the present one have? Earlier plans always conceived the downtown mix as including the region's largest shopping complex as a necessary element. The West Side Master Plan abandoned that notion without explicitly saying so, and introduced the "urban neighborhood concept" with retail as an adjunct to other uses. The retail would be available to the same people it now serves, who are mostly black and poor, but who will be joined, hopefully, by customers from University of Maryland at

Baltimore, the hospital, new downtown residents, and office workers, most of whom will be middle- and upper-middle income.

The earlier plans' failures were in their sponsors not being able to get the support of city administrations and the business community as full partners. This is a real danger today. Mayor Schmoke had announced that he would not run again as he turned the plan over to M. Jay Brodie, the very able but overworked head of the BDC. Councilman Martin J. O'Malley was elected mayor and took office in January 2000. He has indicated his support for downtown initiatives.

Fortunately, the entire West Side is already an urban renewal area due to Mayor D'Alesandro's action in 1957. The BDC's next steps are to conduct the detailed surveys necessary for a redevelopment project, preparation of feasibility reports, redevelopment plans, property acquisition, relocation, demolition, and resale to developers, and get the approval of city council, along with financing.

Three issues dog implementation of the West Side Plan. Issue one: Can a predominantly African-American shopping center be wiped out to be replaced by a predominantly white one? The answer is probably yes, but this may become a political issue. Issue two: Are historic buildings being demolished when they could be restored? The answer to this is yet to be proven. My own belief is that it will not be feasible to restore these buildings to any viable economic use without a massive subsidy and if clearance is not sufficient to allow new buildings, it won't work. The third issue: Does the public purpose of eliminating blighting conditions warrant the use of eminent domain to acquire private property and dislocate minority retail operators in order to demolish the buildings and carry out the plan? My answer is maybe. These are all valid questions, the answers to which have to be argued in a public forum to ensure the validity of any West Side Plan.

Bernard Siegel, the Weinberg Foundation president, said the city was at a rare point where there were many factions working together, but it could all fall apart. Ed Gunts of *The Baltimore Sun* quotes Siegel as saying "right now" everybody's enthusiastic. But the city has to follow through. Unless the city is willing to do its part, everybody is going to drop out.[1]

While now-Mayor Martin J. O'Malley was still a member of the city council and then still-Mayor Schmoke was sponsoring the redevelopment legislation to carry out the West Side Plan, O'Malley voted against it. The more than 100 small merchants who would be displaced voiced strong opposition, and preservation groups organized by Preservation

Maryland and Baltimore Heritage began to be heard. They stressed the high cost of city acquisition and the potential economic benefits in using federal and state tax credits in preserving the majority of the old buildings. Together, they prepared a successful nomination to designate the area on the National Register of Historic Places with a 10-minute film, "Baltimore's West Side Story." In February 2000, the Market Center Historic District was created. Political support came from State Senator Barbara A. Hoffman, who arranged for financing for the renovation of the Hippodrome, which forced the city to minimize demolition.

On January 8, 2001, an agreement was signed between the city and the Maryland Historical Trust, the state's preservation agency, that will preserve more than half the historic buildings in the 28 blocks in the Market Center Urban Renewal Area. Two hundred and seventy buildings out of 400 are to be preserved outright, with another 105 to be reviewed as development proceeds. New construction is to be compatible with the neighborhood. Richard Moe, president of the National Trust for Historic Preservation, says, "This is the largest revitalization plan of its kind in the country."

THE WEST SIDE STRATEGIC PLAN

The new plan, *The West Side Strategic Plan*, which is dated January 2001, also was prepared by The Design Collective, Inc., for the Baltimore Development Corporation. It is a more comprehensive and ambitious plan than before, enlarging the study and action areas to include Mount Vernon, Seton Hill, University Center, and much of the CBD. Actions linking these to the Market Center and the North and South markets become major elements of such substrategies for redevelopment, retail, preservation, public sector infrastructure and transportation, and open space. Urban design guidelines are developed along with phasing.

Full build-out represents $800 million dollars of private sector investment, matched by $100 million dollars of public sector investment over a six-year period. The impact anticipated in taxes and jobs is equally impressive.

How realistic is the new plan? The key anchors in the area now called Market Center appear assured: the Hecht and Stewart department store renovations and the Hippodrome development. The tax abatement proposed for the historic buildings can go a long way toward making rents competitive, but the intrinsic obsolescence of the structures will cost a fortune to overcome. I don't think it will work as conceived, and it will need to be modified with more clearance than currently intended. A racial mix must be achieved to create a climate for economic success, with the demand for market-rate housing still predominantly white in this predominantly African-American city.

And where is the money for the upfront public cost going to come from? Certainly not from George W. Bush's administration. The reality

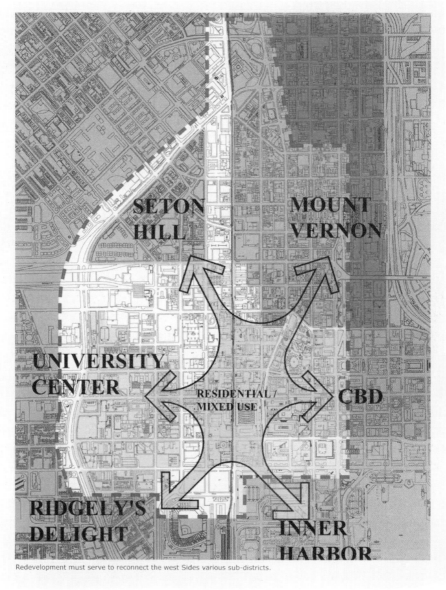

Redevelopment must serve to reconnect the west Sides various sub-districts.

4.7 The West Side Strategy integrates the District into Charles Center and the other areas around it.

behind this story is that in spite of the downtown renaissance, the city is an increasingly smaller, poorer place, less able or inclined to take on big plans, particularly when they don't seem of immediate benefit to the black majority. Baltimore's demographic facts of life are that in the more than 40 years since the 1959 CBD plan, the city has lost more than 31 percent of its population, going from 931,000 in 1960 to 646,000 in 1998. Almost two-thirds white in 1960, the city is now estimated at more than 65 percent African-American. There has also been an out-migration of middle-class African-Americans from the city's inner ring leaving low-income families and single persons in the sparsely occupied housing nearest downtown. Notable exceptions are the near-downtown upper-middle income neighborhoods of Bolton Hill, Mount Vernon, Ridgeley's Delight, Federal Hill, and Little Italy, all of which are still predominantly white. Townhouses on Federal Hill sell for upwards of $1 million if they have a view of the harbor.

BALTIMORE STREET RETAIL AND THE CBD TODAY

Unlike the Howard and Lexington street's region-serving shopping center, Baltimore Street retail on the east side of the CBD was always and is still mainly dependent on the office buildings, City Hall, Courthouse, and government concentrations around it. The blocks toward the eastern end of Baltimore Street were called The Block, an entertainment center. It was a memorable place that evolved more or less naturally as specialty shopping (with the help of the Liquor Control Board), not by planning. It catered to sailors from the nearby port, out-of-town businessmen looking for excitement, and students on a fling. Show-bars, prostitutes, pimps, and pickpockets gave the place an ambience of risk but overt crime was mostly held in check by a continuous police presence.

Forty-five years ago, The Block was a three-block city "institution" of show-bars and night clubs, centered around the vaudeville and burlesque Gaiety Theater. Owners were required to serve food as a condition of liquor licensing. My wife and I liked to eat an early dinner to the music of a blind black pianist at Blaze Starr's club in The Block before the shows started and it got raunchy. Blaze had been Louisiana Governor Huey Long's sweetheart and was an entertaining woman of unbelievable natural endowment. The food was excellent, catered from Marconi's—still one of the city's best Italian restaurants. So when a city hall reporter asked me my opinion of demolishing the club to make way for a detention center for delinquent women, I said I thought Baltimore should hang on to one of the few unusual things that it had going for it.

Unfortunately, the quote appeared the next week in the *Washington Post* in an editorial headed, "Baltimore, City of Sin." When Charles Buck, chairman of GBC, a deacon of the Presbyterian Church and my "boss of bosses" read this, he was livid. I was ordered to a lunch of crow at the old Southern Hotel with him and John Motz. Motz had taken over as chairman of the Planning Council when Hunter Moss's wife, Dora, died and Hunter moved to Miami. I agreed never to let myself be used by the media in such a way again "or else." I did get them to admit that The Block served a useful economic function. And what's left of it still does.

Today the three blocks of show bars have been reduced to one and a half, and Blaze Starr's club is gone. A city department of public works headquarters building chopped off the east end, and the Deutsche Banc/Alex Brown skyscraper on the south side of Baltimore Street with its parking deck on the north side anchors the west end. Live burlesque is long gone and the Gaiety is a porno movie theater, although still with the burlesque marquee. The whole scene has an atmosphere of busy sleaze. At its east end it segues into the Jones Falls Expressway touchdown point, with an attractive new station of the subway to serve the recently opened Port Discovery Children's Museum on Market Place that has replaced the historic fish market north of the Candler Building on Pratt Street in the Inner Harbor.

The Jones Falls Expressway serves as a spoke in Arthur McVoy's express beltway ring-and-spoke system to deliver traffic to downtown and relieve the 1959 CBD's then close-to-capacity street system. The expressway ends today at Fayette Street. While we worked on the CBD Plan, the expressway was being engineered in detail and was a crucial transportation element of the plan, an element largely authored by Henry Barnes. His timed traffic signal and the one-way street system that he had invented in his previous job in Flint, Michigan, had been so successful in Baltimore that pressure for expressways was delayed as much as 10 years.

As another part of Barnes's proposed local street improvement program, he wanted to move downtown Baltimore's two monuments, both smack in the middle of the street, to improve traffic. The Washington Monument in the center of North Charles Street at Mount Vernon Square was the first monument to George Washington built in the nation. The other, the Battle Monument memorializing the victory over the British in 1812, is in the center of North Calvert Street. I remember the meeting where Barnes made his case to a committee that he would move each monument "just to the side of each square" and improve traffic remarkably thereby. When he stopped and asked for opinions, Walter Sondheim finally broke the silence and said, "Henry, I think the answer is no. We'll just have to be satisfied with driving a little more slowly," and that was that.

A landscape and open space element was also a feature of the 1959 CBD Plan. Downtown Baltimore had been built with street trees, but by 1959, the only remaining ones were in parks like Preston Gardens, one of the few major improvements resulting from the great fire of 1904, which destroyed 140 acres of the CBD. The CBD Plan proposed to remedy this situation, and shortly after its submission we invited Sasaki & Associates of Watertown, Massachusetts, to propose an implementation of our landscape plan. In contract negotiations, the city solicitor's office raised the question of the extent that the city's insurance liability would be increased, what with people tripping over roots and so forth. We pointed out that cities like Washington, D.C., had trees in every street. The city's forester added that he estimated that outside the CBD, Baltimore's streets were adorned with some 50,000 trees, and that trees in the CBD would not increase liability very much. When Sasaki got to work, purists who wanted to design trees at specific spacings had to accept trees wherever they could be placed to avoid the ubiquitous tangle of underground utilities.

The landscape element also included recapturing Battle Monument Square from the judges. This was considered to be one of our least practical proposals, as the judges in the adjacent Courthouse had preempted all the central space for parking that was not occupied by the monument itself. Again, Walter Sondheim came to the rescue. He talked to the chief judge, who agreed to relinquish the area for landscape improvement. The intimate park that Sasaki designed is a small oasis in the midst of two lanes of traffic on each side, not much utilized because it's so hard to get to, but attractive to look at from the adjacent sidewalks, and from the cars zipping by.

The area of the Inner Harbor from Lombard to Pratt streets in the CBD Plan was labeled "PENDING FURTHER STUDY," not because we didn't have ideas about it, but because it was not at the center of downtown and we did not want any action to dilute the market for Charles Center. Further, the state highway department's Jones Falls Expressway planners were in the very early stages of design. This is when we should have jumped in to influence their work, but we were warned away from antagonizing MDOT by members of the council as creating an unnecessary adversary and we chickened out.

Today, to cite Rich Burns, the Downtown Partnership's consultant and head of The Design Collective, Inc., development and investment in the CBD has shifted from a traditional north-south axis along Charles Street, to an east-west axis along the Pratt Street Boulevard. It stretches to the University of Maryland campus area—an economic engine on the west— to the cleared Inner Harbor East redevelopment area with a new 750-room Baltimore Marriott Waterfront Hotel. Less than 10 percent of the more than $1 billion programmed for the overall downtown is going to occur in the traditional core of the CBD, Burns says.

At the heart of the CBD core on Redwood Street, vacancy stands at 80 percent along a three-block stretch of historic office buildings, while within two blocks on Baltimore Street new office towers are fully occupied. Lack of adequate parking in the overall CBD is evidenced by consistent reports of more than 100 percent occupancy in parking garages. These and other facts about the state of the CBD were presented to me and others of the original Charles Center downtown planning team as part of the current plan preparation by Burns.

It was small consolation to the Partnership when I pointed out that this was exactly the kind of consequence we had intended in the original chocolate-colored CBD Plan of 1959. In the section of that document entitled "Office Development Program" (pp. 48-53), of the 9.6 million square feet in the supply, 28 percent was to be rehabilitated, 34 percent to be substantially rehabilitated, 38 percent was to be eliminated or converted to other use, and replaced with new, and 28 percent was to be added to the supply by 1980. As is the case in all such forecasts, no one keeps track, but the principle remains and I bet that it more or less happened that way. Unfortunately, Burns and the Downtown Partnership did not have the resources for any such analysis in their most recent effort.

---

1 I remember a similar crucial moment in the city's history when Charles Center was presented. Then-Mayor D'Alessandro turned to his department directors and said, "Let's figure out how we can do this." Not "should we" or "can we." That is what Mayor Schmoke needed to say and mean it.

5

The Jones Falls
Valley Plan

While we were completing the CBD Plan in 1959, the Jones Falls expressway construction was begun. It was a logical next step and we were looking for work. The Planning Council staff were acting as consultants to the city's renewal agency in implementing Charles Center, and in promotion and implementation of our other CBD proposals. We also tried to market our services to nearby local governments and organizations in the same way that the Pittsburgh Regional Plan Association operated, with some limited success. A master plan for Annapolis, Maryland, was undertaken upon the recommendation of Baltimore's director of public works, who was an influential Annapolis resident. Though other prospective clients were assured of my staff's and my professional competence, they were uneasy about what role the lay members of the Planning Council and the GBC's board would have because any contract would be with the GBC. There seemed to be a built-in conflict of interest.

In planning for the Jones Falls Valley, we failed to find the "key to the kingdom," or rather, we were too late. When we were warned away from the Jones Falls Expressway engineers while developing the CBD Plan, we thought we were smart to take that advice and avoid any confrontation, but it's too bad we didn't have the courage of our convictions. It would have changed the way we later approached the Jones Falls Valley planning process and the potential for success. Jones Falls is a meandering creek with a drainage basin that leads from the eastern side of the Inner Harbor northwest to the Baltimore Beltway, and beyond to the Green Spring and Worthington valleys. It is all part of an important and vulner-

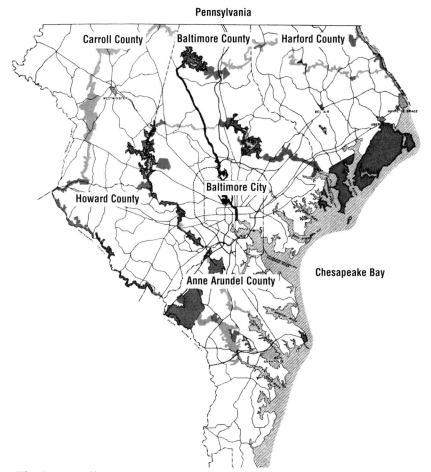

Pennsylvania

Carroll County   **Baltimore County**   **Harford County**

Howard County

Baltimore City

Chesapeake Bay

Anne Arundel County

5.1 The Jones Falls creek leads to the Inner Harbor in the city from the Loch Raven Reservoir, which is almost at the Maryland/Pennsylvania line.

able urban ecosystem that serves as a "spine" connecting downtown's gateway at North Avenue to the suburbs at the Beltway.

Construction of the Jones Falls Expressway that connected the CBD along the Jones Fallsway to the Baltimore Beltway in Baltimore County was already under way. Almost overnight, land and properties that had had limited regional accessibility would be at excellent locations, and the view to and from the new road was going to be very important. Both development and open space opportunities were scattered all along the route, with the biggest opportunity being the creation of a green valley as the dominant visual experience. The engineers designing the expressway had paid no attention to such matters and had missed a golden opportunity. We saw the possibility of taking advantage of their shortsightedness.

I talked to our Planning Council members and was discouraged that neither they nor the GBC would sponsor an urban design study of the route. They took the position that the Planning Council should be run like a private firm and be self-supporting. Our contract with the Committee for Downtown and work for BURHA had spoiled them for any GBC subsidy. We were on our own.

Warren Buckler, a friend of mine and prominent local lawyer, was an active member of the Citizens Planning and Housing Association and also belonged to the Municipal Arts Society, both nonprofit organizations dedicated to good works. CPHA had no money, but Buckler introduced me to the Municipal Art Society's president and principal benefactor, Douglas H. Gordon, who strongly endorsed the idea of a plan for Jones Falls Valley. Forty years before, the society had sponsored a planning study for the Jones Falls Valley that had never been implemented. Together, we approached the board of recreation and parks of Baltimore city and asked them to co-sponsor the study as an update of the earlier effort and the city's overall open space plan, at no cost to the board. Both the GBC and the society recognized that it was unlikely that anything would ever get done without the initiative coming from outside city government.

The Municipal Art Society had a long-term investment in the Fallsway. The society had been created by Theodore Marburg in the late 1800s, and had retained the Olmsted Brothers in 1902 to prepare an open space and recreation master plan for the city. Made famous by Frederick Law Olmsted's plan for Central Park in New York, the Olmsteds proposed three stream-valley parks in the overall plan published in 1904. Their detailed plans for Herring Run Park in East Baltimore and Gwynn's Falls Park in West Baltimore have been largely implemented, but their proposals for the Jones Falls Valley Park were still unrealized in 1960. The Maryland and Pennsylvania Railroad that traversed the valley was still actively promoting industrial uses along the way, as well as serving the mills that had been established in the mid-1800s in the Hampden-Woodbury community that straddles the valley. In 1926, the Olmsted Brothers firm was invited to review and expand on their 1904 recommendations; they were surprised that no action had been taken on the Jones Falls Valley plan. Of course, the Olmsted Brothers had not anticipated the expressway.

5.2 Swett's view of the Jones Falls Valley in 1837 shows the Shot Tower and Gaol on the left and the towers of the old Basilica in the center. Jones Falls was a noisome swamp and was shortly put into an underground sewer.

The expressway now dominates the valley of the Fallsway from its intersection with the Beltway at Brooklandville. There is little sense of the unrealized potential for a connection of the existing major parks along the edge of the valley as parts of a linear park system. Jones Falls begins as an outfall of the Loch Raven Reservoir and is a small stream near Owings Mills, which then proceeds south to the intersection of Interstate 83, the Jones Falls Expressway, and the Beltway. I recently drove south from the intersection on the expressway from Brooklandville in the county to the expressway's terminus at Baltimore Street in downtown. The route follows the Falls past Ruxton where Old Falls Road provides the connection to Robert E. Lee Park and Lake Roland Reservoir. For the areas adjacent, there is an overwhelming sense of isolation except for the constant roar and dominating presence of the elevated roadway.

South of the city line, four large existing city parks are part of the same stream valley ecosystem. They are still unconnected today, but could be easily corrected. From north to south, they are Cylburn Park, Cold Spring Park, Druid Hill Park, and Wyman Park. Each is a local community amenity, but none can play its full major regional open space role because of its isolation. Along the route among these parks, the Jones Falls stream meanders along, almost disappearing from sight, until, in the expressway's last mile—from Penn Station south the stream was put in a box culvert in 1913 because of flooding. Then it reappears as a canal below

Baltimore Street, and is bridged by Lombard and Pratt streets on its final stretch to the Inner Harbor.

Landscape architect/planner Bill Potts headed our planning and design team and he did a superior job. The Jones Falls Valley Plan was submitted in the spring of 1961 to the city and the Municipal Arts Society with thanks and praise, but no initial action. GBC, which should have put its weight behind the plan, had other more pressing fish to fry, and ignored it. However, the Baltimore Regional Planning Council recognized its importance and included the plan as part of their Regional Plan for Open Spaces, which was also published in 1961.

At this point I left Baltimore to return to Philadelphia and start teaching at the University of Pennsylvania. It was fall 1961, and my place at the Planning Council was taken by Potts, who had been a key member of the team throughout Charles Center and the CBD Plan. He also had been the project director of the Jones Falls Valley planning staff, and had begun a quiet promotion of the plan.

In light of the Jones Falls Expressway's completion, our scheme was too ambitious, and we had failed to get key community involvement and approval in its preparation. While we had relied on the CHPA for the latter, we had not directly involved local community groups. As it turned out, that probably would not have helped. When Bill Potts presented the plan to the Baltimore City Council, it immediately drew criticism from several councilmen, mainly to the initial projected cost of $10 million and ultimate cost of $25 to $35 million. However there was sufficient support for the idea of a Jones Falls Valley Park that the city council and Mayor J. Harold Grady referred it to special committee consisting of the "usual suspects"—city officials who would test the political wind. They met and recommended that the GBC revise its plan. The GBC did, issuing the revised version in early 1962. Notice, the plan had become a "GBC" plan along the way, as opposed to a Planning Council or a Municipal Arts Society plan.

Although the revised version did not incorporate many of the changes recommended by the committee, it did back off immediate acquisition of many industrial properties, including the key Arundel quarry, and the Hampden-Woodbury mills. Even so, the mayor's committee decided to prepare its own version. It hired economist Dorothy Muncy, another Harvard classmate of mine, and in late 1962 the committee submitted a modified plan to the mayor, recommending authorization of a $3 million bond issue to be placed on the ballot.

The GBC stood by its revised plan as the irreducible minimum, and criticized the mayor's committee's plan as allowing the industries to remain, thereby eliminating a crucial continuity of parkland. Mayor Grady endorsed his committee's plan, and suggested that the Hampden-Woodbury industrial area be further studied by the urban renewal agency to which the plan was submitted for possible implementation. The committee plan was then adopted as part of the city's Master Plan for Parks and the $3 million bond issue was announced in January 1963.

Placed on the May 7, 1963, ballot, the bond issue was approved and its park purpose was widely hailed by civic and political groups. GBC circulated a mailer enlisting citizen support and the bonds were approved. The Jones Falls Valley Park Plan was to be implemented.

The Baltimore Urban Renewal and Housing Agency's study of the Hampden-Woodbury section of the valley was completed in April 1963. In it, BURHA recommended a linear park along the east side of the valley floor, with new industry on the west slopes. Camp Small, site of a Civil War hospital, was the first property to be acquired in September 1963, with bond issue funds.

In April 1964, a bill was introduced in the city council to acquire vacant industrial property for park purposes, and although quick passage had been expected, opposition to the ordinance mounted. On June 8, 1964, some 200 people from the neighborhoods jammed the city council's chamber to protest the ordinance and the plan.

The Baltimore City Council quickly backed away from the Jones Falls Valley plan. Councilman William Donald Schaefer urged the Board of Estimates to withdraw the ordinance and Thomas D'Alesandro III, president of the city council called the plan "completely inadequate and haphazard." Although the ordinance was withdrawn, work on the plan's implementation continued through 1964.

But in January 1965, the PepsiCola Bottling Company of Baltimore decided to acquire the 13-acre property known as the Shapiro site, formerly the Shapiro rag plant. The plant had burned in 1962, and acquiring the site for part of the park was a key element in the park plan. Instead, Pepsi proposed a new modern one-story building to employ about 400 people.

I was no longer involved, and I owe the account of the ensuing events and ultimate outcome to an unpublished paper prepared by Michael A. Hill, "The Park That Never Was: The Failure of the Jones Falls Valley Park Plan," April 3, 1998. The Pepsi proposal was immediately hailed by politicians and the neighborhoods as vindication of their claims that the land was viable for industrial use and the promise of jobs was unarguable. Further, Pepsi had the right to build without government approval other than a building permit. The zoning had not been changed. The director of the city planning department stated that, short of immediate condemnation for park use, the city could not prevent the construction of the bottling plant.

Not long after Pepsi had announced its plan, Baltimore's Economic Development Commission let it be known that it opposed the park proposals south of Cold Spring Lane in favor of retention of industrial use, and it was in favor of the Pepsi proposal. A tour of the valley was arranged by GBC and the Park Board for the city Board of Estimates. After the tour, the comptroller, Hyman Pressman, City Council President Thomas J. D'Alesandro III, and the rest of the board, except for Mayor Theodore R. McKeldin, announced opposition to the park plan.

Still, the Baltimore Planning Commission delayed approving Pepsi's building permit and the director of planning urged immediate acquisition of the Shapiro property for the park. Finally the commission voted to reject the building permit on March 2, 1965. This led to a wave of protest, not only against the Shapiro acquisition, but also against the entire Jones Falls Valley Park Plan. Mayor McKeldin continued to support the plan, but the city council scheduled a public hearing for April 14, 1965. Again, 200 residents as well as various government organizations, voiced vehement opposition. The hearing was so protracted that Councilman Schaefer scheduled a continuation. Then the city council voted to approve an ordinance removing the park use from the master plan of parks south of Cold Spring Lane, and the Jones Falls Valley Park Plan was dead.

That was 39 years ago. The failure of the Jones Falls Valley Park Plan has always been a major disappointment to me, and perhaps the error was in promoting the plan as a park instead of as part of a multi-use concept. We should have attached ourselves somehow to the expressway planning process—the key to the kingdom.

As I sat down to write this account, to my surprise I find that now, almost 40 years later, there is a considerable amount of citizen activity to create a new Jones Falls Valley Plan. A consortium of sponsors led by the Baltimore Development Corporation, and including the Baltimore Zoo, the Greater Homewood Community Association, the Jones Falls Watershed Association, the Mass Transit Administration, the Parks and People Foundation, and Streuver Brothers, Eccles & Rouse have hired AB

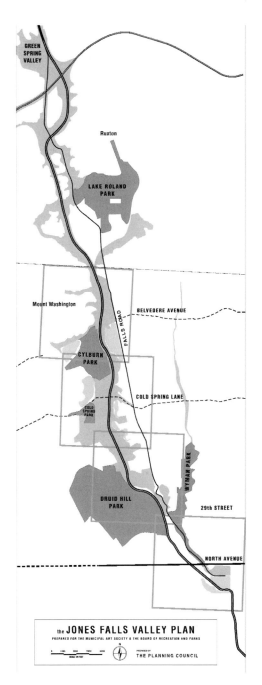

the JONES FALLS VALLEY PLAN
PREPARED FOR THE MUNICIPAL ART SOCIETY & THE BOARD OF RECREATION AND PARKS

SCALE IN FEET

N

PROPOSED BY
THE PLANNING COUNCIL

5.3 The Jones Falls Valley Plan ties the city and county's park systems together in a very persuasive way from an open space and graphic view, but should have been approached from a section-by-section development potential to have succeeded.

Associates, a local planning firm, as the lead consultant of a group that has just produced *First Findings: A Preliminary Report on the Jones Falls Valley.*

Correcting the mistake made earlier, the report sees the need for a multi-function program in its vision statement, planning principles, and summary of area-wide issues, opportunities, and ideas. Specific ideas, many of which are familiar from the 1965 plan, are advanced for each of the 13 subareas or neighborhoods into which the report divides the valley. These were the basis for four forums scheduled through October and November 2000.

The first two forums attracted perhaps 30 people each. In these, three old-timers, outspoken opponents of everything and anything, monopolized the first part of the meetings. They were then followed by a number of young neighborhood representatives who recognized and supported what the planners were trying to do. The PepsiCola plant still employs a substantial work force, but has apparently become a bad neighbor. According to recent reports it allows trash and debris to go uncollected. The Greater Homewood Community Association, headed by Barbara Bonnell, who recently retired as director of research of BDC, has attempted to persuade PepsiCola to cover the massive roof of its plant with earth and landscape, which apparently is structurally feasible, to no avail.

On the good side, a retired biochemist named Michael Beer, who lives adjacent to the valley, has recruited volunteers to clean up along the Jones Falls during the last 10 years. A modern Pied Piper, he has persuaded the Maryland Department of Transportation to close a section of the expressway for four hours on a Sunday morning for the past several years, and last year several thousand neighbors celebrated the event. So I think it may still be too early to say that the Jones Falls Valley plan is dead. There may be life in it yet.

6

Philadelphia: Starting a Private Practice

The GBC's Jones Falls Valley Plan was published in April 1961. Except for our contract with BURHA to help manage the redevelopment of Charles Center and the continuing preparation of the master plans for Laurel and Annapolis, Maryland, the Planning Council was out of work. George Kostritsky had been offered and accepted a partnership by Archibald Rogers. Rogers Taliaferro & Lamb, Architects and Planners, became Rogers Taliaferro Kostritsky & Lamb, soon to be shortened to RTKL.

Harry Cooper left to join Tom Karsten with Blaustein Enterprises and together they became developers. Jerry O'Leary went to Washington, D.C., to work at HUD briefly and then to form Marcou-O'Leary and head that prestigious planning firm for a number of years. John Adelberg joined Hideo Sasaki as an urban design partner at Sasaki Associates in Watertown, Massachusetts.

Bill Potts took over as the director of the Planning Council, where he stayed for the next six years, when he left to join developer Gulf-Western's staff for the new town of Reston, Virginia.

And I became a full professor with tenure, recruited by Dean G. Holmes Perkins of the Graduate School of Fine Arts, joining the Department of City and Regional Planning at the University of Pennsylvania, to start in September 1961. Paul Ylvisaker of the Ford Foundation, whom I had gotten to know at urban conferences and who was watching my career with interest, had arranged for a $10,000 grant from the foundation as an advance on a book about my Baltimore experience. I spent the most frustrating summer of my life, sitting in front of a typewriter in my office in Baltimore, totally immobilized by writer's block. The dedication of this book to Ylvisaker and the Ford Foundation is my coming to terms with this obligation; late but better late than never.

Finding a house and moving to Philadelphia with my wife and step-son saved my sanity, but the book never materialized until now. I gratefully plunged into the life and responsibilities of a member of the faculty. I also continued traveling to Baltimore on a monthly basis to serve as the secretary and a voting member of the Charles Center Architectural Review Board.

We bought a marvelous stone-walled, four-story Norman-French farmhouse in Philadelphia's West Mount Airy. It was part of what is called the French Village developed by philanthropist George Woodward in memory of his son, who was killed in France during World War I. From my study window I could look across Crensheim Creek Park to Chestnut Hill, which is one of America's premier suburban communities; I live there now.

It was a great place to start my new life, developing the courses I would teach and starting a private consulting practice. The house was a 10-minute walk to the Chestnut Hill R-8 west commuter line, then a 30-minute ride to the University of Pennsylvania in West Philadelphia, and another five-minute ride to downtown. I bought a black Triumph TR3 convertible roadster in celebration (just in case the trains didn't run).

Although I was a tenured full professor, I had a relatively light teaching load. I had one lecture course, the Introduction of Planning, which I inherited from William L.C. Wheaton, who had been my dissertation supervisor at Harvard and would shortly move to the University of California–Berkeley. I had never taught such a survey course before, so it took a good deal of preparation. Class met twice a week for an hour, and at first, I was usually only a lecture or two ahead of the class. My other assignment was to teach a planning/urban design studio, a workshop format that met three days a week, all afternoon. But I had all summer off.

I had taught before, for a year at the University of Chicago and at Penn as an adjunct professor while I was at the Philadelphia Redevelopment Authority, so I knew what to expect. But I soon realized that, compared to the teaching pros in the department—like David Crane, Paul Davidoff, or Bill Wheaton—I had much to learn. Denise Scott Brown, who had not yet married Bob Venturi, said it to me succinctly: "You have to decide what it is that you want to teach, and then you must realize that teaching is also show business." All I had to do to see how teaching should be done was to sit in on one of my future partner Ian McHarg's Man and the Environment lectures. Wow! Talk about show business!

I got better, as time went on, and effectively used projects, such as the Lower Manhattan Plan, to teach my philosophy and methods of planning.

In the meanwhile, my consulting practice prospered. During my last year in Baltimore, I had served the Ford Foundation and Paul Ylvisaker as a consultant to Oakland, California, and Cleveland, Ohio. Allan Jacobs and I had taught together at Penn in the 1950s and he hired me to do some "vision planning" for the Pittsburgh Regional Plan Association, of which he was then the executive director. He later become famous as San Francisco's planning director.

Three assignments are the most memorable: Hogates Seafood Restaurant in Washington, D.C., Trenton, New Jersey's, John Fitchway Redevelopment Plan, and Eaton Center in Toronto, Canada.

HOGATES SEAFOOD RESTAURANT

On September 5, 1961, the very day school started, Watson Rulon called. He had been referred to me by my friend Stanley Sherman, who was director of design of the Washington, D.C., Redevelopment Agency. Rulon owned the famous 1,000-seat Hogates Seafood Restaurant on the Potomac waterfront in the Southwest Washington Redevelopment Area. To be more precise, he owned the restaurant—the business, not the building. The agency intended to acquire the building and demolish it, and Rulon had the right, as a displaced tenant, to build a new restaurant in the same location if it was consistent with the redevelopment plan. If he closed the restaurant, he would lose the right.

Rulon was a mechanical engineer who had some years before come on the scene to fix the building's boiler and had parleyed some gratuitous suggestions about improving food service into becoming the restaurant owner. He was an efficiency expert who prided himself in the slogan: "The food you eat was cooked while you wait."

Rulon's other skill was in local politics. He knew a new building would be expensive, particularly on the waterfront, and parking would be essential. He managed to get a friendly U.S. congressman to attach a rider to some bill or other that allowed public parking under his building to be considered as a flood-control measure; ergo, it was paid for as a part of the Redevelopment Agency's cost.

Rulon needed me to help him deal with the bureaucracy, prepare the documents to be selected as the redeveloper, and to provide the necessary steps to design and construct the new Hogates. It was the beginning of a

6.1 Hogates Seafood on Washington, D.C.'s, southwest waterfront is a 1,000-seat restaurant. Planning started in 1962; the restaurant opened in 1973. Designed by Tom Todd, it was the first architectural assignment WMRT completed.

beautiful friendship. When he hired me, it was to do the planning, but at various junctures, Rulon considered his options and continued our services. He couldn't stop the process, or he'd lose the right to be the redeveloper, so he served as our client for the design and construction of the restaurant.

But Rulon was in his mid-60s, and he was not looking forward to running a restaurant in his old age. Construction was well under way, when

6.2 The Marriott Corporation purchased Hogates Seafood Restaurant during construction and it became one of their most successful operations. The restaurant caters heavily to tour buses.

by chance, he met William Marriott, Jr., on the street in downtown Washington, and after striking up a conversation, said, "Bill, do you want to own Hogates?" As Rulon told the story, Marriott and he shook hands on the deal immediately. The only change Marriott made was to eliminate the interior steps to better facilitate cart service. And Hogates for years was Marriott's top moneymaker. It also was Tom Todd's first architectural assignment.

TRENTON, NEW JERSEY'S, JOHN FITCHWAY REDEVELOPMENT PROJECT

While I was with the Philadelphia Redevelopment Authority (1953–1957), I had been active in the American Institute of Planners and had befriended Richard Cylinder, Trenton's planning director. The city had designated the area between the Delaware River and Broad Street from the State Capitol complex south to U.S. Highway 1 for redevelopment. Cylinder hired me to prepare a redevelopment plan for its reuse.

U.S. Route 29 is elevated along the river's edge. The northern section along Assuanpink Creek was the location of the two Battles of Trenton, where Washington trounced the British. Today, the entire redevelopment area is occupied by state office buildings, including the Hughes Justice Center, with the exception of mid-rise housing along its southeast edge. It is an important example of the "urban removal" phase of the nation's redevelopment programs. My role was to facilitate attracting the developers.

TORONTO, CANADA'S, EATON CENTER

You may think I'm not exactly proud of the way John Fitchway turned out, and you'd be right. Toronto's Eaton Center is equally forgettable, at best it was a learning experience.

In early 1963, I was contacted by J.E. Kelly, head of the Don Mills Development, Ltd., a large new community developer in the Toronto suburbs. I can't remember how Kelly came to me, but on January 24, I went to Toronto to meet Kelly and Alan Eaton, head of the Eaton Department Store chain. Eaton's flagship store was in downtown Toronto, adjacent to Toronto's old City Hall, and at the intersection of two recently completed subway lines. Eaton and Don Mills had entered a partnership to redevelop the area around the store into a shopping mall and build a new Eaton's in the process.

Eaton frostily advised me that he was the chairman of the redevelopment authority, so we wouldn't have any trouble on that score. Although

Eaton's was owned by a family trust, it was a patriarchy and he had complete control, so he said. Finally, he said that the plan should include acquisition and demolition of the old City Hall, a Victorian architectural gem. Toronto had a brand-new City Hall and didn't need two. A number of other small properties nearby would be acquired and cleared to make room for the mall. Kelly advised me after the meeting that Victor Gruen had originally been hired, but Gruen had not gotten along with Eaton.

I went home and developed some general, rough concepts that included demolition of the old City Hall, but I suggested that at least the tower should be retained. In our next meeting with Eaton, I gingerly suggested that he might have to recuse himself from the redevelopment authority's actions, and that there might be negative public reaction to the elimination of the old City Hall. Eaton thanked me, then said they would no longer be needing my services.

That was the bad news. The good news was that also in January 1963, Tom Karsten called me to come to Baltimore and discuss the assignment that turned out to be a benchmark in my career.

CHAPTER

7

The Plan for the Valleys

The Green Spring and Worthington valleys are at the northern end of the Jones Falls drainage basin. Ian McHarg's book *Design with Nature* gives a lyrical and somewhat romanticized report on the plan itself, but the article "Diary of a Plan" that I co-authored with William C. McDonnell, which we published in the January 1971 issue of the *Journal of the American Institute of Planners,* is still the best description of the preparation of and initial implementation of the *Plan for the Valleys.*

I have paraphrased from it with McDonnell's approval. It tells the story from the moment Thomas Karsten called me in January 1963, through the plan's development, and the first six years of the plan's implementation until 1970. McDonnell, who had worked with me at the Planning Council in Baltimore, became the ideal head of our Towson office through the preparation of the plan, and then served as the director of the Green Spring and Worthington Valleys Planning Council.

After 1970, there was an hiatus in my involvement with the Valleys until 1977, when WMRT was retained by Baltimore County to prepare a Growth Management Plan for the entire county, including the Valleys. McHarg was not to be involved at the client's request. He had become too identified as an anti-growth advocate to satisfy Marian McCoy, Baltimore County's planning director. In 1980, the firm—by then WRT—was again retained by the Valleys Planning Council, Inc., and in 1989 the result of this work, *A Supplement to the Plan for the Valleys* was published. Both plans reaffirmed the earlier *Plan for the Valleys* concepts and supported the community's continued resistance to either any sewer extension or expressway connection into the Valleys.

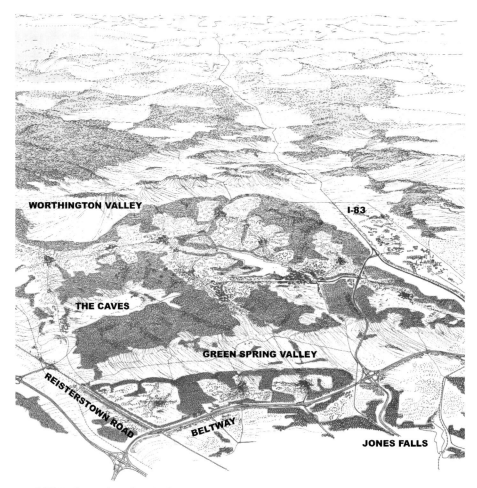

7.1 Bill Roberts lovely Bird's Eye Perspective tells it all. The Baltimore Beltway is in the foreground. It intersects with the Jones Falls Interstate 83, which leads from right middleground northwest to the Pennsylvania line. The three valleys, mostly open or developed at very low density, are clearly the dominant physiographic feature of the region.

It was during the summer of 1963 through early 1964 that McHarg, Bill McDonnell, Bill Roberts, and I prepared the *Plan for the Valleys* for the Green Spring and Worthington Valley (GSWV) Planning Council, Inc. Our office was in McHarg's attic near my own house in West Mount Airy, Philadelphia. We made a study model of the planning area in my basement. The area consisted of three valleys and the plateaus between. The Green Spring Valley is on the south, the Worthington Valley to the north, and the smaller Caves Valley, along with a large plateau area, between the two. All told, the Valleys constitute more than 70,000 acres in the northwest sector of Baltimore County.

The study process began by applying McHarg's new overlay ecological inventory approach that he had developed in studios at Penn. The method first identified land that was performing important natural processes, for example, wetlands, steep slopes, heavily forested areas, and key landscapes. This land was assumed as intrinsically unsuited to and/or imposing severe constraints on development if the natural processes such as water retention, runoff, aquifer recharge, and the like; were to continue undisturbed. Along with areas special to the character of the valleys, they should be left in a natural state.

With these ecologically and visually sensitive areas as a base, I then directed the planning process to identify land suitable for limited development as well as land whose development would not significantly affect natural processes or the unique visual character of the valleys. These were then examined to see whether or not they could meet their "fair share" of metropolitan needs for development and still satisfy the local property owner's economic goals. If development was to be limited on some areas and diverted to others, a mechanism for equitable distribution of gains in land values would have to be devised to compensate those whose property was reduced in development potential.

Together we then developed a program for action and implementation as an integral part of the plan. Most of this program was adopted by the client, the Valleys Council, and has been in place for the past 50 years. However, the key element for full implementation, specifically a real estate syndicate or conservation trust to provide a mechanism for what should have been, in effect, the transfer of development rights and equitable redistribution of capital gains, was never created. As a consequence, the plan has succeeded in preventing growth in the valleys, but the higher density housing and village centers proposed for the plateau area have never materialized. The result is that overall development of the area has not achieved the population density goal set forth. Nevertheless, from the landowners point of view, the plan has been an outstanding success, because most of the residents never really espoused all the goals that were attributed to them by us, the authors. McHarg felt that his objectives of preventing despoliation of the natural landscape had been realized, and I suppose my disappointment is irrelevant.

The county, the Baltimore Regional Planning Council, and the State of Maryland all adopted the plan "in principle." Damaging zoning changes and inappropriate utility and highway layouts have been prevented, or coerced into conformance. But unfortunately the Valleys cannot be considered, as it has been touted, to be the first successful large-scale example in America of humane development and conservation of the countryside by citizen action. I think it is convincing evidence that only through state or federal intervention using the threat of eminent domain will suburban sprawl be averted. And the few examples of successful transfer of development rights in other areas of the country suggest that the concept will be supported on only a limited basis.

PREPARING THE PLAN: 1963–1964

How plans are actually made is rarely reported, but in this case it is relevant to my overall search for why some plans succeed and others fail. When Tom Karsten, chairman of the Green Spring and Worthington Valley (GSWV) Planning Committee, called me at Penn, he stated that the council, formed in late 1962 by 250 property owners in the Valleys area, had approached Baltimore County to ask for a plan, but Malcolm Dill, the county planning director, said he could not assign staff on such a preferred basis. Dill suggested the council hire a consultant to work closely with the county. I had been involved with Karsten when I lived in Baltimore. He had represented Jacob Blaustein, the unsuccessful developer of the first office building in Charles Center. Other members of the council also knew of my work and they felt that I seemed a logical choice. Karsten further emphasized that the objective of GSWV was not to oppose change but to prevent the rape of the countryside that unplanned, disorderly development would surely entail.

Although I already had a number of clients in my budding practice at Penn, I had no employees except students working part-time, and realized that the assignment would require a variety of disciplines. I needed help. McHarg, whom I had known slightly in my class at Harvard, was by then chairman of Penn's Department of Landscape Architecture. He had introduced his new ecological emphasis to the landscape program; I had been impressed by it as a juror on one of his class projects for the New Jersey Shore. McHarg was also principal investigator on an open space research project relevant to the Valleys's problem. I had been named as editor of this research project when William L.C. Wheaton had moved to

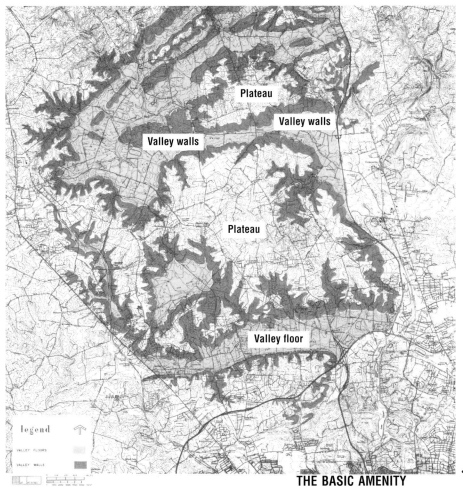

Plateau

Valley walls

Valley walls

Plateau

Valley floor

legend

VALLEY FLOORS

VALLEY WALLS

THE BASIC AMENITY

7.2 The Basic Amenity consists of the valley floors and largely wooded valley walls. Keeping them open is the central idea. This was a landscape concept and what our clients wanted to hear. It was supported by McHarg's environmental analysis, which he developed in later work.

the University of California at Berkeley. At my suggestion, we decided to associate and open an office on the basis of the Valleys job.

Together we visited the site, met with the client group and talked to Malcolm Dill, the county's planning director. I had known Dill from my days in Baltimore and he enthusiastically endorsed our selection. We put together a proposal for a $43,000 fee, which was accepted. We agreed with Karsten that we needed a local office and hired Bill McDonnell as our resident planner. Bill had worked with me at the Planning Council of the

Greater Baltimore Committee, where he helped prepare the plans for Annapolis and Laurel, Maryland.

After signing the contract with the GSWV Council, we retained Ann Louise Strong and William G. Grigsby as legal and economic subconsultants respectively. Both were members of my Penn open space research group. Paul L. Niebanck, at the time one of Grigsby's doctoral students, also would work with us. In Baltimore, M. Gordon "Reds" Wolman, chairman of Johns Hopkins Department of Geography and one of the country's top geologists, and James Piper III, a real estate consultant joined the team. Reds was the son of Abel Wolman, the engineer who would recommend me to Mayor, then later Governor, McKeldin for the Inner Harbor.

We met for the first time with the full GSWV membership. They were an interesting group, with only a few big landowners. Mostly they were homeowners such as Karsten on three- to ten-acre lots that were served by on-site septic systems. They enjoyed looking at the open land of the estates, and wanted to keep it that way. A third category of property owners was the working-class people in small houses on one-acre lots (the minimum allowed by zoning). Scattered helter-skelter throughout the area, they were simply not represented, and at no time did the Valleys Planning Council try to enlist their involvement. The council was and still is an elitist organization. The Baltimore County politicians might have taken a different attitude if the council had been more representative.

In April 1963, McDonnell opened our office at 212 Washington Street, just south of downtown, in Towson, Maryland, after the GSWV sent us a retainer. We had explained that we were impecunious professors and needed the money to get started. I remember the wonderful spring day when we made our first photo reconnaissance of area. McDonnell was enchanted, but appalled at our task, as we all were.

The original proposal had been for 35 square miles based on the early membership in GSWV, but as additional members were recruited from the big Worthington Valley on the north, Karsten insisted we enlarge the area. We finally drew the line at 70 square miles. He and the GSWV promised more money, but it never materialized. When our physiographic survey was completed, the final determination of northern boundary was made at the ridge above the Western Run Valley, an extension of the Worthington Valley.

A CRISIS DEVELOPS

We had no sooner started our survey work than we heard that 100 acres at the southeast corner of the Green Spring Valley was for sale at $7,500 an acre, contingent on shopping center zoning. Worse, it had already been optioned to James Rouse, my old client in Baltimore. I talked to him and pointed out that 75 percent of the property was in a flood plain. While we thought that would make his development difficult, he said it could easily be filled, but he couldn't develop the property without being able to connect to the Jones Falls interceptor sewer.

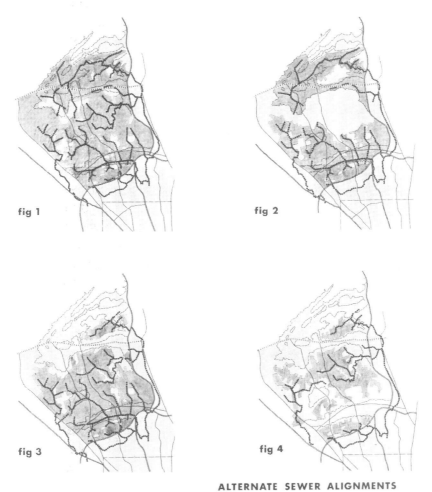

ALTERNATE SEWER ALIGNMENTS

7.3 Analysis of alternate sewer alignments revealed that the most cost-effective way to sewer the region was by the plateaus instead of the valleys. (Figure 4)

The owner of the land adjacent to the 100-acre property was a member of the GSWV Planning Committee. He said even though Rouse's development would increase his values, he'd rather forfeit the increase than have a shopping center as a neighbor. Several other members suggested creation of an area development corporation, so that all owners could share in the development of properties in accordance with the plan we would prepare. Rouse was sympathetic to our work and said the idea of a development corporation or real estate syndicate was crucial to any scheme we might come up with.

The importance of the sanitary sewer issue loomed over everything we did. The huge Jones Falls interceptor sewer, which led all the way to the Inner Harbor, would, in the absence of arguments to the contrary, "logically" be extended by the county's Department of Public Works into the Green Spring Valley and beyond. The only reason it hadn't already been extended was because the existing interceptor and its tributary sewers all leaked and the state Health Department had placed a moratorium on extensions. Lake Roland, a nearby reservoir, and the Jones Falls (stream) along its course were severely polluted. The soil in the Green Spring Valley was not suitable for septic tanks at anywhere near the zoned one-acre densities and the lack of an off-site sewer connection had held development back this long.

Very clearly, the Rouse development could be approved only if there was a sewer extension, and Rouse was a most persuasive person. We advised the council they must sit tight until we had further evidence. Fortunately Rouse's option ran out in December and the pressure would be temporarily off.

THE WORK PROGRAM DETAIL

Our work program had spelled out three parallel tracks of investigation: the ecological inventory and visual analysis with McHarg in charge; predictions of uncontrolled growth that I directed; and alternative plans to accommodate the growth by diverting as much of it as possible to environmentally acceptable locations, which we battled over, and a final synthesis that we jointly prepared. Working with McHarg was never easy and many shouting matches were involved. He was a bully, but never held a grudge after a fight. As we worked and fought, I began to develop a technique necessary to hold my own by challenging his suppositions rather than his conclusions.

The Baltimore County Department of Planning did not like the "uncontrolled growth" label. Its implication was that their work had no real impact except at the subdivision level, which was more or less true, so we stuck with it in spite of their complaints. Our basic approach was to develop a plan based on a "presumption for nature," then see how much uncontrolled growth conflicted with it, and finally prepare a process of guidance and control needed to minimize conflicts and accommodate development demand.

Bill Grigsby and Paul Niebank used the Baltimore Regional Planning Council regional and subregional projections as the data base. As the planner, I had decided on a "handicraft" modeling technique to project "what was likely to happen" after considering various mathematical approaches then current at Penn as unworkable at our level of detail and data. Bill McDonnell and I began a sketch outline of the uncontrolled growth model in five-year increments. First subdivisions already under way, land for sale, and those most likely to be approved were mapped and we assumed they would absorb finite amounts of the projected figures at various lot sizes the market dictated.

The model was reasonably reliable at the beginning, becoming more problematical over the 20-year projection period, while our consultants and we puzzled over how to divert or otherwise control growth. For example, could you market the same size house on a half-acre lot with common open space as was typically on a five-acre lot? In June, Ann Louise Strong produced a memo on "The Development Corporation Conception" that we sent it to members with a legal opinion attached. It noted the possibility of a "syndication" as a limited partnership rather than a corporation to avoid double taxation.

Data on past development and present populations was assembled. The area was 94 percent white, the median income was $8,744 ($6,199 for Baltimore SMSA), and 45 percent had lived in the same house in 1955 and 1960 (51 percent in BSMSA). A recent Baltimore Metropolitan Area Transit Study (BMATS) predicted that by 1980, 65 percent of now vacant or agricultural land would be developed in the near-in valleys. The population would increase from 26,964 in 1960 to 80,000 by 1980 to 110,520 by 2000. Most growth would be on the east, west, and south. We accepted these estimates and economist Morton Hoffman's (1962) sector allocations, which he had done for the Baltimore Regional Planning Council as the basic "attraction rate" or market demand of the Valleys.

Our earlier generalizations about the present population were confirmed by the demographics. It was in three categories: Rich, social people lived on estates and gentleman farms mostly in the Green Spring and Worthington valleys; newcomers had houses on three- to five-acre lots and in expensive subdivisions on the fringes of the big valleys, the Caves, and on the plateaus; villagers, farmers, and tradespeople were on scattered roadside development or in hamlets.

The U.S. Geological Survey had not yet developed its FEMA mapping for the area, so Reds (M. Gordon) Wolman at Johns Hopkins University applied a new shortcut method for 50-year floodplain determination, which we found extremely helpful. It confirmed our own calculations that were based on soil types. Wallace Knight of the U.S. Soil Conservation Service reported that there were four tentative dam sites in the Worthington Valley and others to come. We discovered that most of Caves Valley, a smaller central area all of which was for sale, was a 50-year floodplain. We also discovered by looking at geology maps that the three valleys were underlain by Cockeysville Marble—an aquifer or water-bearing rock that was very possibly connected underground to the Loch Raven Reservoir to the east. While he could not get proof, McHarg asserted that pollution of the underground water in the valleys would affect Baltimore's water supply. Even well-designed sewers leak as much as 20 percent.

The huge effect of the sewer issue hit us. All of these lovely valleys were virtually undevelopable except at very low densities unless a major interceptor was placed in the Green Spring Valley. If it were, the valleys would be developed first, then the hillsides, then the plateau. All that would be left of the area's present character would be street signs and postal addresses.

In July, the council's executive committee met with Rouse for his advice on our planning work. He confirmed that he had dropped his option for the 100 acres. He encouraged the committee regarding its objectives and said, "…it's a tough problem, but more likely to be soluble here than anywhere I know." However, Rouse went on to say that adoption of a plan may foreclose the opportunity for introducing the development corporation idea. "A landowner sees that his property will become a shopping center in the plan, so why should he participate," Rouse added. Nevertheless, Rouse warned against compromising at the outset. He predicted that the overall values attributable to development with a plan will be substantially greater than without a plan. However, the real motivation would be the quality of living that a good plan could provide. Rouse seemed preoccupied and rumors were rife that he had big plans elsewhere, which turned out to be the huge new town of Columbia, Maryland, outside Washington, D.C.

In an August interim report to the membership, the actions of the council were reported as follows: "Highly encouraging and of vital significance to the development of the plan, is the fact that potential developers have, in nearly every area, been seeking our advice and assistance…. Those who have contacted us are withholding their final plans so that their proposals will logically fit our plan." Through these apparent victories, the council had clearly gained credibility and stature.

THE PLANNING PROCESS

The concept of modeling change became central to our planning practice. If you can create a reasonably accurate description of change that is likely to happen under normal market conditions (uncontrolled growth), then you can evaluate that change and develop methods on actions to take to modify aspects you don't like. You can develop normative (prescriptive) concepts, compare them to the uncontrolled growth and see what steps you can take to change the future.

In the *Plan for the Valleys*, the planning problem then was to determine the optimum development of the Valleys area consistent with a high level of amenity and good public policy, then compare it with uncontrolled growth, devise a process to achieve the optimum, and provide a mechanism to enable it to happen. The concept of modeling change became central to our planning process.

The "uncontrolled growth" model that showed development in five-year increments was reasonably predictable in the early stages. It was translated into a pattern of development that we labeled "The Spectre of Uncontrolled Growth." It literally scared the hell out of everyone. The growth modeling idea and procedure, I now see, were the progenitors of the susceptibility-to-change and probability-of-growth modeling that became a trademark of my firm's Lower Manhattan and other central city assignments. As part of the pragmatic process of planning, it represents "What is likely to happen?" and allows the planner to then evaluate "How do you like it?" and "What can you do about it?" For the Valleys plan, a benefit-cost analysis was developed to help answer some of these questions based on three perspectives—the county's, the residents' and property owners', and the developers'.

Planned alternatives included designating the fundamental amenity, the major valleys and wooded areas, as the *genius loci* from which development must be diverted through public control and private persuasion to establish the basis of restrictions, and development of planned "amenity alternatives" as minimum and optimum plans. We then selected an optimum plan and implementation programs.

Once we came to this conclusion, we involved the clients, the county planners, and the regional planners in the development of alternatives. They also were involved in the implementation, feedback, and revision. The role of an Optimum Plan, setting sights high and establishing principles, was central to this process.

THE CAVES VALLEY CRISIS

In September 1963, we discovered that a local developer, Samuel Gorn, in association with a national firm, Gulf American, had an option on 1,355 acres of The Caves, just to the northwest of the Green Spring Valley drainage basin. Gorn had previously approached us to do a plan for him. We had advised the GSWV and Gorn that we had a conflict of interest and could not work for him. But now, with GSWV's approval, we were authorized for a special study of The Caves for $3,500, which Gorn paid. The sewer was again the issue. We concluded that most of Gorn's land should not be developed based on emerging principles of the plan and the natural limitations of his site—a large part of it was a floodplain.

The issue was not that easily resolved. Gorn's proposal brought to the surface the divided nature of our constituency. My observation was that the Jewish community was more residentially segregated in Baltimore than any other city I knew of in the United States—the dividing line went up the Jones Falls Expressway and along Park Heights Avenue with few Jewish families to the east and a predominantly Jewish population to the west. Gorn, who had always built for the "Jewish market" clearly intended business as usual. The Caves Valley would be a geographic extension of the largely Jewish, Liberty-Reistertown Road-Park Heights sector.

The Green Spring and Worthington council's membership was both Jewish and Gentile. Neither group wanted the historic division perpetuated, or at least was not willing to say so publicly. This feeling added impetus to our study of the Gorn proposal.

We conducted a preliminary site plan for the Gorn property, which showed two conflicts of our principles with his ideas. His site would produce less than half as much housing as he wanted, with no "R&D" industry at all, which he said was an essential. The most suitable housing sites were on the northern side of the Caves Valley, where Gorn said he could not begin because it would not be contiguous with existing (and Jewish-owned) housing. We arrived at a stalemate, but the council stood firm and told Gorn it would oppose him.

PRINCIPLES FOR DEVELOPMENT AND SKETCH PLANS

The uniqueness of the GSWV area was clearly in the sweeping openness of the three major valleys surrounded and contained visually by the wooded hillsides. The Gorn experience firmed our resolve that these must be preserved intact if the area's basic amenity was to be retained. We established the following principles as a trial: do not build in the valleys; build at one house per at least three acres on wooded hillsides as the maximum density that could still preserve a majority of the trees; build at a maximum of one house per acre on wooded plateau; and on open plateau and major promontories build at as high density as feasible within market constraints and good design standards. The one- and three-acre densities resulted from empiric observation of how dense development can be and still retain woods. We called the result of these principles applied literally to the GSWV area the Truth Map. It was to become a new kind of zoning based on environmental determinism rather than on economics. We had the courage of convictions, and were still pretty unsure, but we were convinced the result would undoubtedly scare our client as well.

In October 1963, we made the first sketch plans based on the Truth Map. The concept of "testing" the resulting development pattern was evolved. Could the pattern accommodate the housing market as forecast by Grigsby and Niebanck? Because the usual engineering route of sewers up the valleys was out of the question as a method of serving the plateaus alone, was there another way to still efficiently sewer major development on the plateaus? Did the environmentally derived development pattern make sense, or was it chaotic? How did it fit into regional concepts of form (already published by the Regional Planning Council)? How much would current highway plans have to be changed to guide growth toward our development concept? Would the cost of open space exceed the increases in value attributable to greater intensity and efficiency of development?

At this point, Rouse's new town in Howard County was announced in *The Sun* under the headlines "Howard City Plan Stirs Concern" and

Unforested Plateau Development

Forested Plateau Development

Forested Valley Walls Development

7.4 Different intensities of development were recommended for forested valley walls, forested plateaus, and unforested plateaus.

"Howard Project Stirs Wariness." The name for the new town had not yet been selected (it was later called Columbia). This news helped create a climate favorable to the GSWV planning. People began to think bigger, although as usual the general reaction was that Rouse was in over his head. Rouse had by now apparently dropped the 100-acre proposal in the Green Spring Valley.

In November 1963, our sketch plans were complete. It turned out that by extending a major trunk sewer from east of the GSWV, the plateaus could be efficiently served. We began the examination of the sketch plan to see how proposals "fit" implementation devices. Would it also be doable under the current administrative and legal framework? Grigsby's market forecast indicated that all demand from small-lot construction could be met in the next 10 years *without* entering the valleys, but he warned us, "beware encouraging too much development as it will discourage builders elsewhere and accelerate and snowball in GSWV."

We had completed a map of current values and after checking them against sales and with appraisers, we began an estimation of annual values generated by the proposed development based on calculations of increases or decreases in value. We used the English new town planning experience as our precedent. Our concept was the same one underlying the "compensation and betterment" mentioned in British legislation.

As part of our "testing," in November 1963, we met with county planners for the second time on the sketch plans. Initially, we got a good reaction, but the planners obviously needed to be more involved in what we were doing. Nevertheless, we could not let them slow us down at this point or we would lose our momentum and our shirts, so all was not sweetness and light. We clearly represented "project" planning to them at a large scale. It was clear the planners worried that the GSWV would set in motion pressures that would force their hand on allocation of capital projects and resources and in plans for adjacent areas. They felt we were committing them in advance of their "comprehensive plan" that they said was not far off. But when? Who knew?

By December 1963, we received a letter from Baltimore County that stated that the planning staff generally approved the sketch plan and emphasized the need to consider indirect costs and benefits. However, the letter went on to say that our concepts were inconsistent with the regional planners's recently released Metrotown report. We disagreed and showed them that the GSWV area was mostly an "interstice" between two proposed Metrotowns—a further reason for limiting growth to the amount projected for the Valleys by Morton Hoffman, whose forecasting work was our point of departure.

However, the regional planners were by then reported to be enthusiastic about GSWV itself being one of their Metrotowns instead of an interstice. They had been clearly been influenced by Jim Rouse's Columbia New Town and wanted one of their own. (Remember Grigsby's comment about "snowballing.") We resisted this because, by their own criteria, no part of the GSWV area qualified as a Metrotown center. It was clearly and interstice between Reistertown and Owings Mills.

We were not trying to attract more population than would be obtained from uncontrolled or otherwise planned growth. This controversy was an aspect of the usual conflict between project or area planning and the notion of comprehensiveness. We developed from this consideration the position that the GSWV had certain obligations to the region (and county): to accommodate growth with a wide variety of housing types and people; to provide adequate alignments for regional movement east and west; and to produce taxes and support services commensurate with a balanced development. We concluded that the GSWV did not have to, and should not, compete with nearby job and regional shopping centers.

Because the county and regional planners had proposed the nearby centers they could hardly disagree. Also, as a point of fact, the county planners, for all their protestations to the contrary, did not, and would not, have anything like an overall master or comprehensive plan in the foreseeable future. Unfortunately, they did not have the staff for it, nor were they likely to get it.

"ABSOLUTELY IMPOSSIBLE"

Just before Christmas, 1963, GSWV chairman Karsten wrote us a letter "blowing the whistle" on our Optimum Plan. He said, "What gives me the greatest pause is that we are almost certain to be in the posture of going to our constituents with a beautiful plan that is absolutely impossible of achievement." He urged that we tailor specific recommendations to specific subareas and have a strategic "drop-back-and-punt" contingency scheme as well. Recognizing that Karsten was right, we called a conference with our subconsultants and our clients.

The conference cleared the air and by January 1964, a so-called Technical Report was under way. We responded to Karsten on two fronts. With Ann Louise Strong and Bill Grigsby, we worked out a "progressive accumulation of controls," starting with those already available. We also developed several "sub-optimum" schemes that would give the council a way of achieving the "least-worst," if not the best results. Karsten was encouraged, particularly when Bill McDonnell reported the results of the first "financial test." Unplanned growth would generate $33 million in land value increases, $7 million less than the $40 million-plus generated by our plan for the valleys. This great news encouraged Karsten.

The bad news was that in January 1964, we received a letter from Herbert Wagner, a member of the GSWV planning committee and chairman of the finance committee, who said the members were uneasy. He asked for a detailed report on our employees, costs, and what we were up to. He said, "Frankly, the members and subscribers are getting a bit restless, especially since we just sent out the final pledge billing."

Our reply included our current job budget, still not supplemented by the funds we had requested when the planning area was expanded, and our projected expenses and staff. Besides McHarg and myself, we had one full-time (McDonnell), two temporary, and four part-time employees, two professors and five students working part-time as consultants, a geological consultant, and a real estate consultant. The total time spent to that date was between 750 and 800 workdays. I began to realize that the council was treating the contract as cost-plus with an upset limit.

We decided to give the committee assignments to occupy their time and involve them in the work. This became a planning principle we followed in our later work. We suggested that, in addition to our own work, the steps from there on out might look like this: the GSWV should retain a full-time executive director; broadly based committees of the membership should be established to work on various specialized programs; the GSWV should press for adoption, by county and state, of recommended policy and control devices to implement the plan; a development organization (syndicate) and a conservation trust should be created; the program should be widely publicized to enlist countywide support; and planning consultants should be retained to develop detailed area plans as needed.

In February 1964, Strong reported that the "forest zoning," which we had counted on, wouldn't work. Nicholas Muhlenberg, a professor in McHarg's department and a forestry expert said, "No forest is profitable unless it is part of a lumber company's total operation, i.e., restricting land to this use will cause a serious drop in market value." So much for that.

We then met with Gorn—who was still proposing to develop The Caves Valley—and said we had advised the GSWV to completely oppose his efforts. Armed with our information, the council was psychologically ready for the confrontation and convinced they could probably win in a court fight.

In March 1964, the Technical Report was completed and submitted to the executive committee in draft form. Their reaction was that it was too long and that we must tone down the "black-white thing," language that we had included about the need to have an open market for housing as a public policy. We agreed that it was too long and started preparation of the non-technical publication, the *Plan for the Valleys.* The Technical Report length was caused by our desire to record all basic data, steps of analysis

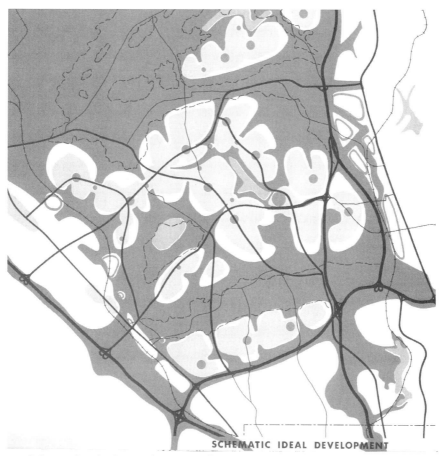

7.5 Schematic Ideal Development shows intensive development along Interstate 80 at the east, and Reisterstown Road at the west, both areas being proposed as Metrotowns by the Baltimore Regional Planning Commission. The dots in the diagram represent hamlet and village centers.

and synthesis, to enable the reader to understand as completely as possible the reasons for each conclusion and recommendation, and the basis for each assumption, be it of fact or value.

On the issue of race, we had said in the first draft that the GSWV area must accommodate a wide variety of housing types and income groups. By inference this meant, inevitably, affordable "town houses," a euphemism for row houses. All housing would be accessible to minority households. Baltimore in general, and a lot of our constituency in particular, were very southern in attitude. Council members cited the usual argument that an important reason for moving to the county was to get away from African-Americans. We pointed out that they could not morally or practically sustain a plan that excluded moderate- and low-income families, and that if they expected their plan to be consistent with public policy they had to accept this fact.

The council's response was to agree with us, but to ask us to "play it down" in the interest of political feasibility. They said they knew that African-Americans and moderate-income housing would inevitably come to the GSWV area, and that our statement for a "wide variety of housing types" denoted a wide variety of income, and therefore minority, groups. We left it at that and said, "The Valleys area must accommodate as full a variety of housing types as possible."

THE POLITICIANS, WMRT, AND SPIRO T. AGNEW

The pace had quickened by April 1964. As publication of the plan proceeded, we continued a series of meetings with county officials and property owners. The comments varied. McDonnell, who conducted most of these meetings, reported on an informal meeting with selected county councilmen, who said, "We will have to go a long way before getting any formal approval or support from council. We will have to force their hand." A frequent reaction was "those rich guys (the valleyites) are going to make a lot of money, so why should we help them?" It became clear that the latent antagonism of the "have-nots" in the rest of Baltimore County against the "valleyites" was formidable. In terms of county legislative action, the attitude seemed to be "Why should we do anything for them?"

Nevertheless, for good or ill, we had completed our contract assignment. At this point, McHarg and I realized that Bill Roberts, who had been working as a consultant, and Tom Todd, who since October 1963 had been working as an employee on the master plan for the Inner Harbor, were invaluable. At first we asked them to be associates; Wallace-McHarg briefly became Wallace McHarg Associates. After much argument about everyone's relative worth, we made them full partners, and the firm became Wallace McHarg Roberts & Todd.

After publication of the plan, Bill McDonnell would leave our employ to become director of planning as a consultant to the GSWV, now called the Valleys Planning Council. He had a budget of $2,000 a month and hung out his shingle as a planning consultant. McDonnell had a well-thought-out program for plan implementation that all of the board did not completely approve, but he had high hopes he could persuade them.

Malcolm Dill, the original director of Baltimore County's department of planning had retired, succeeded by George H. Gavrelis. Gavrelis, chief of comprehensive planning Leslie Graef, and his staff met with us and said they thought it would be ridiculous for us to publish our Action Program. Graef feared the plan and program were too far ahead of planning in the rest of county. McHarg and I noted that the methods we used had wide applicability. The county planners were pessimistic, however.

Reluctantly, the county planners arranged a meeting with County Executive Spiro T. Agnew and members of his administration. Agnew's response was bureaucratic: "If we accept and back this plan, every Tom, Dick, and Harry who ever took a course in drafting will be making plans for areas of the county. The large lot-conservation zone proposed in the plan is completely unacceptable. I even have doubts about the R-40 or one acre lot as possibly being unconstitutional . . . a taking without just compensation . . . little should be said of the guiding role of the county in the development of the plan."

All of Baltimore County, outside urbanized areas all the way to the Pennsylvania state line, had been zoned for R-40 (one-acre) lots a number of years before we entered the scene as a kind of holding action, absurd on the face of it. However, Agnew pointed out one good thing, that our efforts would "force" a closer relationship between public works and planning in Baltimore County. He said that if we could get owners to not develop or to sell development rights to developers voluntarily he might go along. But at least he agreed "in principle." Agnew shortly thereafter went on to become Vice-President of the United States.

In May 1964, McDonnell reported that state roads commission chairman John Funk's reaction to the plan's proposed alignment of Jones Falls Expressway extension and location of the highway access to it on the plateau was positive. Funk said the county should put it on their Highway Master Plan, according to McDonnell.

With this encouragement, we informed the county planners that we were about to release the plan. They panicked, feeling we should be willing to settle for the "sub-optimum" and not oppose several key developments that would violate the plan. We told them we were advising the GSWV to fight for the plan. The county planning office was having particular difficulty with the "over R-40" zoning category. Strong's earlier opinion on their reaction was that ". . . implementation and administrative details were not thought out . . . too tentative . . . and would run serious constitutional risk in the Green Spring Valley."

After his public comments, Agnew agreed off the record to join with the GSWV opposition to the Jones Falls sewer extension to the 100 acres at Falls and Valley roads. However, Agnew reportedly was not sure of his legal position. He is said to have admitted that no owner had a "right" to a sewer, but if the owner was willing to pay for it, he felt that the county must have good grounds for denying it. Agnew informally agreed with us, at least in principle, that since the GSWV had areas for intensive housing, low-density zoning (for three- to twenty-acre lots) might be supportable.

In June 1964, the *Plan for the Valleys* was finally published and distributed. At this point Wallace, McHarg, Roberts, & Todd's contractual relationship with the GSWV came to an end. Our non-professional relationship continued, including happy visits to the running of the Maryland Hunt Cup in the Worthington Valley and tailgate lunches with crabcakes from Thompson's Sea Girt restaurant on Old York Road. From then on McDonnell took over the prime responsibility for implementing the plan.

8

The Valleys Planning Council: 1964–1972

County Executive Spiro Agnew's acceptance of the plan, guarded though it was, enabled McDonnell and the GSWV to act as though it had the approval of Baltimore County. It also enabled McDonnell to nurse a closer liaison with the county staff.

Nevertheless, there was considerable jealousy on the part of the county planning staff. They publicly applauded the efforts of the private sector, while privately indicating displeasure at the proposals, "many of which will doubtless take years to implement, if ever, and some of which are, in fact, their own ideas that for one reason or another they were not able to publicize."

On the private side, a group of large landowners within the GSWV membership, mistakenly or not, perceived the plan as an abrogation of their vested constitutional rights to hold or dispose of their individual properties any way they wanted. As a consequence, some of the active members of the executive committee of the council, which managed the development of the plan with the consultants and staff, reverted to a rather conservative stance with respect to the more influential and wealthy members. This attitude prevailed for several years to follow.

Although the council had followed our suggestion and hired McDonnell as the full-time director, they began to make many decisions secretly, with the advice of various real estate lawyers, out of context of any professional planning advice. Many of the council's members and citizens of the community-at-large had been impressed with the continuing success of downtown Baltimore's Charles Center (now about halfway along in its program) and would have liked to see some immediate phys-

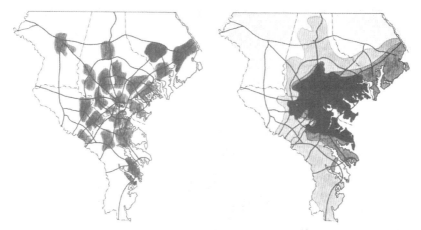

BALTIMORE REGIONAL GROWTH

8.1 Figure 1 (left above) shows the Baltimore Regional Planning Commission's concept of the valleys as a Metrotown contrasted with uncontrolled growth in Figure 2. The *Plan for the Valleys* proposed a third alternative.

ical accomplishment through the *Plan for the Valleys*. They wanted buildings on the ground and in the right places, open space dedication, and total government support at the outset, immediate acceptance of the plan by builders and developers as if it were firm county policy and immediate rezoning to match the plan's land-use proposals. When these things didn't happen, these council members tended to become disillusioned and no longer came to meetings.

In sum, the implementation period began with the leadership bent on success but moving with great caution and deliberate constraints. Had Agnew stayed on the local scene and out of jail, and taken a stronger and more positive position at the start, the council's leadership would have doubtless been bolder in its attitude and the pace would have quickened. Nevertheless, with a reluctant county administration, a conservative stance on the part of local planners, and a negative and warning attitude on the part of a segment of influential members of the council, implementation began. Support would come slowly.

A LONG CAMPAIGN AHEAD

It was clear at the outset that quiet and deliberate moves were needed to gain acceptance of the plan on all fronts. Officers and individual members of the council found themselves "evangelizing" throughout the business day and during leisure hours, supported by detailed weekly progress reports on his grassroots work from McDonnell.

The basic strategy was very simple—and very timid. The president and six-man executive committee were responsible for the management of the council and the planning program; McDonnell reported directly to the president, more often than not on a daily basis, and to the committee in writing each week. Each committee member discreetly spread information to friends and neighbors on request or when opportune.

McDonnell formally and informally presented the plan to every local and state agency and some federal organizations as well, to local developers, real estate operators, engineering professionals, garden clubs, schools, and any interested groups and individuals. Within the first months of operation, much of the initial apathy was overcome.

The county planning board and the local soil conservation district adopted resolutions approving the plan in principle. The Regional Planning Council began its own physiographic studies of the entire region using the techniques established in the *Plan for the Valleys*.

The council committed itself to involvement in two major zoning cases and developed a policy whereby it could assist all parties in an area where a rezoning was requested in making available detailed studies by its staff, consultations with protesters's attorneys, and legal assistance. *Fortune* magazine gave substantial positive coverage to the plan. *Landscape Architecture* devoted a full and praiseworthy article to the plan in its April 1965 issue.

At this point the council had varying degrees of involvement with approximately two dozen proposals for development. Only two went to rezoning hearings. The balance of developers either withdrew or deferred action after consultation with the council's staff. The council presumably rationalized this action with respect to contributions to the council versus the cost of lawsuits, were it not for the fact of the council and its plan, all of these cases (23) would have been heard by the zoning commissioner and possibly through the court of appeals and the enormous costs involved would have been borne by individuals in the area.

Through 1965, the council increasingly hoped that a deliberate "soft sell" program might work. National publicity, acceptance of the plan by local planning agencies, an increase in membership contributions, and successes with a number of hard-nosed developers seemed to support this view. Some still felt, however, that they should "see something." They wanted visible evidence of the, by now, total expenditure of $125,000, at least something beyond "the pretty little green book." The executive committee's attitude toward this was that while visible evidence such as a new community *à la* Columbia was not present, some limited success had been achieved.

To recent settlers of the Valleys, membership on the Valleys Council provided the opportunity to become involved in the affairs of the community. The rewards of participation were similar in kind but greater in degree than those offered by the many local improvement associations. The council stated: "Our responsibilities go well beyond the garden variety improvement association . . . what we have to deal with is the landscape, and the future of the land is our responsibility."

Although the *Plan for the Valleys* at this point had negligible impact on general county development policy, it nevertheless had some influence on routine decisions of county administrative agencies. The wealth of technical information that the Valleys Council made available to the county agencies and its willingness to provide technical assistance through Bill McDonnell were primary sources of the council's influence in the county's administrative decision-making process.

The Baltimore County Office of Planning and Zoning had found in the Valleys Planning Council a valuable constituency in promoting its aims in government administration. The county administration for the first time indicated a recognition of planning by its endorsement of the *Plan for the Valleys*. A number of business firms encouraged their executives to become active on the council. This provided the upwardly mobile executive an opportunity to get in the spotlight without placing an inordinate demand on his time. Commercial and industrial firms that participated in the Valleys program found the plan promised to protect their investment in property.

The Regional Planning Council viewed the council's effort as a valuable experiment in using private agreements to execute sub-regional plans. Speculative builders as well as investors in real estate were among the most generous contributors to the council. Also, many large landowners subscribed to the Valleys Council because they could see the plan promised to protect the value of their property. Their contribution (10 percent of the tax bill on the assessed value of their property annually) was a form of insurance on their property.

By 1966, the council could look to some progress and many developing problems. On the progress side, 600 acres of land in the Green Spring

Valley, the area most susceptible to development, were placed in multi-partite conservation agreements. Their owners agreed not to develop for a three-year period. The county's planning staff asked the council's help in drawing up new land-use regulations, particularly a proposed Planned Development District. The council's development review committee completed studies of a number of plans submitted to the council by developers. The resultant degree of cooperation was very encouraging. Students at the University of Maryland Law School conducted a study of legal problems involved in the creation of the syndicate or development trust and a 32-member committee of the American Bar Association released an article studying in detail the legal proposals put forth in the *Plan for the Valleys*.

By 1967, the council had assumed the complexion of a quasi-public agency, quietly and "gratefully" accepted by the county administration. Some restraint had been placed on what had previously been a hit or miss and somewhat random policy of utility extensions by the county council. School sites in conflict with the *Plan for the Valleys* were eliminated from county plans. The construction of private sewage treatment plants was prevented when several proposals were defeated through the efforts of the council. The county planners and the Soil Conservation Service developed a coordinated program of soils mapping for the county; and the zoning commissioner was obviously impressed with the council's work and prestige as he endeavored to bring developer and council together in zoning disputes. In 1967, the council spent more than half its budget on the review of 28 development proposals, and a quarter in developing the multipartite agreements among members in the Green Spring Valley and continuing detailed planning studies. The remaining 25 percent of its work was devoted to coordinating the plan with various local, state, and federal agencies.

BRUSH FIRES

Facts of geographic and economic life and a conservatively "constructive" approach to specific problems were the council's chief tools in trying to implement the plan. Brush fire after brush fire was put out. The county proposed the creation of a sanitary landfill on 200 acres of farmland north of the Worthington Valley. The issue of refuse disposal had been argued for months in the county council after Agnew's proposal to develop a policy of incineration was defeated. McDonnell began working as a liaison between area residents and the county's engineering staff. The council's position was that a dump is an industrial land use and should be in an industrially zoned region. The council hired an independent engineer and got a grudging 30 days from Agnew to develop an alternate location.

The best the council was able to find was land near a large commercial quarry. The site was previously rejected by the county. County engineers feared that seepage from a dump there might pollute ground water flowing into the metropolitan area's water supply at Loch Raven Reservoir. While the council's engineer believed that this could be overcome by sealing the site against seepage, the county engineer refused to believe it. The council's members showed up 250 strong at a Baltimore County Council meeting when the matter was considered. In the face of this opposition, the county council voted almost unanimously against acquisition of the farm property, and a method was quickly found to seal the bottom of the site chosen by the council.

It was an important victory because it focused the purpose of the entire program of the *Plan for the Valleys*. If the site originally selected by county engineers had been developed as a landfill, it would have caused a mass exodus from the area, with widespread selling of land and speculative buying—precisely the kind of disorder that the Valleys Council was trying to avoid. The incident also showed the council strength.

Because of the apparent success of the operation during 1967, the council's officers decided to continue the minimal program and not to expand. As the decision to begin at all was perhaps the most critical decision, the decision to maintain a minimal program was equally as important in a negative way. "Don't rock the boat" became the policy.

In 1968, John Schmidt in *Baltimore* magazine's May issue concluded that ". . . the most apparent effect of the group's work is that the lava-like advance of suburbia, which had already penetrated from Baltimore to the fringes of the 75 square mile Valley area, had been contained for the most part. The green valley floors show no signs of being transformed into seas of closely spaced, look-alike houses, with the only forest in view consisting of multi-array television antennas. A drive through the Valleys today reveals them essentially as they were in the middle of the 18th century when the area was first settled."

Another fire erupted in 1969. A builder, who also was a resident of the Valleys and member of the Valleys Council, proposed to rezone a 114-acre tract in the mideastern section of the area. The council had been informed of his intentions as early as 1964. His land was designated by the plan as permanent open space, but the council's executive committee felt that they did not have the means to prevent the prospective development. However, the developer needed to extend a sewer to his land, which would also be available to the Green Spring Valley, earmarked as one of the major open spaces in the plan. There was an alternative method of sewering the tract in question, and when apprised of the council's intention to block the extension of the major trunk sewer, the developer indicated that he would not request such an extension if the council would not block his effort to develop his property.

The county engineers informed the Valleys Council that the sewer extension to the property in question could be designed to preclude its further extension—that is toward the open areas of the Green Spring Valley. The council decided to negotiate with the developer in an effort to persuade him to incorporate a high standard of design into his project. The developer agreed, and council modified his initial proposal by reducing the number of units by approximately 10 percent and expending open space from 11 to 30 acres.

His plan still substantially violated the *Plan for the Valleys*. When these "secret" negotiations came to light, many landowners were at once incensed that council had not previously informed them of the prospective development and that council had actually assisted the developer in designing the project. They threatened resignation from the council if it continued its support, and one member said he would write a letter to the county newspaper describing the council's "failure to support its membership." As a result, council opposed the developer in the change of zoning, but the change was granted anyway. Only one member resigned from the council, and the development followed the suggestions of the council's review committee. The developer continued to support the council and regularly conferred with it before undertaking a project in the Valleys area.

The council's actions conflicted with the interests of some of its membership in this case, which illustrated an important issue about the strength and cohesion of the organization. The council felt that its existence was dependent on the ability of its leadership to reach compromises between members' interests and organization objectives in conflict situations. But, by 1969 what was the objective of the organization? Was it survival, or was it something more? It was discovered later that the strongest objector to the development had years before sold the land in question to a developer.

STILL UP JONES FALLS CREEK

State and county health departments had long urged that the Jones Falls interceptor sewer, by 1970 still terminating one mile to the south of the Green Spring Valley, should be extended to serve several existing restaurants and a state highway department building that either had failing septic tanks, or no facilities at all. If such an extension were made, the Green Spring Valley would have immediately become susceptible to development and the Valleys plan for all intents and purposes would be abandoned.

This had been like a loaded revolver at the GSWV Council's head for the previous six years. The council had been able to defer the extension of the Jones Falls sewer and to block all efforts on the part of the county, even to the extent of influencing the county council to reject a portion of the countywide water and sewer plan that is required by state legislation and which would have permitted the sewer extension. That was the first legislative action in favor of the plan since its inception in 1964. Opposition to the sewer was so strong, "garnished" by political support, that the county finally decided to hire an outside engineering firm to study both the council's and the administration's "side" of the question. The report was another cliffhanger.

By 1971, the Valleys Council had expanded from an initial membership of 250 to an enrollment of 355 families. Council membership still constituted less than 9 percent of the total population of the area, but 40 percent of the inventory of *open land* was by then owned by persons paying dues to the council. Moreover, the highest concentration of member land holdings was located in those sections of the Valleys considered to have the greatest potential for development. In one such area, adjacent to the Harrisburg expressway on the east, council members held 67 percent of the total undeveloped acres. Similarly, more than 60 percent of all undeveloped land was held by council members in other highly accessible areas.

However, the character of membership was still not representative of the valley's population and a considerable portion of the lack of general support for the plan was for that reason. In 1971, a drive was initiated to expand and broaden the membership.

The Valleys' population as a whole was never highly organized, politically or otherwise. There were no major organizations or groups that based their operations exclusively within the Valleys except for some 35 improvement associations. The associations of recent settlers in the

Valleys generally served subdivided areas on the periphery, and they considered the *Plan for the Valleys* irrelevant to their interests. Older associations, composed largely of the "villager" segment of the valleys' population, were not represented on the Valleys Council. One such group, the Falls Road Association, was composed of farmers and other early landholders who held valuable real estate in the Green Spring Valley. There had yet to be a major confrontation between the Falls Road Association and the Valleys Council, but the *Plan for the Valleys* was viewed by the Falls Road members as a conspiracy of wealthy residents to secure the development value of the area for themselves. At one point the council's reorganization plan envisaged a Council of Presidents of all 35 associations within the total valleys area, an idea that seems naive.

The countywide Citizens Planning and Housing Association and the county League of Women Voters both endorsed the *Plan for the Valleys*, but had not become involved with the activities of the Valleys Council largely because their principal constituencies were improvement associations located elsewhere in the county.

AGNEW'S GONE, BUT THE MEMORY LINGERS ON

The county administration finally endorsed the *Plan for the Valleys*. Consequently, the county's department of public works and office of planning and zoning were officially on record as supporting the efforts of the Valleys Council. A difference of opinion arose over the county's role in implementing the plan. The office of planning and zoning contended that the county should go beyond mere endorsement of the plan and use public resources and policy to assist in its implementation. The principal means by which the county could assist the Valleys Council, according to the director of planning, was for the department of public works to conform to the pattern of development proposed by the Valleys plan when making its decisions regarding the extension of utilities.

The director of the department of public works continued to believe that such decisions could only be responsibly made by his responding to the demand for utilities such as water and sewer, as they arose. The public works director felt the application of planning considerations to such decision making was of secondary importance, and while they might determine the precise route of the extension of utilities, they were irrelevant in deciding whether or not such extensions should be made.

A FRANK APPRAISAL

During the first six years of its operation with the *Plan for the Valleys*, the council accumulated substantial strength and influence with which public and private groups must contend before undertaking a development project in the valleys. Nevertheless, the council had yet to achieve the level of effectiveness needed to implement the plan. Where the council had become involved, there was a failure to distinguish those cases that were relevant to the plan from those which were not, and considerable time, energy, and money were spent on issues which bore little relevance to the plan. Such cases served the special interests of a segment of council membership rather than the needs of the whole.

The lack of full commitment of the council membership to the objectives of the plan was illustrated by their unwillingness to form the necessary mechanisms for the plan's execution—the real estate syndicate and conservation trust. While the delay in tactics had met with a limited success that far, the council, which lacked a formal control mechanism, and was severely constrained in its ability to achieve the basic objectives of the plan. The council membership's failure to view objectives of the plan as compatible with their personal interests was the most serious threat the Valleys plan's proposal of the pattern of development.

According to projections in the 1970s, development pressures would not approach the interior portions of the Valleys until 1980. A tight money market temporarily delayed real pressure on the outer extremities. If, by 1975, the Valleys Council did not have a formal development mechanism in operation, it was doubtful that the main objectives of the *Plan for the Valleys* could be ever achieved.

A massive public relations effort was required. Full-time legal and technical staff were needed. A prototype of development and conservation should have been built by a syndicate or some similar land development cooperative, to show how compensation and betterment could work on a cross-section of the hills and valleys. This example could have demonstrated how quality development could take place in one area, open space and low-density private ownership could be conserved in another, and the overall capital gains in land value could be equitably distributed to syndicate shareholders.

But the Valleys Council couldn't do it. It is fruitless to talk of a "good" plan that people cannot or will not carry out. If the goals had been set lower, as in the sub-optimum plans, might they have been largely achieved? Perhaps. The Valleys would be developed with a somewhat higher level of coherent amenity than would be the case with "uncontrolled growth." But the Valleys would now be developed, make no mistake.

If the goals had been set lower, however, the plan would not have attracted national attention—attention that has kept the council going, creating a climate of credibility and hope. Without that climate, the council would have long since vanished; so would the open space.

The barriers to the successful implementation of the *Plan for the Valleys* are very clear. First was the intransigent attitude of the department of public works in refusing to use public works as guiding agents of change. Instead, sewers and highways continue to be located in response to developers' demands, often in violation of the plan. The second barrier was the council's unwillingness to take positive action in creating the proposed private real estate syndicate (or syndicates) and conservation trust—the development mechanism. In the meantime, the council was, in effect, encouraging considerably less than the Optimum Plan, utilizing few, if any, of the guidelines and controls available for even sub-optimum results. The council officers only partially filled a leadership vacuum. They were capably enough carrying out defensive improvements and association-type activities but they were not willing or able to mount the offensive. They were winning battles, but losing the war. Nevertheless praise for the plan continued as though it was being implemented in full.

When the plan was published in 1965, renowned author Lewis Mumford wrote:

> This Plan for the Green Spring and Worthington Valley is brilliantly conceived and thoroughly worked out, down to the detailed demonstration of a better community pattern, based on the cluster instead of the row, for the individual housing development. In both method and outlook, this is the most important contribution to regional planning that has been made since Henry Wright's original 1926 report on the Development of the State of New York. McHarg and Wallace have shown by constructing an appropriate many-sided model, what great opportunities for improving the human habitat actually exist, once the forces that are now blindly despoiling the landscape and depressing every human value are guided with intelligence and imagination to more valid goals. The Plan For The Valleys, in both its method of approach and its human aims, should serve as a pattern for all future efforts to conserve life values in a growing community, where uncontrolled or misguided developments may, as in so many parts of California, obliterate the very natural advantages that stimulated this growth. This report should guide, not only the farsighted Council that brought it into existence, but communities all over the United

States that are confronted with similar problems, who have too often been frustrated and deformed by ill-conceived highway and residential settlement plans, and which can be saved or improved only following the strategy that The Plan For The Valleys has worked out.

The basic WMRT fee for the plan was $43,000 including our legal consultant (Ann Louise Strong), economist (William G. Grigsby), geologist (M. Gordon Wolman), and real estate consultant (James Piper III). Of course McHarg, Roberts, and I spent inordinate amounts of unbilled time, and I won't attempt to estimate what the preparation of the plan really cost in current dollars.

While measured by the degree to which the *Plan for the Valleys* was implemented, it was only partially successful, but the plan itself became famous as a chapter in Ian McHarg's *Design with Nature*. When the book was published, McHarg began a full-time speaking tour around the country, and ultimately around the world, promoting his message and using the Valleys as a prime example. The failure in implementation was irrelevant to him.

9

The Baltimore County 1979 Growth Management Plan

By 1977, Baltimore County's Department of Planning was headed by Marian McCoy, who had watched our Valleys plan being developed with great interest. Spiro Agnew had gone on to become Vice-President of the United States under President Richard M. Nixon. McCoy had talked the county administration into retaining WMRT to prepare a Baltimore County Growth Management Program (BCGMP) which applied the Valleys methods to the rest of the county. The county's 612-square mile land area almost surrounds the city of Baltimore; it extends 24 miles from the city's northern boundary to the Pennsylvania-Maryland state line.

In the *Plan for the Valleys*, we had posited that the essential "genius of the landscape" of northwest Baltimore County is in the great open valleys and the wooded slopes that surround the valleys. Further, development was accepted as inevitable for the general area and it must be accommodated. By observing conservation principles to preserve the valleys as open space, the plateau areas around and between the valleys could absorb all prospective growth without despoliation of the character of the countryside.

In our new assignment, we applied the same planning methods to all of Baltimore County. It was classified as to natural characteristics and current state of development. Growth was estimated, then projected by sub-areas to 1995, and the infrastructure and public facility requirements necessary to support the growth were calculated. It was then fairly simple to determine those areas where the growth would negatively impact important natural resources.

Finally, WMRT outlined the actions that the county could take to avoid or minimize the negative impacts of growth and manage the nature and sequence of change to ensure orderly development consistent with environmental principles.

A major component of this new management approach was the coordination of the efforts of various county departments involved in the development-approval process and in setting up a growth-monitoring process for the county. This process was necessary to weigh the county's investment in providing roads, sewers, water, and schools, and other infrastructure needs for new development, as balanced against investment in stimulating revitalization of older centers and maintaining community service levels in existing communities.

This was one of the biggest and most complex jobs that WMRT had accepted. It had a $500,000 contract. I was partner-in-charge, with David C. Hamme—who had been our on-site project manager for the Inner Harbor Project I Redevelopment Plan—as project associate. David Hamme became WRT's managing partner, and he has now retired. WMRT served as the prime consultant for a team of eight sub-consultants in preparation of the Growth Management Plan and its implementing ordinances.

I was the client's point of contact, general director, and enforcer of discipline. We had picked Zuchelli-Hunter of Annapolis, Maryland, as economic consultant both because of my high regard for Don Zuchelli, and because of his friendship with his neighbor, Marian McCoy.

Don was and is a terrific urban economist with whom I had worked before and have since that plan. Unfortunately, in the middle of the job, he had a disastrous skiing accident and was out of commission for almost a year. He was replaced by his partner, Donald Hunter. Hunter turned in an unusable economic report that was to be the basis for our growth modeling. He adamantly refused to redo it, to my consternation, with the excuse that they were already losing money.

As a consequence, I had to substantially redo the economics and rewrite the report. Furious, I sent both Hunter's inadequate version and mine to McCoy to illustrate what I was up against. She chose my rewritten version. Hunter went out on his own shortly thereafter.

The economic projections of growth were the basis for land utilization allocations throughout the county and for fiscal analysis by Tischler Associates. Six types of growth areas were proposed for the county through 1995: town and community centers; existing communities; new urban development areas; fringe development areas; new rural development areas; and rural and agricultural areas. Allocation of projected growth to these areas would have achieved a development pattern that could be efficiently served with community services that would encourage revitalization of older centers. It also would preserve agricultural areas and natural resources.

Almost all of the county, except for the most urbanized portions, was and still is zoned for one-acre lots but cannot be developed at that or a higher density unless public sewers are provided. The Baltimore County Growth Management Program proposed increasing densities within the urbanizing fringe and designating new development areas to absorb the growth that would otherwise sprawl into rural and agricultural areas. The principal difference in cost upfront would be in the savings in the public sewer system not needed for lower density development.

Although Baltimore County accepted and formally adopted the growth management plan, the administration did nothing to implement its features. Rezoning was never undertaken due to the unwillingness of present resident taxpayers to pay up front for infrastructure to guide growth and provide other facilities for newcomers they didn't really want. The county and county residents's attitude was to wait until development and tax ratables were in place so that the new residents could share in the cost. We should have known better. This attitude can be a fatal flaw in managing growth in any metropolitan area.

THE 1989 SUPPLEMENT TO THE *PLAN FOR THE VALLEYS*

Ten years after the Baltimore County Growth Management Program and 25 years after the original *Plan for the Valleys* was completed, Wallace Roberts & Todd was asked to prepare a supplement to evaluate the status of the Valleys area and to determine how the Valleys Planning Council should respond to continuing development pressure. I had partially retired and this assignment was headed up by Antoinette F. Seymour, our senior associate, with my overview.

Growth had occurred much more slowly than had been forecast for the valleys area and the county as a whole. The *Plan for the Valleys* had anticipated a 1980 county population of 800,000; the actual total was a little in excess of 714,000. However, even with less than expected growth, the state highway department was pressing for a major limited access connection between the two growth corridors, Hunt Valley on the east and Owings Mills/Reisterstown on the west, as part of an outer Beltway system. MDOT's surveys showed that if there were such a connection, it would be heavily utilized and therefore MDOT assumed it should be built.

Our examination of the area showed that, although it would be heavily used if built, the area would be adequately served if it were not, and there did not need to be such a connection. We retained Kellerco from Arlington, Virginia, who conducted traffic studies, which demonstrated that such a connection actually generated traffic demand that did not exist without the connection. And of course such a link between the two corridors would have been the death knell to the retention of the valleys as open space.

The 1989 supplement reconfirmed the validity of the 1964 plan and gave the Valleys Council ammunition to continue their preservation fight. The report emphasized the importance of using zoning and planning and programming of public improvements to reinforce the major mixed-use centers of Owings Mills and Hunt Valley by discouraging competitive development around them, providing light rail systems to serve them, and to link them to downtown Baltimore. Also, among many other actions, we again urged that a transfer-of-development-rights (TDR) program to make open space preservation economically feasible be put in place similar to the TDR program being undertaken by Montgomery County, Maryland. TDRs would allow Baltimore County to do implement the development "syndicate," which was mentioned in the original *Plan for the Valleys.* However, despite the evidence of a successful example, the Valleys Planning Council continued in its limited conservation role.

THE CAVES VALLEY GOLF CLUB

If you include The Caves, as its called, there are actually five major valleys within the 70-square mile Valleys area. The Worthington and Western Run/Belfast valleys on the north area are still almost entirely rural with many large estates and farms in excess of 500 acres. The 1930s-era movie *Rebecca of Sunnybrook Farm* was filmed in the Worthington Valley. The greatest threat to these are the five- to fifteen-acre ranchettes that defile the landscapes of so many metropolitan regions. They are sewered onsite. So far, these valleys have largely escaped the ranchette's influence, but proposals to "improve" Butler and Belfast roads into an outer-outer east-west beltway are always on the horizon.

On the southern end of the Valleys area, the Green Spring Valley, centered on Green Spring Road, is still intact as a visual experience because many estates have been converted to one or another kind of institutional use. The valley is also intact because Baltimore County resists pressure to extend the Jones Falls interceptor sewer into the center of the valley. Development has been minimal and the Valleys Planning Council appears to have won this battle.

But the greater war goes on. In the middle of the plateaus between these two vast valley landscapes is the 1,000-acre valley called The Caves. The Caves Valley has always been at the center of development pressure. Named for its limestone sinkholes over the Cockeysville Marble aquifer of its underlying geology, it is surrounded by houses on two- to ten-acre lots interspersed among the woods and served by onsite septic systems. The Caves had been optioned by Sam Gorn during our *Plan for the Valleys* work in the '60s. Thomas Karsten, our client, lived on the Caves Valley's forested slope, overlooking the open meadows at its base.

By the late 1980s, Kingdon Gould, a developer from Washington, D.C., had purchased the property from Gorn's estate and The Caves became the subject of a bitter rezoning fight. As usual, official sentiment favored development. To sewer The Caves would necessitate extending a major collector through the Green Spring Valley from where it still terminates at the end of Jones Falls.

The idea of buying The Caves from Gould and developing a golf course on part of it is generally credited to Les Disharoon, currently chairman of the Caves Valley Golf Club. At the time, Disharoon was head of the Monumental Life Insurance Company, one of Baltimore's major employers. In this capacity, Disharoon had become increasingly aware of the difficulty of recruiting upper-level managers from out of town without being able to promise them memberships in the region's ethnically restrictive and oversubscribed local golf and country clubs. He enlisted the assistance of other corporate executives—most notably Andre Brewster, managing partner of Piper and Marbury—one of the top lawyers in the city, and together they raised the money to buy Gould out.

The overall Caves property dates back to the early 1700s as an original land grant from Charles Calvert, the fifth Lord Baltimore, to Charles Carroll of Carrollton, a noted barrister, patriot of the Revolution, senator, and author of the State's Declaration of Rights. Originally nearly 3,000 acres, the property was owned by the Carroll family for some 200 years. In 1906, Janon Fisher bought the central 1,000 acres, and in 1936 sold 100 acres to the Breed family from New York. The Breeds built a fine Georgian Colonial mansion that has been renovated as part of the main clubhouse.

Thirty overnight sleeping facilities are in the main clubhouse and five guest cottages were built as part of the clubhouse "campus."

When Disharoon met with the other founders and Tom Fazio, the golf course architect, at the Breeds's mansion, the view of their 940-acre purchase was unhappily dominated by a high-tension power line. Putting that power line underground was a major financial decision reaching into seven figures, but Disharoon reported within several weeks that he had gotten agreement to bury it, so today you wouldn't know there was a major power line there.

More than 450 acres were set aside as a conservation easement. The remainder of the property was developed with a lake, the championship golf course, and home sites for 34 residences on very large lots. Nobody on the board really wanted the housing, but it was argued as necessary for the financial plan, and all reluctantly agreed. Parenthetically, the market for housing disappeared in the early 1990s. The club and course were developed without the added income, and the housing turned out not to be essential to the club's development. Today, the club's leaders wish they had not compromised the area with the residential lots that are now completely built out.

The course is laid out on 200 acres divided among open pasture, forested ravines, and hillsides. More than 7,000 yards from the black tees, it is a true championship course. It hosted the USGA Mid-Amateur Championship in 1995 and the USGA Senior Open in 2002.

The club was to be established strictly for golf and represents itself as a "business" club, and does not discriminate by age, race, creed, or gender. Caves Valley opened in 1991, limits itself to 600 members, and is modeled after Augusta National in Augusta, Georgia. It has club members from throughout the United States as well as Belgium, Italy, England, France, Holland, Bermuda, Hong Kong, and the Virgin Islands.

Although I was not personally involved in the development of the golf club, I cite it as an example of the creative response to problems that I have observed throughout my Baltimore experience. The upshot of the *Plan for the Valleys* and the Baltimore County Growth Management Plan was to propose a boundary for suburban development similar to that in the so-called Portland system for regional growth management in Portland, Oregon, as popularized by architect Andres Duany, the prominent proponent of New Urbanism. Duany, who is from Miami, says the system isn't really working in Portland as the outer line for development keeps getting moved out as growth takes place. He cites Miami-Dade County's natural constraints of the Everglades as the kind of publicly owned barrier necessary to prevent urban sprawl.

10

The Baltimore Inner Harbor

The Caves and the Green Spring and Worthington valleys are at the northern end of the Jones Falls watershed; Baltimore's Inner Harbor is located at the south. Jones Falls flows southward through the city of Baltimore with its creek meandering back and forth under the expressway until the stream disappears in a culvert at Penn Station, then empties into the Inner Harbor south of Pratt Street. One part or another of this hipbone, thigh-bone, ankle-bone, toe-bone connection has been my planning turf since 1957.

In contrast to the considerable, but still only partial, success of the *Plan for the Valleys* and the failure to date of the *Jones Falls Valley Plan*, the *Inner Harbor Master Plan* has succeeded beyond my wildest dreams. Starting with a sow's ear, the city has ended up with a silk purse.

THE INNER HARBOR MASTER PLAN

To cite David Barton from the 1964 Inner Harbor master plan's introduction,

> Twenty-five years ago Baltimore was a city with an inferiority complex, haunted by memories of a golden past, alarmed by threats of a bankrupt downtown, uneducated in the ways and means of urban redevelopment. Many other cities were already on the move. Baltimore, suspended between a heritage it could not resurrect and a destiny it had not yet envisaged, was beset with the problems of obsolescence. Approaching the 1960s, Baltimore was a city without a plan, and worse, a city without a dream. Then came Charles Center as a calculated risk, and with it, the most intensive period of self-education Baltimore has ever experienced.[1]

As chairman of the city planning commission and from an old Baltimore family, Barton had the license to say such things about his city. He went on to say, "What makes some plans surge ahead and others lag is not so much their design—important as this is—but the quality of the public and private leadership with which these plans are implemented."

Charles Center had been conceived in 1959 as the first step—or tactic—in the longterm strategy of downtown revitalization. By 1963, Charles Center's evident success established an investment climate substantial enough to warrant proceeding with the University of Maryland's downtown campus expansion to the west; it also set the stage for the Inner Harbor redevelopment to the south.

In the spring of 1963, shortly after we had started to work on the *Plan for the Valleys*, Bill Boucher called me. He said he was acting for Jim Rouse and the GBC, and, with the approval of then-Mayor Theodore R. McKeldin, for the city. He reported that civic leader Abel Wolman had returned from a trip to Stockholm's harbor and advised McKeldin that the time was ripe to redo Baltimore's Inner Harbor. The city had decided that

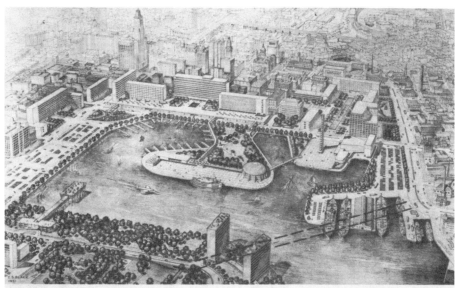

Artist's illustration depicting a possible plan for renewal of the Baltimore inner harbor.

10.1 Shortly after I had moved to Baltimore and begun work in January 1957, Arthur McVoy, the city's planning director, sent me this "artist's illustration depicting a possible plan for renewal of the Baltimore inner harbor." For all I know McVoy may have drawn it himself, but whoever the artist, he or she had some interesting ideas, for example, the building cornice line framing the space.

MDOT had finalized preliminary plans for the Jones Falls and East-West expressways and we could accept their plans as "givens." WRMT would have a budget of $50,000 for what turned out to be a $150,000 job. We started work in early fall under contract to the GBC. We hired Tom Todd, who had been working at the Philadelphia City Planning Commission, on the strength of the contract. He started work October 7, 1963.

How wrong the city was about the Maryland Department of Transportation. The MDOT engineers had adopted literally—and without much detailed analysis of alternatives or impact—a regional expressway concept originated by Arthur McVoy, the city's planning director, in the early 1950s. The engineers, Greiner, Inc., under contract with MDOT, were planning an inner beltway around downtown, a key section of which was to be an elaborate interchange at the harbor's narrow throat in front of Federal Hill. The highways spread spaghetti-like over most of the water but they had avoided Federal Hill. Tom Todd's diagram of "Problems and Opportunities" shows how awful the results would have been.

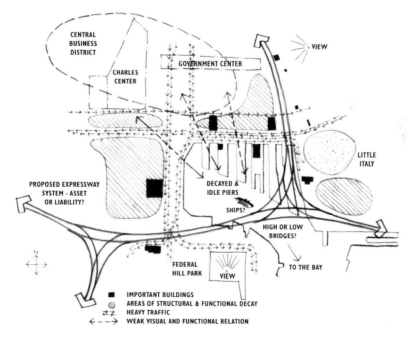

MAP OF PROBLEMS AND OPPORTUNITIES

10.2 Tom Todd's Map of Problems and Opportunities is a good urban design summary of what we were up against.

It wasn't the first time the harbor and Federal Hill were in jeopardy. As open space it has always attracted highway engineers. Federal Hill is largely man-made, composed of clay and sand dredged to deepen the harbor during the eighteenth century. By 1838, Dr. Thomas H. Buckler, ancestor to our Jones Falls Valley plan's sponsor, Warren Buckler, proposed using it to fill in the Inner Harbor, thereby eliminating both the Hill and the Harbor as barriers to the north-south street system. When the proposal was introduced to Baltimore City Council, Benjamin Latrobe, (architect of the White House in Washington and of Baltimore's Catholic Basilica) estimated it would cost $764,346, not including damages. Fortunately the bill was defeated due to opposition of shipyard and shoreline owners. Still, it was a narrow squeak. During the Civil War, Baltimore was known as "mob-town," because of rioting gangs. Cannon were mounted on the Hill to fire on the anticipated unruly mobs across the water in downtown.

We also can thank Henry Barnes for preserving the Inner Harbor until we got there. Barnes delayed the whole expressway program by at least 10 years when he synchronized the downtown traffic signals to improve flow, reduced congestion, and quieted the public clamor for street improvements. I once charged Barnes with this and he admitted that if the expressway program had moved as fast in the 1950s as it did in other cities such as Norfolk, Virginia, or Seattle, Washington, we'd have had an elevated ring over and around the Inner Harbor by 1963. So by indirection, Henry Barnes also saved Inner Harbor.

When we began planning, Tom Todd, our chief of design, and I tried every way we could to realign and redesign the expressway short of getting rid of it altogether. We finally came up with an idea we reluctantly adopted, which was to move the interchange to the east and south from over the water and out of the Harbor's neck. We proposed hiding as much of the elevated roadway as possible by building an extension of Federal Hill in front of the old one. As you can see from the illustration, this became part of the published plan. We also moved the interchange itself away from the Pratt Street piers and the water, designing such attractive—looking housing towers on the piers that everyone on the steering committee immediately saw the potential and MDOT reluctantly agreed to move the spaghetti eastward.

Extending Federal Hill in front of the expressway still did nothing to solve the main problem: the bridge clearance over the Harbor's entrance. Further, the structure would have forever separated the harbor from

10.3 The Inner Harbor in 1957 as seen from my window in the (then) Olin-Matheisen tower. The Inner Harbor was polluted, ringed by parking and traffic, and surrounded by warehouses and small industrial uses, but one could still see the pearl in the oyster of opportunity.

South Baltimore. Even after the Inner Harbor Phase I Redevelopment Plan had been adopted in 1967, the expressway issue still was not resolved. By then we were preparing contract documents for the water's edge and disposition plans for the adjacent land area, and it had become painfully evident that if the expressway was to go over the Harbor's throat, not only would it act as a barrier to the south, it would preclude access by water except for very small boats. The owners of the U.S.F. *Constellation*, the ship we wanted to locate next to Pratt and Light streets, would not allow her to be anchored there if the expressway were built, and other tall ships could never visit.

Martin Millspaugh, president and CEO of Charles Center/Inner Harbor Inc., brought in Lev Zetlin from New York, one of the country's foremost structural engineers, to see if he could come up with an acceptable design solution for a high-clearance bridge. We had always seen the *Constellation* as the centerpiece of the Inner Harbor, both in symbolic and visual terms. Her topmasts reach 185 feet above the waterline, and that was the challenge Zetlin tried to rise to. With a lower bridge, the

Constellation would have to unstep its masts to be refitted, and all other tall ships and most visiting naval vessels would have been barred from entry. As a practical matter the nonprofit corporation that owned and operated the *Constellation* flatly stated that it would not berth her in the Inner Harbor if there were a low bridge.

Using MDOT's engineering design criteria, we had earlier struggled unsuccessfully with the idea of a high-level bridge. Zetlin's heroic effort to make what at this point was a 14-lane bridge look elegant had all the delicacy of a brontosaurus, and, much like that dinosaur, the concept died of its own weight. To give Zetlin credit, he said that if he had been able to study it at the next level of design with computers, he could have slimmed it down considerably. Tom Todd, Bill Roberts, and I finally presented the concept to State Roads Commissioner John Funk, who demolished our arguments with the disdainful statement that MDOT "didn't build bridges." I remember riding home with Todd and Roberts, and doing a sketch of the three of us in the car's back seat with kiddie steering wheels and Funk up front doing the driving.

Ian McHarg, in his usual way, embroidered on this event in his autobiography, *A Quest for Life*. I have no memory whatsoever of the story McHarg tells about his intervention with Lady Bird Johnson, which resulted in Funk being fired to save the Inner Harbor from MDOT's plan. Ian was a great embellisher of facts that, in this case, just didn't happen.

10.4 Charles Center-Inner Harbor hired New York engineer Lev Zetlin to design a multilane bridge to cross the neck of the harbor with 185-foot clearance. Lev claimed that if he had had enough money to put it in the computer he could have slimmed it down considerably. Fortunately SOM's design concept team relocated the expressways to a tunnel at Fort McHenry.

In the end, the solution for the harbor was to get rid of the problem. During the 1970s, Archibald Rogers, still a member of GBC's Planning Council, had become a design adviser to MDOT. The department was being attacked across the state for neighborhood-unfriendly designs. He and Millspaugh persuaded the new State Roads Commissioner, Jerome Wolfe, to hire a "design concept team" with urban design architects to take charge of the state's urban expressway program. Skidmore Owings & Merrill (SOM) of Chicago, headed by partner Nathaniel Owings and project director/urban designer Norman Klein, became the managers and lead designers of the team for a $4 million overview of the whole system.

They found that a 16-lane interchange was needed in the Harbor's throat, the result of three interstate expressways all coming together. Even the engineers agreed this was an impossible idea. So two expressways were shifted to the south where they cross the harbor at Fort McHenry and the third (Jones Falls) ended in downtown Baltimore. SOM managed to get MDOT and U.S. DOT to accept an expressway spur from the west as part of the interstate delivery system to serve downtown. This violated the U.S. DOT's usual stance that spurs were part of the local street network and therefore not federally fundable. Two of the interstates now run east-west under the water in tunnels at Fort McHenry. The Inner Harbor was saved again.

The third, the Jones Falls Expressway (Interstate 83), had been planned to turn east and follow the water's edge to Fells Point and beyond, but it has never been extended south beyond Baltimore Street in the central business district because Barbara Mikulsky, then head of a community group and now a U.S. senator, used the information from the design concept team's impact analysis to mobilize public opinion and kill it. The Inner Harbor East, Fells Point, and Canton neighborhood areas were saved from an elevated monstrosity that would have imperiled the revitalization under way today.

THE *CONSTELLATION*

The fact that a nonprofit corporation owns a former flagship of the U.S. Navy, the U.S.F. *Constellation*, is an interesting part of the story. The navy decommissioned the *Constellation* in 1954 and would have broken her up except for the *Constellation* corporation's intervention. Otherwise, the *Constellation* would still be in the Navy and kept in the Norfolk Navy Yard just as the U.S.F. *Constitution* is anchored in the Navy Yard in Charleston, Massachusetts.

The original *Constellation* was the first ship commissioned by Congress for the young U.S. Navy. It beat the *Constitution* into the water by several months. Plans drawn by Joshua Humphries of Philadelphia had been sent to John Stoddard's shipyard on Harris Creek at Fells Point, just east of the Inner Harbor where she was built. However, according to one theory, Stoddard and Thomas Truxton, the *Constellation's* captain, radically redesigned her during construction. According to the story, that is why the *Constellation* looks like an 1850s frigate. Her as-built drawings are unfortunately not available, having been destroyed in the Washington Navy Yard fire set when the British burned Washington, D.C., in 1814.

A more likely theory for the ship's mid-nineteenth century design is put forth by the Navy's principal historian, Howard Chappell. He says that the original ship was stripped to the keel and completely rebuilt in an 1840s refitting as a way to get around Congress's unwillingness to finance new ships. Chappell argues that only parts of the original keel were used, and therefore she is really an 1850s frigate and "only an old boat." That is why the U.S. Navy decommissioned the *Constellation* to save the upkeep, and it would have broken her up if the present owners hadn't come along.

No matter which side of the argument one takes, she's a handsome and authentically historic ship, flagship of the Atlantic fleet during World War II, native to Baltimore, and with a great naval history if the first theory is correct, and a less-great, but still important, place in history if it's not. So the *Constellation* became the centerpiece and symbol of the rebirth of the Inner Harbor.

INNER HARBOR REDEVELOPMENT PROJECT I

The *Inner Harbor Master Plan* envisioned redevelopment that would require a major city investment, although one that would return many times over what it would cost. Our urban design approach in its preparation had included a study of the intensity of development that would be necessary to generate sufficient residual land value to pay for all redevelopment costs. We knew what we were up against. When Tom Todd and I attended a key meeting of the steering committee arranged by Mayor McKeldin, at which we presented our proposals. Jim Rouse played the crucial role, as he had in the earlier Charles Center days. While he admitted to being skeptical about our numbers, then he said, "Gentlemen, we must not fail to do this." All agreed it would be a prudent investment. Nevertheless, until Baltimore had the initial funds, it couldn't proceed, so for a year nothing happened.

In 1964, two months after the *Inner Harbor Master Plan* was announced, the voters approved a $6 million bond issue, with $2 million earmarked for implementation of the plan. The preparation of the *Inner Harbor Project I Redevelopment Plan* was authorized, and WMRT was hired to assist the Charles Center Management Office, whose name was changed to Charles Center-Inner Harbor Management, Inc., (CC-IH) to reflect the new assignment.

Based on the 1964 Master Plan and a number of special feasibility studies, the *Inner Harbor Project I Redevelopment Plan* was prepared in 1965 by CC-IH and David Hamme, who moved to Baltimore and was our project director. The plan was approved by the city and the federal government in 1966. It dealt only with the one-block deep area along the harbor's edge. In conjunction with CC-IH, we established the design parameters for the first Inner Harbor projects to include the location and

10.5 The model of the 1964 Master Plan illustrates the urban design principles that have largely stood the test of time in the harbor's development: public access to the water and along its edge; Light Street and Pratt Street expanded as boulevards; a continuous cornice line of buildings to create a frame for the open space; the western promenade aligned with Calvert Street and the waterfront area used for both open recreation and small commercial activities; housing on the piers to chase off the highwaymen; and if a bridge was ultimately necessary put it as far south as possible.

character of the water's edge; we divided the land area into various disposition parcels, and developed basic urban design guidelines for each which would illustrate the city's objectives as part of our urban design concept. Most of the guidelines were not made part of the redevelopment plan, so CC-IH would have flexibility in using them as negotiating instruments with developers rather than as legislated straight-jackets on development. They are usually followed, but not always.

We arrived at the overall concept in the master plan through an exercise of the urban design process. Earlier concepts were examined, including Arthur McVoy's. He clearly had the idea of a continuous cornice line, but his horizontal buildings would have only partially framed the harbor. His proposed water's edge was capriciously changed from its historic shape, and the harbor was to be surrounded on three sides by surface parking.

After a series of analytical and parcelization studies, our overall design concept choices boiled down to two clear alternatives. The first concept developed buildings within a loose zoning envelope with random heights and no controls other than the envelope itself, each block self-sufficient in providing parking for its development. The outcome would inevitably result in a variety of visually unrelated towers on parking podiums or towers and attached garage decks with street commercial limited to where the each tower came to ground. The result would have been really no coherent concept at all and very suburban in character.

The second alternative was to frame the harbor with a required build-to cornice line, a line that would extend the length of each block, with first floor commercial uses on at least three sides of parcels. The resulting buildings would act as a backdrop to and a frame for the harbor's edge. Parking would be under-supplied at the front row of blocks, to be supplemented by higher parking ratios away from the harbor's edge to provide an adequate overall supply. The mandatory cornice line was designed to hide the visual chaos of downtown buildings and give an order and sense of design coherence to the harbor from the water. This was the concept adopted.

Our major design decisions have largely stood the test of time. They included the nature and location of the water's edge and Constellation Dock, with the West Shore Promenade as a pedestrian extension of Calvert Street to the north, thus tying it to the central business district. The major tower Tom Todd showed anchoring the harbor's northwest corner was developed as the U.S. Fidelity and Guarantee Building. It was one of

Baltimore's few corporate headquarters. When U.S.F.&G finally fled to the suburbs, it was succeeded by Legg Mason, also a homegrown corporation. The other isolated tower, the one with its "prow" symbolically in the water, was developed as the World Trade Center, home of the Maryland Port Authority. It is the only large building outside the harbor frame—designed by I.M. Pei—and it mirrors Tom Todd's concept quite literally.

The residential towers placed in the master plan on the piers to help ward off the engineers with their expressway spaghetti proved not to be economically feasible at the time. The piers are now occupied by the National Aquarium at Baltimore and the Christopher Columbus Center. Each structure is designed as an "object in space" as opposed to a "space-defining" object. The Aquarium by Cambridge Seven Architects is outstanding. The Columbus Center by Toronto architect Zeidler/Roberts is a less successful design and the commercial portion recently failed as an enterprise.

The harbor's frame is still incomplete. If you stand on Federal Hill, you can see that on the west where the McCormick Building has been demolished and its site awaits development. On the north, the two-block stretch between Gay Street and the Candler Building is a gap in the frame. It was at first underdeveloped in the 1970s by Baltimore Community College. Now the college has moved and the site was awarded to the Kravco Corporation from King of Prussia, Pennsylvania, with architects Cope Linder. I had hoped that the architectural review function and design control would continue to be enforced. During Mayor Schmoke's administration, the board was abandoned and the design review function was placed under the aegis of the director of the department of city planning, advised by a design consultant from Philadelphia, a well-qualified architect named Emanuel Kelly. The board is now composed of local architects and academics.

The experience in Inner Harbor East, where Stanton Eckstut's plan is being abandoned, and in Charles Center, where the covenants are expiring, does not augur well for the future, but I was heartened to learn from Gerald Cope some time ago that his design for the developer Kravco Corporation's hotel/office complex on the old Baltimore Community College site would conform to the plan's design controls. This would complete all but one of the framing cornice lines along Pratt Street. The recent recession has put construction on hold. But Kravco has sold out to Trammel Crow, and in the new design specs there is no hotel, the cornice line abandoned, and the height limit is exceeded by 30 percent. The steel frame is already up as I write.

The original architectural review board that had been set up for the Charles Center project had its jurisdiction expanded to include the Inner Harbor. After much deliberation the board agreed that there needed to be an approved concept, and adopted the one we recommended. The mandatory build-to cornice line was established at 145 feet, which matched roughly the cornice of the old McCormick spice factory on the west shore.

Ironically, the fact that McCormick's was still there at the time to act as a benchmark as we developed the Master Plan was largely due to a crucial decision by Richard Steiner, Robert Embry's predecessor as head of the Baltimore Urban Renewal and Housing Agency. Steiner was a tall, slow-speaking, enigmatic bureaucrat's bureaucrat who had served as federal urban renewal commissioner under President Dwight Eisenhower. Steiner owned a sheep ranch in upper Baltimore County, which he operated as a hobby. When the 1964 Plan model was in preparation, and the buildings not yet glued down, Steiner had lifted the McCormick piece off the model, studied the result, and slowly replaced it. He said it was too big, too expensive, had too much employment, and paid too much in taxes. I agreed and felt that the building was an important part of the city's past that should be preserved.

McCormick's spice manufacturing gave off various marvelous aromas throughout the Inner Harbor, depending on what was being made each day, until the company was bought out and its manufacturing was moved to Hunt Valley in Baltimore County. The property was acquired and the land is owned by Central Parking System of Nashville. I had always hoped the building would be converted to a residential tower, but it was demolished and the site awaits redevelopment while providing surface parking. Proper development of this property is crucial to completion of the harbor frame on the west.

Three elements made our 1964 Inner Harbor master plan and subsequent project redevelopment plan different from many urban design efforts for the harbor and for other similar projects throughout the country. The first was the fundamentally sound economics on which the plan was based. The second was the readiness of a success-hungry city to back a winning program that would clearly change its image. And third, Tom Todd's very believable urban design and conceptual graphics and the design principles they expressed were elegantly persuasive.

In our concept, the continuity of the harbor's frame was to be interrupted at the intersection of Pratt and Light streets with a major vertical lynchpin tower. The tower was to be an object-in-space anchoring the harbor frame from the west and north, and to serve as a visual landmark linking the southern edge of the central business district to the harbor. This tower concept was carried out literally, albeit in a somewhat heavy-handed manner by Vlastimil Kubeck of Washington, D.C., as architect for the USF&G's corporate headquarters. Further, the plan proposed that the central business district was to be bounded by Pratt Street Boulevard and extend no further south to prevent dilution of its intensity, a key factor in making the mass transit system work and a policy component of the 1959 Central Business District plan that had been produced after Charles Center was initially planned. Pratt Street Boulevard would create a dynamic street address for the central business district on the north side, and a location for the Baltimore Convention Center on the south.

On the north shore in the 1964 plan, a short gap in the continuous frame along Pratt Street was to provide for a linear park extending the

10.6 This model shows how the design concept evolved as part of the 1967 preparation of the Urban Renewal Plan for Project One. Pressure for commercial activity resulted in the three rather awkward pods connected across Light Street to larger buildings. These became the basis for the Rouse Company's Harborplace.

harbor's open space north, creating a visual link from City Hall to the harbor at Commerce Street. The park was to be called the Municipal Mall, with the World Trade Center (WTC) to be a vertical focal point at its southern end. Unfortunately, the city has ignored this feature that would have helped link the harbor to the central business district.

I remember when world-famous architect I.M. Pei was commissioned by the Maryland Port Authority to design the World Trade Center in 1969. At our first meeting, Pei's reaction to our plan was to say he must redesign the whole harbor. Like all good architects, he was first questioning the concept in which his building was to play such an important role. After he got through his initial analysis, he realized we had done it right, confirmed our master plan, and the World Trade Center sits with its "prow" in the water just as envisioned by Todd in the plan. Pei's was only one of a succession of challenges and later confirmations of our overall concept. The City Hall Mall is the only element that has never been implemented.

In doing the planning, water uses were just as important as land uses. With the *Constellation* as the centerpiece and no bridge at the harbor's entrance, a logical theme for the water's use was Chesapeake Bay and Baltimore shipbuilding and maritime history. After much study and visits to in-water museums around the country, we and the CC-IH's Millspaugh rejected the concept of an expensive-to-maintain in-water maritime museum, such as Mystic Seaport in Connecticut. Instead, active ships and boats of all sizes were favored, and only the submarine U.S.S. *Torsk*, the Coast Guard Cutter *Taney* and the Light Ship *Chesapeake* are on permanent exhibit, along with the *Constellation*.

DESIGN OF THE HARBOR'S EDGE

The design program for the harbor's water activity is a consequence of water depth and edge accessibility. The deepest water is on the north and northwest, the shallower water on the south. It was important to put large "exhibition" vessels, such as the *Constellation* and visiting destroyers, as close as possible to the passing motorists near Pratt and Light streets to heighten the viewer's sense of drama and immediacy.

After approval of the Project 1 Redevelopment Plan in 1966, WMRT signed a contract to design the harbor's edge, the promenade, and *Constellation* dock. The contract was later amended to include the Pratt Street Boulevard, all landscaping and street furniture outside the shell of buildings, and the pedestrian bridges. After studying many alternatives, we recommended a strong, simple water's edge to reduce cost and to allow as much flexibility as possible for later activities. This meant a plain design. We wanted as much land as we could get on the west shore between Light Street and the water's edge, but we didn't want to reduce the water area.

Not everyone involved saw the design assignment in the same light. Over-design was a frequent temptation. I saw the area between the streets and the water south and east of Harborplace as a flat stage that should be able to accommodate the widest variety of city events as "theatre-in-the-round" as well as "proscenium" events. Mine was the least expensive concept, which was the reason I prevailed.

Never underestimate succeeding generations' temptation to complicate life and screw up a good thing. Sometime in the late 1980s, the city held a landscape competition to which WRT was notably not invited. It was won by landscape architect Martha Schwartz from Boston who developed a really weird scheme for the western edge based on obscure symbolism. Fortunately it was never built, but was a good example of over-design. My friend Walter Sondheim told me that when he entered the room as one of the jurors to help select Schwartz, his reaction to her entry was to say, "Well, that is one we won't pick." Hotter heads outvoted him.

Shoreline changes were nothing new to the Inner Harbor. Until 1784, the harbor had extended a block north of Pratt Street to Water Street with marshes at its edges. In 1784–1785, the area north of Pratt Street was improved by cutting 20 feet off the ridgeline along Lexington Street three blocks to the north where the courthouse now stands, and using the soil to fill to about the present line of Pratt Street. At the same time the marsh south of the new Pratt Street was dredged and the finger piers that were present until 1970 were constructed.

In those early days, the entire edge, north, south, and west, was used by industry, coastal shipping such as the Old Bay Line, and shipyards. There have been 51 shipyards in the Inner Harbor since the first was constructed in 1773, built 44 years after the city's founding in 1729. None remain today. The Bethlehem Ship Repair Yard was the last, replaced with developer Richard Swirnow's Harborview, a luxury apartment tower on top of the old dry dock that he converted to underground parking. There is a yacht club and marina adjacent to the site. Harborview is mostly condominiums, but my friend Walter Sondheim rents an apartment on the 18th floor. An hotel/condominium has been planned to the north on the remainder of the Bethlehem site. I saw the plans the other day, and it fits nicely on the site from an urban design perspective, but unfortunately is in the French Second Empire style and looks like Baltimore's post office rather than a resort hotel. The economic recession of the early 2000s has put that development on hold.

Prior to the 1970s redevelopment, the shoreline on the west had been rebuilt and the shipping removed after a 1950 hurricane drove water over Light Street and flooded the McCormick spice factory's first floor. At a cost of some $7 million, the Old Bay Line terminal and other buildings were demolished, a northbound Calvert Street was added adjacent to and east of Light Street, and a concrete parapet over which one could not see the water from the street was put along the edge. The Inner Harbor had disappeared from ground view.

Our redevelopment plan allocated various portions of the water area to appropriate activities. Large, more or less stationary historic maritime exhibits were to be on the northern edges—the U.S.F. *Constellation*, the submarine U.S.S. *Torsk*, a Chesapeake Bay lightship, and MDOT's harbor tour boat. At that location they have a close dramatic connection with people on the promenade and are easily seen from passing vehicles. Small, rented paddleboats also use this protected area. Visiting ships up to 20 foot draft are berthed along the northern portion of the West Promenade. Shallow-draft visiting ships and working boats, such as the *Pride of Baltimore,* are along the southern portion of this promenade and in the Small-Boat Harbor placed in the center of the West Promenade.

The decision about materials whether the edge and the promenade should be faced with brick or granite became a major controversy. G. Holmes Perkins, then dean of Penn's Graduate School of Fine Arts and a member of the architectural review board, was from Boston, a granite town, and he was in favor of a granite vertical facing to the edge to express permanence. Tom Todd and I were in favor of brick because Baltimore is a brick city, and the edge is not solid but actually hollow, a so-called relieving platform. It is an apron that sits on piles and goes no deeper than the water at low tide, and to make it of stone would imply otherwise. We built a full-scale section of each, and Martin Millspaugh, then president and CEO of CC-IH picked brick with granite trim. It was a crucial design decision.

The water's edge at the west promenade is located on a line with Calvert Street and gives the viewer a sense of the harbor's interrelationship with downtown. The Battle Monument is in view on axis at the top of the rise at Fayette Street. The 150-slip marina on the south embankment is outboard of a granite sloping edge that lets people go down to the water. Here, the edge is solid and not a relieving platform and granite was appropriate. The stones came from the seawall of the old piers at the north edge that were demolished. The marina became very successful in spite of conventional wisdom even as late as 1972 that a marina would never work because the water was too polluted and the number of slips too few. Our response was that as the harbor's development flourished, the sources of pollution would be eliminated.

CC-IH brought in hydrologist Donald Pritchard from Johns Hopkins University. His study was instructive. The Inner Harbor is like a bathtub, its water sloshing in and out, with only a one-foot tidal change. The wind and varying surface and bottom temperatures slowly move the water around. Storm runoff from city streets was and still is the major source of pollution. With these facts in mind, Kenneth Wilson, publisher of the *Afro-American* newspaper, was very courageous when he responded to fellow

10.7 The properties in the Project 1 Urban Renewal Area were being acquired, businesses relocated, and land assembled as the harbor's edge was cleared to become a stage for recreational and entertainment activities.

boater and then housing and community development commissioner Robert Embry's challenge in 1973 to be the operator of the marina. It has turned out to be almost too successful, very popular with the sailing and boating community.

The decision to have no railing at the harbor's edge was based on an extensive study of alternatives, and trips to similar harbors both in the United States and abroad, such as Toronto's Inner Harbor. The fact that ships would dock, load, and unload at any place along and across the edge finally determined the decision. Instead of a railing, granite copings at the edge warn pedestrians to beware of the danger in a fashion similar to a railway platform. In fact, Maryland law says that a body of water is its own warning, but in spite of that, the city, the contractors, the engineers, and WMRT have been sued twice for negligence as a consequence of drownings. The suits were settled out of court, and thank heavens the 10-year statute of limitations is now in place.

Because the northern edge was not to serve big ships, we established its elevation at only four feet above mean low tide to allow a Pratt Street passenger to see as much water as possible from the car. The western shore was to be a working edge, and it is at an elevation 7-$\frac{1}{2}$ feet above the water at mean low tide. Its alignment is a continuation of the eastern building line of Calvert Street to the north. The Battle Monument is close to the centerline of the west promenade. The 1814 monument was dedicated to General Samuel Smith, the commanding general in the 1814 defense of Baltimore against the British force that landed at Sparrows Point. Apparently the battle was over by the time Smith got there.

Speaking of General Smith, one of my efforts was to try to encourage the city to put his statue back in the harbor next to Tom Todd's McKeldin fountain. The monument is on Federal Hill, where it was moved during the construction of the new landscape at the intersection of Pratt and Light streets. I wrote a letter to the mayor and council that enclosed buttons I had made that said "Put Sam Smith Back." We had originally planned to put him atop a Corinthian column from the old east front of the U.S. Capitol, which we could have gotten through George M. White, the Architect of the Capitol and a former client of the firm. All I accomplished was to infuriate Walter Sondheim, who had been in charge of relocating Sam to Federal Hill. Sondheim wouldn't speak to me for several months until I apologized humbly for going over his head. Mayor Schmoke just ignored my letter.

SPECIAL DESIGN ASSIGNMENTS

In the 1964 plan, the widening of Pratt Street into a tree-lined boulevard had been proposed as a major design statement to deal with the traffic and also to mark the southern edge of the central business district and extend the harbor's influence to the west. It was an idea first suggested by David Barton, who wrote the introduction to our master plan. The boulevard has 70-foot landscaped parks on either side west of Light Street, and on the north side only to the east. In these parks, three-feet high, 20-feet wide planted earth berms separate pedestrians from traffic.

The Pratt, Light and Calvert street intersection—the old Sam Smith Park—has been the knottiest design problem both from a vehicular traffic point of view as well as for pedestrians. With free traffic flow from Calvert onto Pratt, it could be downright dangerous. Neither we, nor anyone else who has studied it—including Cooper Robertson in a current effort—has come up with a solution that is both feasible and attractive, so it must be bridged for pedestrians. What was Sam Smith Park has been renamed McKeldin Plaza; Tom Todd designed its marvelous cascade fountain to serve as a "steppingstone" for people on the bridge that crosses Light Street from the Hyatt Hotel to Harborplace. I think its one of the best fountains in the country. But it lacks Sam's statue as a focal point.

When Millspaugh and Embry asked WRT to prepare a schematic design concept for the fountain and a pedestrian bridge at this intersection, a local landscape firm, Land Design Research (LDR) of Columbia, Maryland, also submitted an entry, unbeknownst to us. After Tom Todd and I had presented Todd's concept to a committee consisting of Embry, Millspaugh, and M. Jay Brodie, then Embry's deputy, a long moment of silence ensued. Finally, Brodie said, "At the risk of seeming enthusiastic, I think it's pretty good." Knowing Embry was no fan of ours I could have kissed Brodie for his support. In any event, we were commissioned to go ahead with contract documents and didn't learn about LDR until later when their head, Cy Palmier, was reported to be claiming authorship of Todd's concept.

Credit for the Inner Harbor and its parts was always in jeopardy. I would quite frequently walk into a selection committee in a distant city to present our credentials only to be informed that LDR, RTKL, or the American City Corporation, a subsidiary of the Rouse Company had just claimed authorship of the Inner Harbor's plan or development or both. Setting the record straight was always fun. It involved finding out from the committee a lot about our competitors, then documenting our own work, being careful to give each other firm the credit they really were due.

We designed four pedestrian bridges to cross Pratt Street. The first is from the Hyatt Hotel to Harborplace via the McKeldin Fountain. The second WRT-designed pedestrian bridge crosses from the Convention Center to the Equitable Bank Building where a group of shops at the upper level originally included a branch of Hutzler's Department Store. This bridge ties in with the Charles Center walkway system to the north. A third WRT-designed pedestrian bridge connects across Pratt Street east of the World Trade Center from the Renaissance Hotel to the north pavilion of Harborplace. The fourth WRT-designed bridge connects the Inner Harbor Center, an office building designed by RTKL as its own headquarters, to the plaza in front of the National Aquarium at Baltimore. RTKL's building, which should have had a setback to allow the start of the City Hall Mall, unfortunately blocks that concept from achievement.

These bridges tie into the overall elevated and on-grade pedestrian walkway system that begins at Charles Center's northern edge, and continues south through the Convention Center to the harbor. They are crucial to the proper operation of the parking principle adopted for the Inner Harbor. The plan supplies almost no parking on the water side of the harbor's surrounding streets, and makes up the deficiency by a parking oversupply on the outboard side. Up to a point this principle can work without the preemption of other uses by parking on these valuable blocks. Beyond that we anticipate the development of satellite parking on the east, west, and south of the harbor, served by small buses or "elephant-train" people-movers such as those in Washington, D.C.'s, Mall.

Fortunately the Inner Harbor's biggest parking demand—now generated by Rouse's Harborplace, the Aquarium, the Science Center, and the other retail including all the restaurants—peaks at times when the nearby central business district office parking supply is most available.

VARIOUS DEVELOPMENTS

The 150,000 square feet of commercial space of the kind now in Harborplace had been part of the 1969 urban renewal plan. When Rouse and Millspaugh had their first discussion of the Rouse Company's involvement in 1977, Rouse indicated his unwillingness to use Millspaugh's first suggestion of the old power plant at Market Place south of Pratt for retail because it was too far away from the center of the action. Rouse came back with a proposal to develop an L-shaped building at the northwest corner of the harbor, which would have blocked the key view corridor from the water to the central business district. A hue and cry immediately arose from people who had come to enjoy the openness of the partially completed project area. Although the proposal for development along the water in the plan had been part of a public document since 1969, and retail had always been proposed next to the water, the recreation buffs as well as residents had come to look on the open space as permanent.

Rouse and Millspaugh agreed on a compromise—which Rouse much preferred—in which Harborplace would be located in what came to be called the "crotch," on either side of the view corridor that linked the USF&G Building to the water. However, the city was challenged by a petition and to settle the issue, there was a citywide referendum. Rouse and the Harborplace plan narrowly won. But there was also agreement that the area to the south of the Harborplace's western pavilion would stay as permanent open space.

Rouse hired Ben Thompson from Cambridge as his architect, but before Thompson started to work, WRT was asked by Millspaugh to do a feasibility study to test the location and develop special design guidelines for negotiation of the site with Rouse. Thompson's ultimate design follows those guidelines except for where he builds across the proposed

10.8 By the early 1970s we had built *Constellation* **Dock and the sistership to the U.S.S. Constitution was in place as the centerpiece to the Inner Harbor.**

view-corridor extension of South Street, which would have required Rouse to have three buildings instead of two. His reasons for having only two buildings were persuasive and we reluctantly gave up on that view corridor. Rouse again tested the city and CC-IH to see if he could close the "crotch" and have only one building. Fortunately Millspaugh held firm and maintained that this most crucial view-corridor was designed to be used as an open air theater.

Harborplace turned out to be exactly the year-round activity generator needed for the Inner Harbor: More than 18 million people visit Inner Harbor each year.

Most of the harbor's developers and/or their architects were persuaded by Millspaugh to follow the concepts and standards and controls, usually after a preliminary challenge. Bud Hammerman, a local developer, had plans for a hotel to be at the southwest corner of Light and Pratt streets. Hammerman's architect was world-famous Louis Kahn, whom I knew well as a colleague on the Penn faculty. The financial package was to be backed by the Ford Foundation. I presented our design guidelines to Kahn at the start of his work and he affably agreed to our form concept

10.9 A view of the pedestrian bridge over Pratt Street Boulevard from the Convention Center (foreground) to the (former) Equitable Bank Center. This is one of four bridges WRT designed.

10.10 Viewed from *Constellation* Dock, the IBM building on the right follows the build-to cornice line and the USF&G tower anchors the northwest corner of the harbor.

of wrapping the hotel around the parking, with retail along the streets. This was the concept we had developed in the 1969 Redevelopment Plan. I pointed out where the concept had been carried out very successfully in Montreal's Place Bonaventure project. I should have known better.

When Kahn presented his scheme to the architectural review board—without warning to me and without explanation—he had developed a towers-on-a-parking platform solution that violated the frame idea, and put parking facades instead of retail on all the streets. He also closed the Camden Street view-corridor that focused on the *Constellation*. Nobody, including me, dared criticize the scheme openly because Kahn was such a world-famous architect. I'm sure Kahn would have ultimately made his concept into an intrinsically attractive design, but it was the wrong building mass and program for that location. I was incensed, but saw that my position in expressing my opinion as a voting member on the architectural review board was in conflict with my own firm's work that would come before the board. So I resigned from the architectural review board.

Kahn might have brought it off, if not for his developer. Hammerman got in some sort of trouble, much to the embarrassment of the Ford Foundation. The proposal was withdrawn.

In its place, the Chesapeake and Potomac Telephone Headquarters, designed by local architect Richard Donkervoet of Cochran Stephenson and Donkervoet, and the Hyatt Hotel by George Pillorge of RTKL, have been built on the site. The C&PT headquarters was constructed in conformance with both the cornice line and frame concept, but the Camden Street view-corridor had been given up earlier in the negotiations with Hammerman. The Hyatt's cornice is at the right height, but does not adhere to the build-to line, and its reflecting-glass facade serves to weaken the purpose of the frame. However, the city and CC-IH felt that the first hotel was so important in getting the harbor redevelopment under way, they would have accepted any decent design that conformed to the cornice line of the "frame." They also agreed to Hyatt's offer that it be a "non-convention" facility. The city, with an Urban Development Action Grant (UDAG), became an equity partner in the hotel as well as in Harborplace. The Hyatt became the chain's best-performing facility immediately upon its opening.

The Inner Harbor has had at least three examples of its luck in financing. The first occurred on November 4, 1964, only two months after the master plan had been made public. A bond issue for construction of a new schools administration building was voted down, but the $2 million intended to start the Inner Harbor process was approved as part of another issue and we were off and running.

INNER HARBOR WEST

The second example of luck in financing occurred in June 1975, when Housing and Urban Development Assistant Secretary Lawrence Cox approved a $19 million grant reservation out of discretionary funds for Inner Harbor West to expand the successful first project. The money allowed the development of the Otterbein Homestead Village and new housing, and provided sites for the Convention Center, the Garmatz Federal Courthouse, and the Equitable Bank office building, and the two stadiums. Cox's approval reportedly was made against the advice of his principal assistants. Baltimore had already gotten a big grant that year and the staff felt that too much money was being given to one city. Cox

10.11 Have plans, will travel: David Wallace and Tom Todd in front of the north pavilion of Harborplace. The *News American* **building in center rear is now demolished. RTKL's headquarters is on the right.**

said that he approved the money for three reasons: first, the excitement of the project and its intrinsic merit; second, Baltimore had shown, thanks to Embry, Millspaugh, Sondheim, and many others, that it had the capability of really carrying out such a project well; and third, Baltimore, like other cities from Maine to Florida had lost a major industry—coastwise shipping—and needed special help. Trucking had taken over and the cities' waterfronts were left in a desperate condition, with harbors too shallow and constricted to allow them to convert to oceanic shipping. Cox's decision was the beginning of federal support for urban waterfronts all along the East Coast, such as in Camden, New Jersey, Norfolk, Virginia, Charlestown, South Carolina, and many others.

With new federal planning money available, CC-IH held a national competition to select the designer. This was another benchmark in our work. WRT was selected again and prepared the *Inner Harbor West Redevelopment Plan*, a plan that included a very good urban design concept that was successful in getting the money from HUD for the city, and getting the redevelopment process started. However, to start the plan's implementation CC-IH held another national competition and the team that won included world-famous Kenzo Tange from Japan to do a new urban design plan. Embry, who was always attracted by big names, asked Tange to ignore our plan and create a design that was to be the basis for parcelization and development.

Unfortunately, Tange's plan turned out to be unworkable and was not able to be implemented in the American market. While Tange's concept met the fashion of the day with interesting sculptural shapes, its form was overwhelming with concrete masses of housing perched atop a two- to three-level continuous parking podium. It was not at Baltimore's residential scale, and was clearly not economical. After considerable delays and abandonment of Tange's plan, the offering by the city of a $30 million city mortgage fund attracted a new developer with Louis Sauer of Philadelphia as the architect for the residential portion. Baltimore then proceeded more or less with our plan. Sauer prepared the designs with WMRT as the architect of record for the very successful housing that is built today.

The failure of Tange's plan had a good side. It allowed Embry to have second thoughts; he came up with the brilliant idea of an Urban Homestead Village for the restoration of the old townhouses in the southern portion of the Inner Harbor West redevelopment area that had been condemned in the early 1960s in the path of the original East-West expressway alignment. The shells of the buildings were auctioned off in a raffle, and the winners paid $1 and guaranteed to restore them and live in them for at least two years. The rest of the Inner Harbor West redevelopment area was committed to the new convention center and the Sheraton Hotel, which could not have happened if either Tange's, or our plan for that matter, had been implemented.

The third lucky financial break was in Embry getting the funding for the aquarium. The city had built and operated Friendship International Airport (now BWI) for many years. Embry proposed that the State of Maryland buy it. A condition of the sale was that Baltimore use the money for a worthy public venture. Embry had observed Boston's new aquarium with envy when he was visiting Harvard. He immediately retained its architect, Peter Chermayeff of Cambridge 7, for a feasibility study. On his first visit to the harbor, Chermayeff was shown a site to the south of

Harborplace's south pavilion on the west shore north of the Science Center. He turned and pointed to the pier just east of the World Trade Center and said, "That is where it should be." And that's where it is, one of the truly outstanding landmarks in the Inner Harbor.

Preparing the sites for other developments often required relocation of existing uses. The old Hanover Street Market occupied most of the Inner Harbor West area and the Maryland Food Distribution Center in Anne Arundel County had to be created so that the Convention Center could be built. But Baltimore's leadership was always equal to the task. Their time and efforts have paid off handsomely, not only in the two redevelopment projects cited—Charles Center and the Inner Harbor—but also in their influence on the revitalization of the whole downtown.

In the meantime, the Inner Harbor and the new downtown seem to suit Baltimore very well. In fact that there is a considerable euphoria and a real danger of overdoing it. Success could kill the magic quality of the place, its *genius loci*.

No small part of that spirit was exemplified by Sandy Hillman, for a number of years the city's outdoor activities organizer. Hillman initiated and ran the myriad events that took place in Baltimore each day. In 1976, Millspaugh conceived of building the *Pride of Baltimore*, a full-scale working replica of a Baltimore Clipper in the Inner Harbor using 1812 methods and tools. Al Copp directed the construction. The original *Pride of Baltimore* was lost at sea in 1986, and it made people realize how much of their hearts and emotions were part of the clipper and the harbor. The replacement, *Pride II*, was put to sea in 1988.

In the economic recession of the 1990s and early 2000, a number of Inner Harbor developments have been put on hold. In January 2002, the Baltimore Development Corporation initiated preparation of a new Inner Harbor Master Plan. The RFQ called for an emphasis on physical design guidelines for modifications to existing development and to address "specific planning, design and development issues and or projects and review them in the context of the overall development goals of the Inner Harbor area."

Studies of all proposed new developments were to be examined, including undeveloped sites, piers, expansion plans for the Science Center and the Aquarium, Rash Field, the western shore area and the marina. Proposals for the light rail extension and the Maglev high-speed train, both of which would have an immense impact on the Inner Harbor, also were to be studied.

10.12 The *Pride of Baltimore* sails the world over as an advertisement of Baltimore and the Inner Harbor. The Maryland World Trade Center is in the middle background.

In other words, as the politicians would say, everything was on the table. Although the detailed scope of the work was not clearly articulated in the RFQ, the call for a complete review of the current framework for the Inner Harbor's future, and none too soon.

AN INNER HARBOR UPDATE

As early as 1984, twenty years after the *1964 Inner Harbor Master Plan* was published, the major components of the plan were largely in place. Office and hotel development lined Pratt Street Boulevard, with several parcels still undeveloped as the national economy blew hot and cold. But by the year 2000, new projects increased in number and scope.

To cite Martin Millspaugh again, in this case from his article about the Inner Harbor:[2]

> By 2000, upwards of 60 new projects were either built or recycled: 15 office buildings, 12 hotels, 10 museums, and 17 other attractions, plus the Charles Center Subway Station, a new police headquarters building, and the campus of the Living Classroom Foundation. The residential market slowly awoke, starting with the conversion of vacant old loft buildings and the new, in-fill housing in the Otterbein neighborhood . . . ."[3] (with WRT as planners and landscape architects.)

10.13 Mayor William Donald Schaefer, two-time Governor of Maryland and now State Comptroller, was against the Inner Harbor when he was a Baltimore City Councilman, but became its biggest supporter and booster when elected mayor.

Within the Inner Harbor "entertainment zone" two difficult-to-develop historic structures, the Fish Market and the Power Plant, failed in their first recycling, have succeeded dramatically as Port Discovery, an interactive children's museum, and a Hard Rock Café, Barnes & Noble bookstore and the first ESPN Zone sports bar.

Looking ahead, the downtown of the old central business district centered on Redwood Street is being rediscovered as a place to live, with some 20 residential projects under way. In Charles Center, new commitments are being made to replace the expired renewal plan covenants. With tourism understandably down in 2002 and 2003, the Baltimore Area Convention and Visitors Bureau has adopted a new approach to respond.

THE 2003 BALTIMORE INNER HARBOR
MASTER PLAN FRAMEWORK DRAFT

In 2001, the Baltimore Development Corporation hired Cooper Robertson and Partners of New York City to review the achievements to date and to prepare the first overall new plan since 1964. I received a copy of the graphics sent at Jay Brodie's request on May 14, 2003. The written text and the transportation section are expected early in 2004.

After detailed review, I am outraged at the plan. I contained my anger and dismay and sent Jay Brodie the following response:

May 15, 2003

Mr. M. Jay Brodie
President
Baltimore Development Corporation
36 South Charles Street
Baltimore, MD 21201

Re: Baltimore Inner Harbor Master Plan
Framework Draft Report

Dear Jay:

Thank you for asking Shubroto Bose to send me a copy of the above which I received on May 14, 2003. I have reviewed it, and while a written text would have helped, I think I understand it and would like to bring the following comments to your attention:

1.   **Design Recommendations: Streets and Streetscapes**

1.1 Realignment of Light Street Northbound from Conway to Pratt Street

This realignment has very negative traffic consequences, a minimal pedestrian improvement, and **requires the elimination of one of the outstanding urban fountains in America. (Tom Todd's McKeldin Fountain)**

In our planning of the present street alignment, we considered the alternative now proposed, and rejected it as unworkable.

1.2 Bicycle Path Concept

A continuous bicycle path is proposed around the Harbor, adjacent to the nearest street. As shown, it intersects with each pedestrian intersection at the point where pedestrians gather to cross the street.

2. **Design Recommendations: Open Space**

2.1 <u>Proposed Underground Garages/Rash Field and Children's Playground</u>
The proposed underground garages (2-level) will cut off views of the harbor from Key Highway and from the south 200 feet of the upper surface. The serpentine mounds along the promenade do little to reduce the negative impact, and unless the Concert Tent is located here, there is little market for what will be extremely expensive space.

2.2 <u>Bullseye S/W Shore Piers</u>
This Bullseye shows in all the drawings and is a major departure from the simplicity of the Harbor's edge. If more pier space is needed, I would recommend extending the piers from the north.

3. **Design Recommendations: Development Parcels**

3.1 <u>Piers 5 and 6</u>
These piers are very close to being overbuilt, what with the recent construction of the Cordish garage and office building built in contradiction to the current master plan.

3.2 <u>Pratt Street / Market Place</u>
It appears that the developer of the old Baltimore Community College site has been allowed to violate the setback line by 30' and the 145' cornice line by 30%. With the building under construction, this is a fait accompli, but regrettable.

3.3 <u>President Street Urban Design Proposals</u>
President Street is upgraded to boulevard status, and heights are allowed that are out of scale with Little Italy to the east.

I hope these comments are useful in the forthcoming dialogue before the Master Plan is adopted.

Sincerely yours,

David R. Wallace

My mild letter of objection to various elements that were proposed in Cooper-Robertson's Plan for Inner Harbor went unanswered.

In early November 2003, I called Shubroto Bose, the Baltimore Development Council's chief of design. He had originally sent the draft to me. Brose reported that the final draft was expected soon, and he would send me a copy of that as well.

I really wanted to know what Brodie thought of the proposals, particularly the demolition of the McKeldin Fountain. In the meantime, I found out from Martin Millspaugh that the Greater Baltimore Committee had been given the assignment to determine what to do with the management of Inner Harbor. Their study showed that it was in poor shape and needed to be in the care of an organization like CC-IH. Their report had been held up at the mayor's request, but had been recently released. Millspaugh felt that this was a sign that Mayor O'Malley may be planning to implement it.

Millspaugh thinks that there may never be a final Cooper-Robertson Inner Harbor report, and even if one is produced, it will simply sit on the shelf. Ed Gunts, a reporter on the city beat of *The Sun*, also believes this. Gunts says that Otis Reeley, the new, young planning director, fired the urban designer that was the planning commission's liaison to Brose on

10.14 Harborplace is at the lower right; in the middle, Light Street zigzags east to connect to Calvert across Pratt Street Boulevard. Cooper-Robertson's plan proposes straightening northbound Light Street to Pratt Street Boulevard, which would result in the demolition of the McKeldin Fountain and a severe reduction in traffic flow to Calvert Street.

the project, and the architectural review function has been all but abandoned. Gunts also says that Cooper-Robertson's $250,000 fee is exhausted and there is no money for a final report, according to the project's director, Brian Shea.

I finally caught up with Jay Brodie in mid-November 2003. Brodie was cheerfully unapologetic about not answering my letter or phone calls. He has an Olympian detachment in regards to the Cooper-Robertson report, and says that the BDC neither approves or rejects their recommendations. "The report is far from an official plan," Brodie says. Cooper-Robertson, however, labels it "Baltimore Inner Harbor Master Plan Framework."

The Pratt/Light Street realignment is currently being tested for traffic impact and Brodie says it would be unfortunate if "your favorite fountain had to be demolished." I haven't told Tom Todd about any of this; maybe I'll wait until this book comes out.

As to the proposal for a parking deck under Rash Field, Brodie says the Parking Authority is doing a supply/demand study to see if it can be justified. When I mentioned Cooper-Robertson's proposal to move the Music Tent from its pier to Rash Field, he laughed and said the Federal Hill community probably wouldn't like it and a more likely relocation site is the Allied Signal site in Inner Harbor East.

The proposal for a "water feature" at the South Shore/West Shore water's edge is a terrible idea. I asked how the Cope-Linder-designed office building was allowed to violate design controls, particularly the cornice height limit. Brodie said that the State of Maryland had bought the site, which had been occupied by Baltimore Community College. It did not go through the urban renewal process, the controls were not in their title when the property transferred. The state then leased the property to Kravco, without the renewal controls in effect. Brodie said the steel for the new building was already up and commented, "I don't think it will look too bad."

Finally, I wonder what happened to the proposal for an LRT extension eastbound from Howard Street along Pratt to Fells Point and Canton, and westbound on Lombard Street back to Howard Street. Nobody seems to know.

---

1   WMRT, "Inner Harbor Master Plan," p. 2, 1964.
2   Martin L. Millspaugh, "The Inner Harbor Story," *Urban Land*, April 2003, p. 40.
3   Along Pratt Street, north of the Inner Harbor, the Rouse Company built the Gallery, a 1.2-million-square-foot mixed-use project, which helped trigger recycling of old build-

ings in the heart of the central business district; Inner Harbor East expanded hotel and commercial development with five major buildings and an hotel; to the south Harborview Apartments, a 2,600-unit development by Richard Swirnow, is in its second phase; and to the west the Ravens stadium followed the fabulously successful Oriole Park at Camden Yards.

11

Looking Backward

On Friday, December 1, 2000, the former staff of the Planning Council of the Greater Baltimore Committee held a reunion at One Charles Center, in Peter Angelos's law office board room. Hunter Moss and Archie Rogers were invited as the sole surviving members of the council. Hunter lives in a retirement community outside Philadelphia and couldn't make the trip, but Archie showed up for lunch at the Center Club and welcomed the staff to a review of how Charles Center and the central business district have fared over the years. Jay Brodie, head of the Baltimore Development Corporation, gave a short speech on the status of development under way and plans for the future, and Walter Sondheim was there. He expressed his regrets about not having been a member of the council in the early days. As chairman of BURHA, Sondheim had represented the city as one of our clients.

George Kostritsky had organized the event with Martin Millspaugh, Barbara Bonnell, and Harry Cooper. George had stayed with RTKL for a number of years, then left the firm to act as a consultant to the United Nations, where he served notably in Sri Lanka and Nigeria. Today, he is a wonderfully alive octogenarian whose voice always seems about to break into laughter. He is retired and lives in suburban Baltimore. Barbara Bonnell, assistant director of Greater Baltimore Committee until Millspaugh recruited her to join the Charles Center Management Office during the Charles Center days, is recently retired as director of research for Baltimore Development Corporation. Barbara's early days as head of the National Junior League still show in her elegant demeanor and deportment. Harry Cooper hasn't changed a bit. Bearded, fat ,and jolly, he lives in the same house with Cici, his wife. He and Tom Karsten left

11.1 The Planning Council staff in 1958 from left to right: Hiroshi Matsumoto, Japanese internist who ended up a senior housing administrator in Tokyo; George E. Kostritsky, later the K in RTKL; David A. Wallace; economist Harry B. Cooper; landscape architect William Potts; architect John Adelberg; and planner Jeremiah O'Leary. Not shown are Millicent P. Gordon, research assistant, who later married Bill Potts; and Ruvelle "Mickey" Falcone, secretary.

Blaustein and have been developers of projects across the country and I suspect he has a lot of money.

Jerry O'Leary is also rich and somehow looks it. He is the epitome of a "black Irishman" with a ruddy complexion, square-cut features, and a twinkle in his eye. He and George Marcou sold Marcou-O'Leary, the firm he created after leaving the Planning Council, to the Westinghouse Corporation. President Jimmy Carter had challenged the Westinghouse CEO to do something about cities and do more than just sell appliances, so Marcou and O'Leary sold out and worked for five years for Westinghouse on everything from a Lincoln New-Town-in-Town in Washington, D.C., to a new community in Iran. As O'Leary cheerily noted, neither project materialized, but many others were successful. Fortunately he was paid for the firm in cash rather than Westinghouse stock, and invested the nest egg in a number of new businesses, including a national bank that he and his wife, Barbara, still own. Jerry says that if he'd chased Barbara around Greater Baltimore Committee's filing cabinets today the way he did when they were courting, he'd have been guilty of sexual harassment. They live in Rehoboth Beach, Delaware.

John Adelberg left Sasaki Associates in 1985 to form his own firm, Architectural Associates, Inc. They specialize in small housing projects in and around the Boston metropolitan area. John said he got tired of the traveling life of an architect/urban designer with a national and international firm, and loves the hands-on scale of his present work. Bill McDonnell, who was WMRT's local planner for the *Plan for the Valleys,* had worked with the Planning Council after I left, preparing the city of Annapolis plan and another for Laurel, Maryland. He continued and still acts as a local planning consultant for organizations such as Black & Decker, whose national headquarters is in Towson, Maryland.

Bill Potts continued on with the council for six years after the rest of us had left, when, as he put it, he unfortunately took a job as landscape designer and planner with the Gulf-Western Corporation. The corporation had purchased the planned new town of Reston, Virginia, from its founder, Robert Simon. No sooner had Potts joined the group than they sold out to an organization that was going to retail the property and he was unemployed. Bill had married Millicent Paco Gordon, who was the first research assistant that I had hired when I started with the council. They decided to retire and now live on the southern coast of North Carolina where he is very active with the Episcopal Church.

Martin Millspaugh left Charles Center-Inner Harbor, Inc., in the late 1980s to join Jim Rouse's Enterprise Development Corporation, which Rouse had formed when he retired from the Rouse Company. As was the case with other developers who market their services around the world, Millspaugh has been on teams that have planners that are in competition with us as planning consultants. At our reunion he described some of his latest projects, then showed his pictures of the Baltimore Charles Center and Inner Harbor planning and development without once mentioning the role that WMRT or WRT had in the process. I realized then, as I have many times in the past, that developers like Marty see themselves as initiators, authors of, and responsible for development. Their architects, landscape architects, and planners are merely the draftsmen of their ideas.

Ah well, unfortunately I had left for a train before he was finished with his reminiscing, so I never got around to claiming credit and reporting to the assembled staff what happened to me after I resigned from the Planning Council and moved back to Philadelphia. I tell it here as a necessary part of my story, hitting highlights to give the reader enough of my resume to serve as background for my work in Baltimore and elsewhere.

What happened afterward has been a wonderfully rich and rewarding career that began with the two benchmark projects, the Inner Harbor and the *Plan for the Valleys*, and is ending with my spending one day a week, retired from partnership in the firm, writing these memoirs as an employee of Wallace Roberts & Todd, LLC, in a small space in the firm's headquarters in downtown Philadelphia. I eat lunch with the current principals to keep up-to-date with what WRT is up to and how it's doing. It is doing just fine.

12

The Lower Manhattan Plan

Philadelphia and Baltimore were tremendous training grounds for my career. As I formed WMRT and tested my philosophy and skills in practice, I felt that my partners and I were ready to take on the world.

As it turned out, WMRT's first major project after the Inner Harbor and the *Plan for the Valleys* was with New York City to prepare the *Lower Manhattan Plan*. This plan filled the area between the pier-head and bulkhead lines offshore and proposed new residential communities on it. The method that we invented to develop and test the plan became a WMRT trademark in downtown planning for a dozen cities. The plan itself set the framework for subsequent Lower Manhattan development. Concepts such as the water's edge walkway system became the model for the Hudson River waterfront walkway in New Jersey and elsewhere.

The plan is as relevant today, post-September 11, as it was when it was published. Alexander Garvin, recently appointed vice president of the Lower Manhattan Development Corporation, indicated his interest in developing the Lower Manhattan Plan's Fulton Street "cross-town artery" from Battery Park City to the South Street Seaport, among other ideas.[1] The Lower Manhattan Plan is the clearest prototype for the theme of his article in *The New York Times*.

Our entree to the world of New York planning was thanks to Robert B. Mitchell, professor of planning and chairman of the department of city and regional planning in Penn's Graduate School of Fine Arts. Mitchell had been executive director of the Philadelphia City Planning Commission before Ed Bacon and he was a consultant to the New York City Planning Commission. Mitchell was impressed by our work on the Inner Harbor and he recommended WMRT as the only firm qualified to

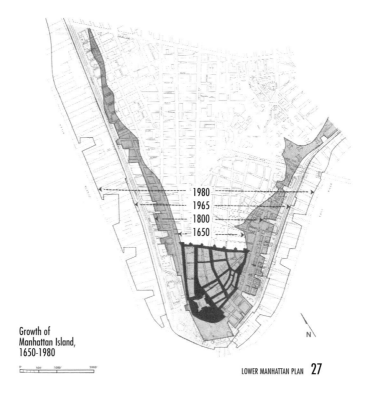

Growth of
Manhattan Island,
1650-1980

LOWER MANHATTAN PLAN **27**

**12.1 Growth of Lower Manhattan Island, 1650–1980. The land area along the
East River has not yet been filled.**

undertake the Lower Manhattan assignment. I never did understand the
Byzantine politics of the selection process, but when we were told we had
the job, we also were informed we had to associate with a New York firm
of our choice to keep the local architectural world happy. I picked
Whittlesey & Conklin.

I had known Julian Whittlesey, the senior partner with the firm, from
my Philadelphia Redevelopment Authority days. He was more sympathetic to urban design and planning—which most architects think they
know all about, but don't. By March 1965, we had drawn up a joint venture agreement and were under contract to the city. Julian shortly retired,
and William Conklin became the lead partner. He and James Rossant
headed Whittlesey, Conklin & Rossant. Both Conklin and Rossant were
excellent architects, but knew little about urban design or planning,
although, of course, they thought they knew a lot. Fortunately, they were
quick studies.

We set up an office near Union Square. We hired Paul Willen, a local architect, as project director mainly for his knowledge of New York, and Marvin Richman as senior planner. Scott Killinger and Michael John Pittas, among others, were later taken on to develop and illustrate the plan; Charles D. Laidlaw in Philadelphia was our economist. Ultimately Killinger was responsible for the East Side Case Study, which became the prototype for offshore development. Tom Todd developed the plan's overall concept, and Pittas did the detailed plan illustrating the concept under Rossant's direction.

While I was in Baltimore, I had met and worked with a traffic engineer from the National Highway Traffic Safety Board named Alan M. Voorhees. He had some fascinating ideas about developing micro-assignment computer models of traffic flow. By 1965, Voorhees had formed his own transportation and planning firm with David W. Schoppert. We hired them to develop and apply their theories to Lower Manhattan, which, as a discrete area, lent itself ideally to their node/link network system analysis. Their micro-assignment modeling methods, of course, have since become standard throughout the transportation planning world. Their ability to forecast the transportation consequences of plan projections was crucial to our overall plan development.

The cast of characters on the city side was important. Jack C. Smith was a Mitchell protege and was a special consultant to the commission. He was the key person acting as our client in day-to-day contact. Infrequently we met with Richard K. Bernstein, executive director, and Alan K. Sloan, assistant executive director. Voorhees and his guys worked with a street technical committee and particularly with Joseph McC. Lieper and Arthur Wrubel as project manager for transportation. They all made significant contributions to the product, particularly Smith, who was responsible for signing off on our billings and representations as to percent complete. Getting paid and keeping solvent was always problematical.

When we started, the project had already considerable history. Back in 1957 and 1958 the Downtown-Lower Manhattan Association, under Warren T. Lindquist as acting executive vice-president, and with Skidmore Owings & Merrill as principal consultants, had completed reports on Lower Manhattan recommending various land-use, redevelopment area designations, and traffic improvements. SOM also had done an occupancy survey in 1961. Their backlog of data and concepts became a strong underpinning for our work. Lindquist—acting both for the asso-

Building
Life
Expectancy

Legend:

▨ SHORT-TERM
■ LONG-TERM

12.2 The Building Life Expectancy map shows long-range and middle-range givens based on property evaluation. The open areas invite new development if the market responds or public policy intervenes.

ciation and as a principal advisor to David Rockefeller, chairman of the association's board—became a good friend and key participant in our planning and design process.

So what was so unusual about the planning and design process—aside from the relevance to September 11 planning—that warrants recording here? I submit three elements for the reader's consideration: applying the concept of modeling change to development as well as to transportation; the use of a case study to test alternative concepts against development goals; and the end product concept plan as a prototype generator of change.

I have described the modeling of land-use change to illustrate the "spectre of growth" in the preparation of the *Plan for the Valleys*, so modeling was on my mind when we started work on Lower Manhattan. The

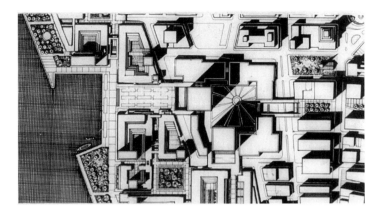

Waterfront
Development:
Worlk Trade Center

0'   300'   1000'

12.3 Excavation for the World Trade Center waterfront development was under way when we started planning. We classed it in a Probability I category with the adjacent buildings as Probability II in our growth modeling procedure.

idea was that while the first step in our planning needed to be a description of the existing conditions, these were under continuous change. The next step should be a definition of current problems, and a projection of what is likely to happen if the market mechanism is allowed to operate without any intervention. Then we could compare this eventuality with our goals to determine what we "liked" and "didn't like" about the outcome, and marshal ways to influence what we didn't like to conform to what we wanted—in other words, design the future. I discussed in a very general way the application of this modeling method to the Baltimore Metro/Center in Chapter 4, illustrated by what we called CBD East. We used it to good effect in a number of downtown studies, including the Downtown New Orleans Growth Management Program in 1975. The following describes the steps of the method in enough detail to provide the professional reader a blueprint for replication.

I was the only member of the team who had ever prepared a downtown plan—Baltimore's Central Business District Plan of 1959—so the

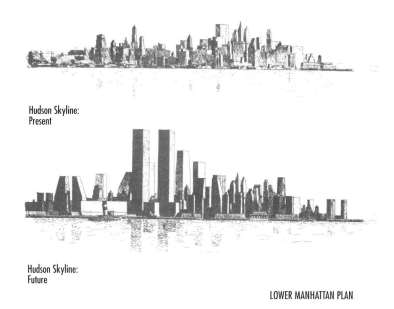

Hudson Skyline:
Present

Hudson Skyline:
Future

LOWER MANHATTAN PLAN

12.4 The present and future Hudson River skyline. Events of September 11, 2001, sent us back to the past.

programming and directing of all our activities fell to me, in consultation with Tom Todd and Bill Conklin, who took the lead role for WC&R.

DESCRIBING THE EXISTING SITUATION

Marvin Richman and Paul Willen knew Lower Manhattan well and quickly provided us with not only the background and setting, but also a clear sense of change, stability, and trends. Space utilization, employment, property values, historic structures, recent remodeling, vacancies, all were recorded and their patterns studied. The movement system with particular analysis of subway stations and pedestrian flows was analyzed. This was all necessary to the modeling procedure that we initiated.

DETERMINING THE SUSCEPTIBILITY TO CHANGE

Put in simple terms, buildings that are big, expensive, new, occupied with important functions and many employees, are historic, and/or create special places are established on maps as "givens." They constitute the base of "least susceptible to change." Cutoff points were not arbitrary; for example, pre-1965, non-fireproof buildings with low-speed elevators less than 12 stories were considered expendable, all other things being equal.

Future
Development
Opportunity Areas

12.5 Future Development Opportunity Areas combined with long- and middle-range givens provide the matrix for the plan's Probability II and III development.

But if they had cast-iron fronts, that put them in a special category, usually historic.

In the normal actions of the market, the least susceptible building will continue and development will occur in areas most susceptible, except for another consideration that I called "hot-cold." Some areas are the focus of speculative activity that cuts across the least-most susceptible classification. Real estate brokers were contacted to identify areas where land assembly was under way, and where new development could afford land costs unrelated to the normal market economics. An example of this would be a corporate headquarters of banks such as J.P. Morgan, where there is a "non-market" choice.

The resulting pattern I called a "figure ground," an urban design term, whose negative portrayed where development was, or could be, most likely. The next step, the probability of change, was conceived as a sub-model for the overall growth modeling procedure.

THE PROBABILITY OF CHANGE

New development must depend largely on favorable market conditions for the urban designer to have a space program. For Lower Manhattan, our economist Chuck Laidlaw observed that in the early years the World Trade Center and the World Financial Center were going to absorb the majority of the market. Nevertheless, Manhattan's long-term growth was typically 500,000- to 1 million-square-foot buildings with at least 30,000 square feet on each floor. The two World Trade Center towers, each of which had 40,000 square feet a floor, were an anomaly that would not be repeated.

The probability-of-change model provides a view into the future that starts out with specific and detailed development that is under construction (such as the World Trade Center) or in late planning and financing. This we labeled Probability I.

Probability II consists of private and public proposals that are in early planning, but may or may not occur, and may change their character when they do.

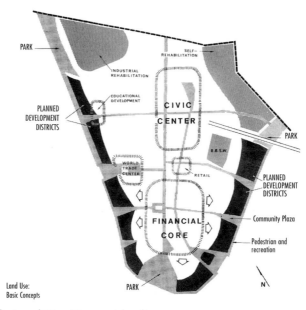

12.6 The Basic Land Use Concept in diagram.

The results of the above were laid out in reasonable design detail, and evaluated in terms of a set of goal criteria established in parallel step.

Probability III consists of possible development; here the urban designers must not be inhibited by the economists's inability to project more than five or ten years with any assurance. Laidlaw noted that even though he could not forecast space demand, life would go on and we could assume that an attractive and vital Lower Manhattan would become a magnet for a variety of uses in addition to office space.

In effect, Laidlaw gave us *carte blanche* regarding the amount and mix of uses, assuming Lower Manhattan's office core would expand and office employment would generate its own market for retail, community facilities, and most critically, for residential housing. At the time we were planning, there was almost no housing to speak of.

GOALS FOR LOWER MANHATTAN

The purpose of our planning was to provide a framework, which would be an organizing concept that acted as a guide to public and private actions and established a public policy. That was necessary to enable private response. Thus, in a real sense, a compelling visual concept was essential.

We were, within several months of starting, convinced that our programmatic vision for Lower Manhattan would in many respects copy mid-Manhattan, but without the theater and entertainment districts. The strong office core already existed and was growing, thanks in large part to David Rockefeller and the Chase Manhattan Bank's decision to consolidate their headquarters in the core. Therefore, the use most lacking, and most possible was considered to be residential.

DEVELOPMENT OF CONCEPT PLANS

Collectively the partners outlined our approach to concept planning. First we all agreed that an open space system would encircle Lower Manhattan, providing continuous public access to the Hudson and East rivers. This linear park should be connected at intervals to the office core and subway entrances by pedestrian walkways. Between the waterfront and the core, high-rise residential communities should be developed based on extensions of the old Lower Manhattan street grid.

Tom Todd received the assignment to do the first overall concept plan. Based on the above program, his concept clearly established the optimum development. He put the Hudson River and the East River elevated

12.7 The Circulation System becomes the armature of the detailed plan.

expressways in underground tunnels with the encouragement of Al Voorhees and Dave Schoppert, our transportation planners. They knew it could not be done, however, without federal financing, or so they thought.

THE EAST RIVER RENEWAL CASE STUDY

We decided to select one of the new communities in this concept plan as a case study to test the principles. We picked the area between Wall Street on the south and Fulton Street on the north from the bulkhead line to Water Street. The objective was to show that a new community that would meet good design standards could be developed, and would generate enough in land sales to offset cost of acquisition, demolition, relocation, site preparation, and construction of a section of a new sub-surface expressway.

Scott Killinger was assigned the job of developing this critical case study under Jim Rossant's design direction and my urban renewal overview. A sequence of maps (not included) indicate the thought process and design steps involved. I quote from the Lower Manhattan Plan:

> The purpose of this special study in depth was to test the principles of the Concept Plans and Program, to study the special problems of integration of in-shore and off-shore development, to determine the preliminary costs and implications for such development and to design a prototype for the perimeter of the peninsula. It also served as the basis for outlining a development process whereby that part of the Plan can be carried out.
>
> The area selected is bounded by the pier-head line on the east, Water Street on the west, Fulton Street on the north and Wall Street on the south. Reasons for picking it have been discussed briefly before. First, it is the area of present expansion of the financial Core and has been under active site assembly and speculation, particularly between Water and Front streets. This is both an advantage and a disadvantage. It is a disadvantage in raising site costs, but an advantage in that it is an area of great investment interest.
>
> Second, the area, while still in multiple ownership, has been assembled to such an extent that only a relatively few owners are involved. This simplifies dealing with them for coordination and planning.
>
> Third, 42 per cent of the area from Water Street to South Street is already in public ownership in the form of streets, excess taking from the recent Water Street widening or occupied by public buildings. If South Street itself and the bulkhead-to-pier-head area are included, public ownership rises to 81 per cent. With this large proportion of (land) in public control the City's role in this development is easily apparent.
>
> A fourth reason for selection of this area is that much of the land is vacant, occupied by deteriorate and/or small structures and with few important activities. The land-side is very probably eligible under state (and federal) legislation for renewal activity. In addition, the pier area will also qualify in all probability as a renewal area, a potential aid to assembly and site improvement.
>
> Finally, private renewal, although not yet at full speed, is proceeding apace on a small-lot, fractionalized and un-integrated basis. Clearly the opportunity for development in accord with a master plan is here and now; otherwise it will quickly be dissipated as private development occurs. It is reasonable to assume that a planned result will be superior to what might take place without some concerted action.[2]

Suffice it to summarize by saying that the East Side Renewal Case Study proved to be feasible from all points of view; policy, market demand, program, and development process all combined to show how waterfront development could occur. The case study became our prototype for application to the entire Lower Manhattan waterfront.

However, when the State of New York took the lead in creating the development entity as we recommended, the area of the waterfront adjacent to the economically struggling World Trade Center was chosen as the site to begin. The Battery Park City Authority hired Cooper-Eckstut of New York to develop the master plan. It was a good plan, but unfortunately it backed away from depressing the expressway. The opportunity was lost to knit the new development to the core although it is a very viable residential community, relatively untouched by the September 11 disaster.

OPTIMUM DEVELOPMENT AND NEXT STEPS

The Lower Manhattan Plan set no particular time schedule for implementation, and as I write, 38 years later, it would be useful if the Lower Manhattan Development Corporation were to replicate the process we

LOWER MANHATTAN PLAN

12.8 Tom Todd translated the Future Land Use into three dimensions in this first cut at an urban design plan. This plan is on the cover of the 2002 reprint by Princeton Architectural Press.

developed and compare the results with the following: If all the choices of alternate land use are selected over time in accord with the recommendations of the plan, the resulting land-use pattern will be as shown in the proposed land-use map. It must be borne in mind that there is an interdependence to many of them so that a decision for a different use—in the Washington Market Area, for example—affects adjacent areas.

The core itself is expanded somewhat in geographic extent. Office space has increased from the present 50 million net square feet to a total of 72 million net square feet, (including 10.165 million net square feet in the now demolished World Trade Center). The process of change anticipates retirement of 9 million net square feet, an addition of 31 million net square feet for a net gain of 22 million net square feet. Government and related business services are not estimated separately, but are included in the total change in office space. Residential space increased from approximately 4,200 dwelling units and 15,000 people today to 45,000 dwelling units and 112,000 people.

The new park at the Brooklyn Bridge accounts for 11 acres, Battery Park for 25 acres, and the new park south of Canal Street on the Hudson for 23 acres. The remaining 31 acres are in the strip park and open space at the water's edge. Regional open space has become a major use, occupying 90 acres along the water's edge.

The northwest area is shown as still in its present industrial use, to be designated for some other use some time in the future. No attempt is made to add up all land uses to the total area of Lower Manhattan because of the interlocking and mixed nature of many of the uses.

Land-use plans are primarily of value as devices for translation of programs and principles into zoning controls—which are necessary, but a negative and limiting kind of concept. Since it is anticipated that zoning will be used in new and creative ways, it is necessary to spell out in three-dimensional terms the principles to be followed and objectives to be sought. Otherwise zoning arrives at what is wanted by preventing what is not wanted—what developers can't do rather than what the city would like them to do.

LOWER MANHATTAN AS AN INVESTMENT

The opportunity for developing Lower Manhattan as shown in the plan floats like a dream unrealized, except for Battery Park City and the World Financial Center along the Hudson River. Yet the city is literally sitting on a gold mine of opportunity. The loss of the World Trade Center has forced

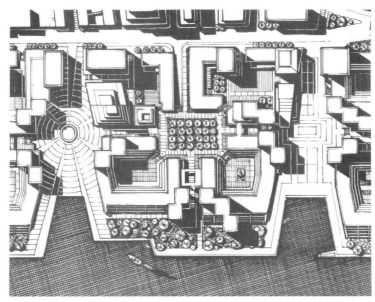

12.9 The East River Renewal Case Study. Prototype Development Sequence: IX, Optimum Development. This prototype was then extrapolated for all of the other communities along both East and Hudson riverfronts.

the city to think about what should replace it, but the scope of planning should reach beyond the center's 16 acres to all of Lower Manhattan.

Costs to the city for creating these new residential communities will be substantial, but carefully scheduled and geared to the market absorption, the area's development will be largely self-supporting.

We have gotten used to big figures from the costs of war in Iraq and the increase in the national debt, so $5 billion as the total new investment in Lower Manhattan shouldn't scare anyone.

Roughly $4 billion would be for residential, and $1 billion for office development. These figures include the cost of infrastructure—the relocation of the expressways, new land fill, public parks, utilities, and other considerations. I won't place an estimate on the increase in real property taxes as well as income and other ratables to the city, but they would be enormous.

Subsidy for middle-income housing would make it possible to get a broader economic and racial mix (and incidentally accelerate the absorption and shorten completion as I found out in Baltimore's Charles Center). However, to do this, a land subsidy also would be necessary, as the land costs envisioned here are above what can be supported under the Mitchell-Lama program. The result of the subsidy would be to lower rents and thus broaden the range of families, incomes, and ethnic groups rather than reduce the intensity or nature of use.

THE FORM OF THE FUTURE

The final test of the investment, however, will be the quality of the environment, the improved transportation, economic diversification, a change in the whole quality of working and living in Lower Manhattan, a change which will result in a more intense and valuable business community.

The sketches at the end of the report (by Tom Todd and James Rossant) are designed to offer a hint of this future downtown—a new type of "total community," composed of 500,000 workers and some 85,000 residents, with interpenetrating residential, office and recreational activities, for which Lower Manhattan is uniquely suited.

Historic streets like Wall and Broad, now reconstituted as pedestrian ways, carry people directly to waterfront plazas at the city's edge. Residential towers rise to look out at the river and back at the great business power they adjoin.

The waterfront plazas are physical extensions of the canyons within, lined with shops and restaurants, low-rise apartments above; the junction-place of business lunches and residential shopping. Along the water's edge are areas for strolling and play, which are suitably interspersed.

STEPS FOR IMPLEMENTATION

The Plan for Lower Manhattan represents a formidable undertaking—requiring a degree of administrative coordination and public consensus rarely seen in New York. Yet it should be remembered that the plan was, first and foremost, a guide for decision making rather than a set of specifications for a series of projects.

Published in 1966 by the New York City Planning Commission under the administration of Mayor John Lindsay, and later included as The Manhattan Community Planning District #1 component of the *1969 Plan for New York City* (published by M.I.T. Press), the plan established WMRT as expert in both waterfront and downtown urban design and planning. However, this was almost the last New York job WMRT had. I found that getting work in New York very difficult because of the New Yorker's

12.13 Tom Todd's view of the East Side Case Study area shows new development with the Brooklyn Bridge in the background from the waterfront walkway.

belief in their local firms being the best—unless the firm has the kind of reputation we earned from Baltimore's Inner Harbor.

---

1   *The New York Times* Metro section, Wednesday, March 20, 2002, p.B2.
2   Wallace et al., *The Lower Manhattan Plan*, prepared for the New York City Planning Commission, 1966, p. 91.

13

Lower Manhattan: 1966-2004

We almost got another New York job shortly after the Lower Manhattan Plan. We were invited by the city to prepare a Model Cities plan for Harlem during President Lyndon Johnson's administration. The plan was to be completed in six months and had a budget of $500,000. The assignment was ill-conceived and we were the wrong firm for the job: We weren't black, no one outside the Pentagon could intelligently spend $500,000 on urban planning in six months, and with the city's propensity for slow pay, we'd be bankrupt before it was over. We turned it down, and the young black architect who took it on went bankrupt.

NEW LIFE FOR THE BATTERY

However, in 1967 we were still riding the high of our award-winning *Lower Manhattan Plan* when the New York Stock Exchange announced that it was seriously considering leaving New York for New Jersey. I had become friendly with Anthony Peters, head of the prestigious real estate firm of Cushman & Wakefield, and together we came up with the idea of putting the Exchange over the air rights at the entrance to the Brooklyn-Battery Tunnel. It was a free and prominent site.

Our idea also included relocating the city's main television tower in Battery Park. At the end of the *Lower Manhattan Plan* work, when the State of New York was still negotiating with the television networks for the right to put the main television antenna—with a rental fee of $1 million a year—at the top of the World Trade Center, the Lower Manhattan Plan Joint Venture had toyed with the idea of a tower at Battery Park to accommodate it. As a joint venture we decided a tower there would be diversionary. So with engineer Lev Zetlin, WMRT combined the Stock

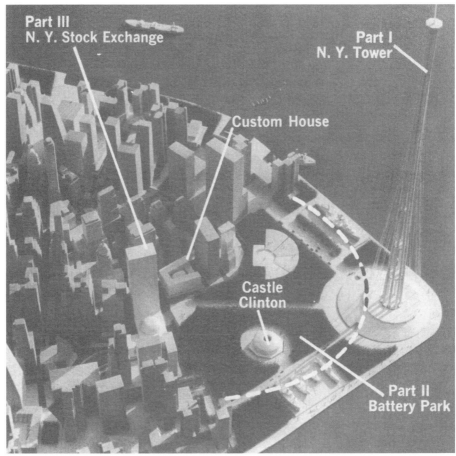

13.1 In 1967 WMRT, Cushman & Wakefield, and engineer Lev Zetlin proposed locating the footloose New York Stock Exchange over the entrance to the Brooklyn-Battery Tunnel, and a 2,500-foot tower with television antennae, restaurants and so on, at the tip of the Battery.

Exchange proposal with a 2,500-foot television tower/rotating sightseeing and restaurant complex. We presented the project to Mayor John Lindsay on June 5, 1967. I would say he was mildly interested. Unfortunately, that day the Six-Day Arab-Israeli War broke out and we were lucky to make the last page of *The New York Times*. It was just as well; when I showed the tower to a senior Eastern Airlines pilot who flew into La Guardia Airport every day, he said that even though it was not in the flight path, he was sure FAA would never permit it. That was our last New York job.

I saw in the Metro Section of *The New York Times*, on Wednesday, May 1, 2002, that television executives are pushing a 2,000-foot-tall tower with a restaurant and observation deck on top, modeled on the Space Needle in Seattle as a replacement for the broadcasting antenna that was lost when the World Trade Center towers fell. President George W. Bush's recent decision to give Governor's Island to the City of New York for a possible City College of New York facility has opened up this as a potential site for the tower, although some broadcasting officials are said to prefer the Liberty Science Center in Jersey City.

THE WORLD TRADE CENTER

At 110 stories each, the World Trade Center's twin towers were briefly the tallest buildings in the world, and were an out-of-scale phenomenon in Lower Manhattan. Their height was made possible by the creation of lobbies partway up where people bound for the top changed elevators. Otherwise, the number of shafts necessary for the traffic would have filled the entire lower floors, precluding rentable space. The towers were crude and ugly. But as time wore on and people got used to them, they became a popular, if not admired, icon for New York, eclipsing the Empire State Building.

Completed in the early 1970s, the towers were slow to fill. After all, 10 million square feet is a lot of space. The principal tenants at first were state office workers occupying some 1.6 million square feet in the South Tower. Those offices were located there after pressure from Governor Nelson Rockefeller—it was clear he was helping save his brother David Rockefeller's decision to put the Chase Manhattan Bank's new headquarters nearby. Ultimately both towers filled, and the center's tenants resembled a cross-section of downtown and national businesses. The towers became the anchor for development of the 1980s World Financial Center to the immediate west and for the decision to create the new community of Battery Park City.

At our suggestion, the dirt from the WTC's excavation was conveniently used to fill the 91 acres of waterfront between the pierhead and bulkhead lines from north of the center to the Battery. New York City set up the Office of Lower Manhattan Development in 1967 to prepare guidelines for use of the newly created land and to implement other features of the Lower Manhattan Plan. In 1968 the state created the Battery Park City Authority; in 1969 a plan was prepared for its detailed development.

Also in 1969, the City Planning Commission put together composites of all plans for sections of the city and published them as the *Plan for New York City. Volume 4: Manhattan* spoke of mid-Manhattan and Lower Manhattan in glowing terms. "An unprecedented boom in new office construction—sparked by such projects as the World Trade Center, the New York Stock Exchange, and Battery Park City—is adding dramatically to assessed valuation and employment. By 1970, 19 million square feet of new office buildings will have been completed, 9 million square feet of it between 1965 and 1970."[1] With such developments as Chase Manhattan's 60-story tower, which was added in 1955, Lower Manhattan was attracting a substantial share of this growth.

Through the boom and bust cycles of the 1970s and 1980s, growth in Lower Manhattan continued apace. So much so that in 1993, under Mayor David Dinkins, the Department of City Planning published another *Plan for Lower Manhattan* that recognized in fact that the *1966 Lower Manhattan Plan* had succeeded. To cite Ann Buttenweiser's review of downtown's future, published in the fall 1991 issue of *Seaport*, "Wall Street—despite ups and downs—was flourishing, foreign banking and service jobs had replaced maritime and blue-collar industries. The residential population had grown from 833 in 1970, to about 14,000 people, and tourism had become a major source of economic activity. Since then, the northern residential section of Battery Park City has been steadily adding apartment towers. Its park area is almost fully developed, and it is linked to the state-funded Hudson River Park that continues up the west side to Fifty-ninth Street. New esplanades and bikeways have been built piecemeal along the East River, and there are plans for further consolidation. Battery Park City and the World Financial Center had transformed what the 1960s planners had described as obsolete and often dilapidated piers, the blight of the elevated expressways, sprawling parking lots into a vibrant community. From the North Cove marina, yachts, tour boats, ferries, water taxis, and recreational sailboats define a new image of the waterfront."[2]

My own involvement with the WTC in the years following 1966 was to use their observation deck from time to time to take pictures of WRT's Jersey City and Weehawken projects across the Hudson, and once in a while eat at Windows on the World.

SEPTEMBER 11, 2001, AND AFTER

I had turned our television on at home for the morning news just in time to see the North Tower smoking from the first terrorist attack, and sat in horror as the second plane hit the South Tower. My and my wife's reactions were a mixture of disbelief, fear, and anger as the ensuing disaster played itself out and the towers collapsed. For hours, we listened dumbstruck to news anchors and analysts speculate on who was responsible and why the nation was under attack. Our lives would never be the same, although it would be sometime before that realization would sink in. My wife and I are sick at heart for the thousands directly involved, then and now in the war on terror, and we suffer a subliminal anxiety for the future of our country.

COMPETITION FOR REBUILDING THE WORLD TRADE CENTER SITE

As a professional planner and architect, I have watched the competition for rebuilding the WTC site with great interest as reported almost daily in *The New York Times* and on television. The first studies done by my old friend Jack Beyer of Beyer Blinder Belle were hampered by programmatic requirements and were almost universally scorned as pedestrian. The Lower Manhattan Development Corporation then invited applicants from around the world to submit credentials and selected six finalists who would be paid $50,000 each for their entries.

The team led by Polish born architect Daniel Libeskind was selected with a scheme that I like the best of the bunch. He reportedly spent $500,000 in the competition. His proposal is actually quite modest and practical, although who is going to pay for the world's tallest spire (1,760 feet) remains an open question. Governor George Pataki is reported to be a candidate. For that matter, developer Larry Silverstein owns all the rights to build on the site. He appears to have commissioned David Childs, head of Skidmore Owings & Merrill, a disappointed finalist, to design the first office building, I suppose in conformity with Libeskind's concept. Because Silverstein doesn't have a prime tenant, and is unlikely to start construction without one, I won't hold my breath. In the meanwhile, the competition for the memorial on the site proceeds. As they say, stay tuned.

THE HIJACKING OF THE 1966 LOWER MANHATTAN PLAN

The local Skyscraper Museum, displaced from its gallery space on Maiden Lane by the events of September 11, mounted an exhibition of the World Trade Center Towers at the New York Historical Society that ran from February 5 to May 5, 2001. Following this Carol Willis, the Skyscraper Museum's director, conceived the idea of reprinting the *1966*

Lower Manhattan Plan for that event. Unfortunately, she never contacted me or Bill Conklin, the principal authors. The following exchange of letters took place.

From David Wallace to Carol Willis, January 23, 2003

Dear Ms. Willis:

I recently received a copy of a reprint of *The Lower Manhattan Plan* put out by the Princeton Architectural Press. Your name appears as Editor on the cover, spine, and frontispiece, with the clear implication that you edited the entire document, not just the first three essays.

In fact, I was the partner-in-charge of the entire Lower Manhattan effort, designed and oversaw the work program, was the principal author of most of the text, and my partner Thomas A. Todd was the principal urban designer of the basic concepts and many of the illustrations including the plan drawing on the cover of the reprint.

I am astonished that you, as an experienced architectural historian, should not have contacted me in the process of publication, and should be responsible for such slipshod and improper accreditation. You have your professional reputation at stake.

I feel that my rights have been violated, and ask what you and the Princeton Architectural Press intend to do to correct the situation.

From Carol Willis to David Wallace, January 27, 2003

Dear Mr. Wallace:

I received your irate letter this afternoon, and it made me feel both apologetic and defensive, on a number of levels. I am truly sorry that you have taken such personal offense at the effort I made—without any payment to me or to The Skyscraper Museum—to make available again the admirable out-of-print publication with which you were involved some thirty-seven years ago. Certainly, I regret the very fast cycle of publication that we were forced into as we endeavored to bring the report back into print—which we did so that the *Plan* might contribute to the debate about planning Ground Zero. I would have greatly enjoyed the luxury of days of research, but because I squeezed this project into an already full schedule of work at the Museum, I relied, perhaps too much on the recollections of Paul Willen. His view of principal authorship is different than yours, but in any case, that question was not the subject of my essay, which was, rather, an attempt to understand, post 9/11, what was important about the bold planning efforts of the 1960's generally, not just about the *1966 Plan* itself.

I am quite frankly astonished at your complaint about my name appearing as the editor on the "cover, spine, and frontispiece" (obviously I did not design these) and your assertion that there is a "clear implication" that I edited the entire document. In fact, the back cover, frontis, and my essay all make clear that the book is a facsimile reprint, untouched except for a reduction in size. The credits for the original document are, simply, the ones given on the original title page. I fail to see how anyone could misapprehend this. I would also point out that if I had not decided to insert the cover letter that accompanied the particular book I borrowed, it seems that your full name would not have appeared in the reprint at all.

Again, I do deeply regret that I did not have the opportunity to interview all of the members of the original team, as I would certainly have wanted to do if this had been a normal research project. I do, however, resent your charges that my actions were improper and unprofessional. I did verify with Department of City Planning that the *1966 Plan* is a public document, and therefore without copyright; they did, however, specifically grant permission to make this reprint.

I congratulate you, as a member of a team of professionals, on an impressive piece of planning, commissioned by and prepared for the City of New York. I am delighted to have, finally, been able to make this rare document more widely available than its original 100 copies. I would have hoped that you, too, would have been pleased.

If you would like to volunteer, as Paul Willen and Jim Rossant did, to write an account that details your own recollections of the planning process, I would gratefully include it in the Museum's archive along with our copy of the original *Plan*.

Carol Willis

THE WAR ON TERROR: MY PERSPECTIVE

Historian Barbara Tuchman has written the wonderfully insightful book *The March of Folly: From Troy to Vietnam.* In it she records examples through history of misguided emperors, monarchs, and presidents who followed their own drummer to disastrous ends. The September 11 events galvanized a lackluster President George W. Bush into a truly crusade-like response. Is it a march of folly?

Bush and his administration first focused on Osama Bin Laden and Al Qaeda as not only the perpetrators of the World Trade Center attack, but also the leading edge of an Islamic assault on the entire Judeo-Christian civilization. The war on the Taliban in Afghanistan, then Saddam Hussein in Iraq, and the establishment of the Department of Homeland Security with the Patriot Act legislation make sense only if Bush's premise is correct.

THE NEW GROUND ZERO

On Sunday, August 31, 2003, the *Sunday New York Times* devoted eight pages of the Arts & Leisure section to an update on plans for "The New Ground Zero." Architect David Childs turns out to be the *eminence grise*, not just of the World Trade Center site, but all of Manhattan, according to the *Times*.

I remember Childs when he was brought to Washington, D.C., during President Gerald Ford's administration by Skidmore Owings & Merrill's political partner, Nathaniel Owings, to open their Washington, D.C., office. Childs's principal assignment was a master plan for Pennsylvania Avenue sponsored by U.S. Senator Daniel Patrick Moynihan. With the plan a success, Owings had President Ford appoint Childs as chairman of the National Capital Planning Commission (NCPC), where I met him.

WRT was in the process of preparing the Master Plan for the U.S. Capitol which, as a Congressional Precinct, was not under NCPC's jurisdiction, but we wanted their informal concurrence. I was very impressed with Childs. He thought in big terms like an urban designer. SOM's Washington, D.C., office was never financially successful and Childs was shortly reassigned to head up SOM's New York office. There he has been eminently successful, both as a business and intellectual leader. I have watched his career with interest from afar.

Shortly after moving to New York in 1984, Childs attended a lecture series at New York University by real estate developer Larry Silverstein. They struck up a friendship. When Silverstein leased the World Trade

Center Twin Towers shortly before September 11, 2001, he hired Childs to take a look at updating the towers and had scheduled a meeting for a first discussion on those plans for September 12, 2001. The meeting turned out to have a quite different agenda than planned. Silverstein and Childs spent the day figuring out how to rebuild.

Julie Iovine's article portrays Childs as "the Invisible Architect," one who "doesn't have a signature style," but is "changing the look of New York." She misses the point that Childs is first and foremost a superb urban designer who is as much concerned about the framework and context of his buildings as he is about the buildings themselves.

As the other articles in the section suggest, Childs has his work cut out for him. Michael Kimmel writes thoughtfully about how the need for a memorial is being met, and how different the challenge is from Washington's Vietnam Memorial. Philip Nobel considers what cultural institutions and functions might be included, and Herbert Muschamp votes against a Museum of Freedom. Hugo Lindgren reports on a small group that wants to rebuild the Twin Towers as they were, possibly Larry Silverstein's favorite solution. Childs is reported to have not liked the WTC anyway. Iovine quotes Childs as saying, "It was a place I went out of my way to avoid."

Meanwhile, Daniel Libeskind, the winner of the design competition with arguably the most exciting concept, hovers over David Childs's shoulder to try to ensure that the architecture fulfills his rather weird dream. Although he pushes himself to become the design architect, he has no relevant experience in that position, and SOM and Childs appear firmly entrenched. Libeskind will be a design consultant.

The challenge is both in program and design. Libeskind's high-rise buildings have unusual shapes and sizes that don't conform to Manhattan's zoning geometry or building code. How SOM (and Libeskind) can design competitive rental space for what will be speculative office buildings and still make them look anything like Libeskind's model is going to be interesting to watch.

I think that there will be a "taming" of the concept. Buildings with public sponsors will have big-name architects and will not be driven by economics. They can be as free-form as a Frank Gehry might devise, and Libeskind may feel that they are a threat to the integrity of his concept. But buildings that must be rentable and meet a financial bottom line will look less and less like Libeskind's fantasy and more and more like David Childs's Manhattan as time goes on.

1   *Plan for New York City. Volume 4: Manhattan*, p. 22.
2   *Lower Manhattan Plan*, 2003, p. 23.

14

The Developing Practice

We successfully used the *Lower Manhattan Plan* as the basis for promoting the firm as downtown planning and urban design experts. I used my teaching position and planning studios at Penn to refine and further develop the modeling process as the basis for a design approach to urban redevelopment.

In 1968, we won a competition for a downtown plan for Buffalo, New York, quickly followed by being selected for downtown plans for Los Angeles in 1970, New Orleans in 1973, and Miami in 1974. Having the credentials for such work was necessary, but not sufficient to win. In each case there was a key to the kingdom. I forget what the trick was in Buffalo, but in Miami, I was a fellow board member of the American Institute of Planners with George J. Acton, Jr., the local planning director. In Los Angeles, Hal H. Holker, the client group's executive director had been a WRT client in our first Camden, New Jersey, job. In both of them we were up against national competition and opened up local offices as part of the agreements. We sent senior associate Donald Brackenbush to Los Angeles. He ran the firm's branch office for the succeeding 10 years until he decided he wanted to become a developer. We closed the Los Angeles office when he left because we discovered that Brackenbush was the essential ingredient in getting work and was not replaceable.

The *Downtown Miami Plan*, with me as partner-in-charge and Richard Huffman—whom we had recruited to head up our New Orleans work—as project director was very successful. Miami was a city in transition from predominantly Anglo to predominantly Hispanic in the early 1970s, and by 1976 when our *Miami Comprehensive Neighborhood Plan* was published in two languages our Miami office was well established. We had

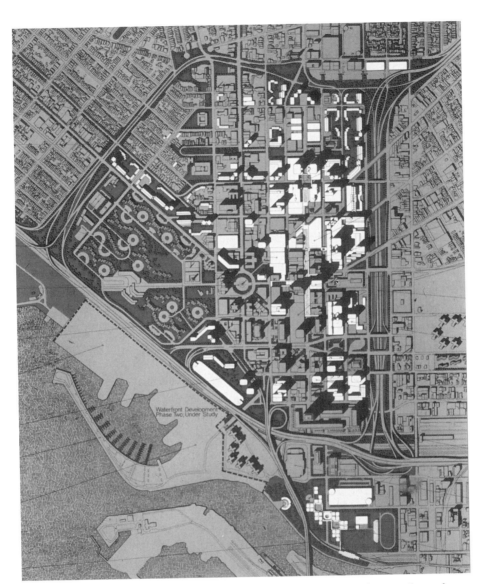

14.1 The Plan for Downtown Buffalo, New York, was one of a number of downtown plans prepared under either mine or Tom Todd's supervision or together.

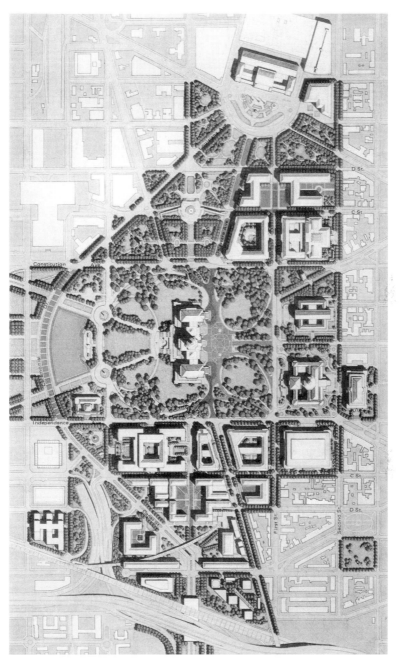

14.2 The Master Plan for the United States Capitol, Washington, D.C., which Tom Todd and I prepared together for the Architect of the Capitol. It proposed an environmental capacity for development on Capitol Hill based on movement system limits. Today WRT is heading up a team for a new master plan for the House of Representatives.

moved Boris Dramov and his wife, Bonnie Fisher, from our San Francisco office to manage the production of the comprehensive plan. Boris and Bonnie returned to San Francisco, and they now own and run ROMA, a notable planning and design firm based there.

The Miami office is now located in Coral Gables, and has been run by John Fernsler and Alyn Pruett since the Dramovs left. We had hired them straight out of Penn's graduate urban design program to help prepare the 1976 Comprehensive Plan. The office has been responsible for many notable plans and landscapes. Today, Fernsler specializes in comprehensive plans and recently completed a notable one for Kansas City, Kansas. Pruett specializes in college and university master planning; he is currently working on one for Georgia Tech.

Tom Todd and I were the partners principally responsible for the various downtown and urban design plans, such as the very successful AIA award-winning master plan for the U.S. Capitol in Washington, D.C., in 1976 for the Architect of the Capitol and the U.S. Congress. I managed a huge project in San Francisco on the waterfront called Mission Bay for the Santa Fe Railroad. Mission Bay was an award-winning design in *Progressive Architecture* magazine, but was rejected by the city and never was built. We were retained by Robert Mosbacher, later Secretary of Commerce under President Ronald Reagan, to prepare a plan for the 6,000-acre Cinco Ranch in the suburbanizing area just west of Houston. Mosbacher reportedly had a falling out with his partner when he refused her proposal of marriage, so they sold the ranch. They had paid $15 million for the ranch, and sold it to US Homes for $85 million based on our plan. This took place in the late 1980s, and shortly thereafter the economy took a dive.

In the meanwhile, Bill Roberts was building a specialty in master plans for barrier islands such as Sea Pines on Hilton Head, South Carolina, and Amelia Island, Florida. He worked for developer Charles Fraser. We were selected because of McHag's reputation, but Fraser unfortunately quickly became disenchanted with McHarg. Roberts became the principal partner for Wye Island's plan on the eastern shore of Maryland for the Rouse Company. The Wye Island plan was finally rejected as too urban by the county in spite of its very persuasive and environmentally sensitive elements—an example of smart growth.

In our business, while you cannot expect to win them all, we had more winners than losers. Roberts had one of the most successful in the master plan for Sanibel Island, Florida. Sanibel was the Florida base for

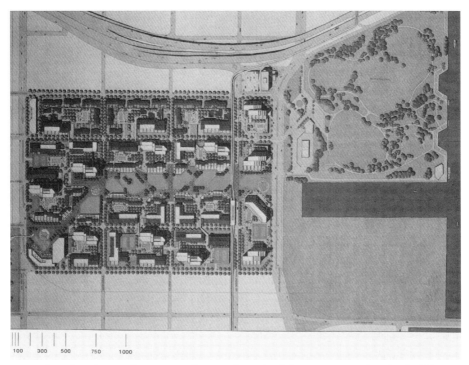

100   300   500   750   1000

14.3 The Plan for Park West at the north end of downtown Miami, Florida, with Biscayne Bay at right. This followed downtown and citywide plans and became the basis for WRT's award-winning Overtown project and subsequent housing developments.

the CIA during the Bay of Pigs fiasco. In 1977, Lee County had zoned the island for wall-to-wall development. In protest the citizens of Sanibel Island incorporated.

They went through a consultant selection process, had conducted interviews, and were all set to proceed when Charles H. Page, the cousin of the mayor and a former student of mine at Penn, told the islanders that they must include WMRT in their consideration. Mayor Porter J. Goss (now a U.S. Congressman) and the newly elected city council interviewed us belatedly, and WMRT, with Bill Roberts as principal, was unanimously selected. The resulting plan was based on the environmentally derived capacity of the island to sustain development—most notably to evacuate the population across a two-lane bridge with four-hours notice of an oncoming hurricane. Rapacious developers from Chicago whose property on the island had been drastically downzoned sued Sanibel Island

and the firm, but the court ruled in our favor and the plan has stood the test of time.

METROPOLITAN REGIONAL PLANNING

In the early 1970s the firm's work expanded to a metropolitan regional scale. My training at Harvard had included a semester's studio on California's Central Valley and my doctorate is in regional planning, but nothing had really prepared us for the metropolitan assignments we won.

Meanwhile, Ian McHarg had taken a sabbatical leave from Penn and from the firm in 1968. He wrote *Design With Nature*, which was published in 1969. It was a summation of the studio workshops he had been teaching, the *Plan for the Valleys*, and a lecture series he had called "Man and Environment." He shopped the "dummy" of the book around to various publishers, both text and graphics, as he told it, and every publishing house was interested, but everyone wanted to change it in some way. One publisher wanted an $8\text{-}1/2$ inch by 11 inch format instead of his 11 inch by 11 inch format, no color, fewer graphics, whatever. McHarg wanted it his way. He finally decided that—with minor reproduction help from WMRT that he quickly repaid—he would publish it himself, and made a minor fortune as a consequence. He had it printed by a local press and then sold the completed product to the Natural History Press, who distributed it.

Design with Nature's publication was a defining event for him, for WMRT's reputation, and for the landscape profession as a whole. McHarg's speaking fees rose dramatically as he went around the country promoting the book, his method, himself, and the incidentally, the firm. He quickly became a famous personality and a national celebrity. Students flocked to Penn to study with him and the landscape department flourished and expanded into an environmentally based version of regional planning. McHarg's personal emphasis remained on his method of layering ecological observations and his putting his concern for nature and natural process first. Unfortunately, after the *Plan for the Valleys*, he never again successfully integrated his results with physical land planning in a real-life project.

But at the firm, integration of the two emphases became a trademark. Constance Lieder, one of my old contacts in Baltimore, was the head of the Maryland State Planning Commission and in 1972, the commission chose WMRT to prepare a plan for a study of the Chesapeake Bay. The result was essentially a "plan for a plan" whose programs included not only a McHarg-type environmental inventory but also were supplemented by, among other inventive features, a so-called "water budget" to show water's crucial role in the system, which was designed by our associate Richard Nalbandian. An atlas that allowed for instant enlargement of any element anticipated the present Geographical Information Systems (GIS) by a number of years. Later, in 1994, with David Hamme as partner-in-charge, WRT headed a team to apply these programs in producing a Governor's Plan for the Chesapeake Bay for Maryland's Department of Environmental Resources.

Also in 1972, WMRT was chosen by the Washington Metropolitan Area Transportation Authority (WMATA) to prepare an environmental impact evaluation of the first of their subway lines to be built. WMATA and the various other entities involved in the route selection and design

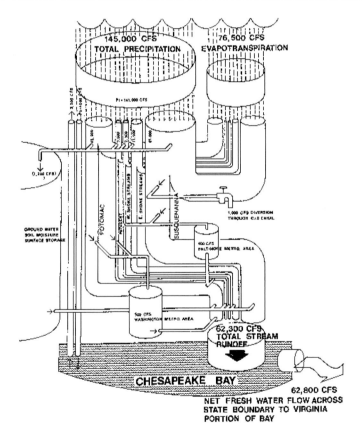

14.4 At my insistence and with much scientific reluctance, WMRT's associate, geologist Richard Nalbandian prepared this water budget for Chesapeake Bay. This could be translated into a computer model as an effective analytical and planning tool.

found the result that I had prepared so useful that we were hired for similar evaluations and route selection criteria, leg-by-leg, for the entire system. We completed the last assignment in 1997, 25 years later. Each partner successively took on one of these assignments, which became a training ground for regional qualifications.

As a consequence, transportation-related regional planning became an additional specialty of the firm. In 1973, when the Denver Regional Transportation District (DRTD) was looking for an engineering firm to design their system, Bill Roberts persuaded the board that they should know the kind of region they wanted before they chose the hardware to serve it. We proposed ourselves as the prime contractors who would help them select the engineers after we had completed a regional transportation plan. This (albeit rather soft-headed argument) appealed to a board dominated by environmentalists who were all too conscious of Denver's daily smog levels. But the clincher in our selection was Harry Parrish, an executive director, who was enchanted with the idea of a fully automated Personal Rapid Transit system (PRT) at any cost, and he wanted a consultant who knew less about transit than he did. So we were hired.

On the environmental side, this was an opportunity for McHarg to apply his inventory method at a regional level, and he developed more than 80 marvelously colored eight-foot long maps that were to be the basis for a regional plan. However, our assignment was to prepare a transportation plan, which we did, relying on personal rapid transit. PRT was still in its experimental stage nationally. It was operating and installed in Morgantown, West Virginia, but it dominated the Denver plan. Although the plan we produced looked great on paper—and mass rapid transit stations were to be the basis for organizing growth—the Urban Mass Transit Authority in Washington, D.C., would have none of it. The plan was never adopted and was soon superceded by hard-nosed engineers. I sometimes wonder what has happened to all of McHarg's gorgeous maps.

That same year, the San Francisco Metropolitan Transportation Commission (SFMTC), influenced by our Denver work still in process, conceived of setting up an environmental impact assessment procedure whereby all physical, social, and environmental phenomena, at whatever scale available, would be mapped. These maps would then be accessible, through computers, to serve as background for any agency to array their alternative plans on to make a quick assessment of impact. Unfortunately, without the computer capability of a GIS model, (still being developed

14.5 WMRT prepared environmental impact evaluations for all of the Washington Metropolitan Area Transit Authority's routes, which became important factors in the choice of alignments and stations.

during this time, the early 1970s) the result was another set of 80 beautiful regional maps, which produced information overkill and was little used.

McHarg and I had worked together on the San Francisco Bay plan with increasing friction about how to utilize the environmental and other information in the physical planning process. He clung to his graphic overlay system in spite of its illegibility when more than a few factors were combined; I proposed cell and a number-retrieval method that I had developed with Richard Nalbandian, one of McHarg's former students. I remember an embarrassing meeting with the SFMTC board where McHarg presented his maps and then publicly denigrated Nalbandian's product and my method.

As a consequence, when the firm was hired by the Minneapolis-St. Paul region in 1975, I refused to work with McHarg and he was the sole partner involved. In 1978, he was hired by the Toledo and Detroit regional planning commissions and on both he went ahead without any other partner involvement. He still ignored what by then was the growing GIS computer network capability. His standard procedure was to spend the

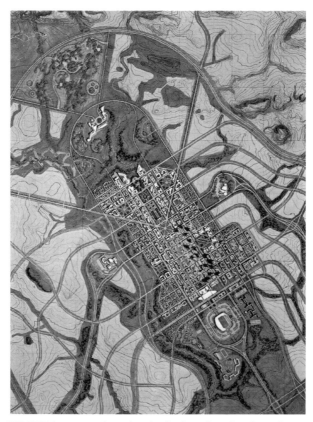

14.6 In 1978, WMRT became the physical planning leader of a team that prepared a regional plan, city plan, and central area plan to Nigeria's new capital, Abuja.

majority of the fee preparing the environmental inventory, leaving little for any plan preparation. All three projects lost money, the latter two dramatically. In addition, the firm narrowly avoided a lawsuit by the city of Detroit for failure to complete the work satisfactorily.

The most interesting and exotic experience we had in regional metropolitan planning was in preparing the master plan for Abuja, the new capital of Nigeria. I was contacted by an old colleague, Abraham Kruskov in the fall of 1975. Abe had been on my staff at the Chicago Housing Authority in 1950, and he was now head of Archisystems, Inc., a subsidiary of the Summa Corporation, a Howard Hughes operation. Kruskov was organizing a team to make a proposal to the Nigerians. Archisystems, WMRT, and the PRC Corporation formed a tripartite joint venture partnership, the International Planning Association. PRC was responsible for transportation planning and engineering, WMRT was responsible for physical planning, urban design, and architecture, and Abe was the point man with the Nigerians.

Tom Todd went to Lagos to present our credentials the day after Christmas and we signed a contract for more than $2.5 million and started work in 1976. We set up an office in a rented house on Ikaye Island in Lagos. Todd and Walter Hanson of PRC were in charge of the planning and design of the new city.

The Nigerian Federal Capital Authority had selected a general location in the center of the country analogous to the U.S. District of Columbia, but much larger. Within it we were to prepare regional metropolitan and central area programs and plans for a city of three million people. Water supply, utility systems, location of an airport, and capital government facilities were key elements, as was the nature of the environment and the Nigerian culture.

The ultimate concept used Washington, D.C., as a model for government layout with the President's Palace adjacent to a monolithic granite outcropping, Aso Rock. Alyn Pruett, now a WRT principal, was responsible for the prototype community plans and Todd designed the central area.

As we were completing our work in 1979, architect Kenzo Tange from Japan was brought in to design the government buildings. He threw out the central area plan and where Todd showed boulevards, Tange instituted elevated expressways much as he had proposed for Tokyo Bay. Tange's plan was abandoned, and in the 1990 publication *Abuja: So Far, So Good* by the Federal Capital Territory Authority, the International Planning Association, and all Todd's and Hanson's plans are reproduced as the official master plans.

We finished the job in 1979, with some $800,000 due as our final payment. As Tom Todd tells it, our invoice was sitting at the bottom of a pile on the Secretary's secretary's desk. Our PRC "representative" knew the Secretary's secretary had a longing for an English tea set, so he flew to London and had a complete service flown back, and magically, we were paid.

By 1978, my growing disenchantment with teaching at Penn had gotten to the point that I began to consider myself a practitioner who taught on the side, rather than a teacher who practiced on the side. I found myself making commitments for the firm and my jobs that competed with my academic responsibilities. This tension and a department rife with inside politics made me decide to simplify my life. I resigned my professorship. It meant a substantially reduced income, but the firm prospered, and I more than recovered.

It was also an end to a chapter in my life that had enriched and rewarded me enormously. Ideas and attitudes from students and fellow faculty members had become an important component of my professional life.

15

McHarg and Pardisan

I come reluctantly to the plan for Pardisan and McHarg's departure from WMRT. Pardisan—the name means paradise in Persian—was a proposed 721-acre recreational and educational park on a tract of barren desert at the northwest edge of Tehran, the capital city of Iran. The idea was conceived by Eskandar Firouz, the Shah's minister of the environment, as a place to explain the Persian culture to the world, and to replicate all of the world's major environments to help bring Iranians into the twenty-first century. Proposed facilities would range from an aquarium to a zoo, with a museum of science and industry and a wide variety of other cultural and educational facilities in between.

WMRT was first contacted in 1972 by the Iranian Embassy. Bill Roberts conducted a preliminary feasibility study to outline the scope of the work needed for a master plan, and we were selected. It was a "natural" project for McHarg to run, and Roberts agreed somewhat apprehensively to turn the project direction over to him. McHarg and Firouz hit it off from the first as reported in McHarg's autobiography, and the resulting master plan, published in 1975, was an outstanding professional achievement. In Firouz's words, the park "must transform Iranian attitudes toward the environment," and "it must help modern Persians to solve modern problems." The master plan and accompanying movie by consultants Charles Eames and Glenn Fleck promised all of the above within the theme of a Persian Garden.

Unfortunately for WMRT, McHarg had exceeded the budget and incurred an actual loss of $60,000. That was a huge loss for us. No amount of pleading succeeded in getting relief with the client's project coordinator, Jahangir Sedaghatfar. Sedaghatfar assured us that we would be able

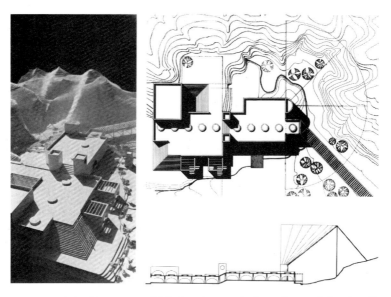

15.1 A segment of the Bazaar and Birds of Prey Aviary, Part of the Pardisan Master Plan.

to easily recover our costs when we proceeded into the landscape design contract for the next phase. Ah, how many firms have been lured by such promises?

The overall fee basis for the design and construction contract was to be a lump-sum contract in the millions of dollars, with interim payment on percent completion. We were required to set up an Iranian corporation with an Iranian architect partner, open an office in Tehran with a principal-in-residence, and the "major part" of the work was to be done there. All reports and documents were to be both in Farsi and English. Disputes were to be settled solely by the project coordinator. No arbitration would be allowed. Payment of outstanding invoices was in Iranian rials, promised on a timely basis, but no penalty was to be paid for money in arrears. Sedaghatfar promised that he would require only a "very general" design-documentation level of detail, because workers's skill levels would be primitive. As we saw later, this promise was made to keep the overall estimate as low as possible.

The client was to provide a survey of the site before we began planning, a provision that it ultimately failed to carry out in spite of Sedaghatfar's demands that we proceed with design anyway. We were also required to take out an "irrevocable letter of credit" for $100,000. That letter of credit sounded like a generous advance, but it turned out to be a hook whereby they could demand repayment at any time for any or no cause at all.

The whole arrangement was a formula for disaster. I strongly argued for rejecting the assignment and swallowing the master plan loss. Bill Roberts and Tom Todd were on the fence, and were finally swung to McHarg's side when he agreed to take any ultimate loss incurred from his own capital account. Ultimately, on a three-to-one vote with me still against it, they decided to proceed. Our senior associate, Narendra Juneja, agreed to move to Tehran and be the managing principal for WMRT/IRAN, Inc. Juneja was an associate professor who taught with McHarg at Penn. He was reluctant to take on the assignment because he was an Indian national and was afraid of losing his green card, but he was unable to refuse McHarg. Juneja also was single and would not have to uproot a family.

Juneja was a marvelous conceptual designer imbued with an environmental emphasis, but was not a strong personality and had no construction experience on the scale that was required. For that matter, McHarg's own experience did not qualify him for such a major undertaking. To offset this lack of experience, we set up a design team to include Roberts, Todd, and our construction-expert partner, Charles B. Tomlinson, to keep things under control. Our Iranian partner, an architect named Nader Ardalan who had co-authored the master plan, rounded out the top staff.

By 1978, we had spent the $100,000 advance and had had $300,000 in invoices outstanding for more than six months. We were well beyond the schematic phase into design development, and still had not received the site survey from the client. Rather than requiring only general detailing for design documents, Sedaghatfar insisted on elaborate documentation and our budget was soon in deep trouble. In the meantime, construction was under way for a 16 foot-high perimeter wall whose plans and details were developed at significant cost to us without recognition as an extra outside the original plan's scope. The wall was needed, it turned out, to keep other Iranian departments from expropriating the site for their own purposes. And then in October 1978, the Iranian revolution struck and the Shah fled the country.

Events from that time all happened in a blur. The Anglo-Iranian Bank that handled our account was burned to the ground, fortunately along with the original of our irrevocable letter of credit. The renewal date passed and we were able to reject our client's pleas to reinstate it, pointing out that they owed us far more than $100,000. Juneja, who hadn't wanted to go to Iran in the first place, managed to get on the last plane out before they closed the airport, only to die of a heart attack a short while later, which may have been brought on by the stress from managing a project under such difficult circumstances. Minister Firouze, who had been related to Shah Pahlevi, had been replaced by a new minister, Manichour Feili, who demanded we continue to carry out our contract, but refused to pay any of the $300,000 owed. Ironically, the purpose of Pardisan—to acquaint Iran with the world and vice versa—was in direct opposition to the Ayatollah Kohmeni's declared desire to isolate Iran from the world. Notwithstanding, when we said we could not continue, Feili declared us in default, and had us tried for breach of contract in absentia in an Iranian court. The court condemned us to unspecified penalties.

The project showed a total cost of some $500,000 in invoices and "work-in-process" over income received when we had called a halt on any further work. At this point, McHarg reneged on his promise to accept Iranian losses, declaring that he could not be responsible for what he called a *force majeure*. Roberts, Todd, and I decided that after Toledo and Detroit—and now Pardisan—enough was enough. McHarg, who had always been trouble to have as a partner, but arguably was worth it, had become more trouble than he was worth. In an unforgettable partners' meeting, we asked McHarg to leave and he simply stopped coming to the office. He claimed in his autobiography that we changed the lock on his office door and denied access to his records and files, but that is not true.

Only a lucky chain of events prevented WRT from going bankrupt. In 1976, Todd had started the preparation of the master plan for the region and the city of Abuja, the new national capital of Nigeria. The resulting positive cash flow became a life saver. In Tehran, the Iranian revolutionaries laid siege to the American Embassy; President Jimmy Carter froze all Iranian assets in American banks; the United Nations referred settlement of all claims against Iran to the International Tribunal in The Hague; and the U.S. State Department selected our case as a prototype for "small claims" and provided us with free legal help. When Roberts went to The Hague and presented our massive documentation and other evidence before a three-judge panel in the Netherlands, we were awarded the $300,000 for outstanding invoices plus accumulated interest, less one-fifth of the total because Juneja was an Indian national.

We each independently received $187,500. This fortunately avoided the problem of how to get agreement from McHarg on dividing it. Although the total equaled $750,000, we still had a loss of $200,000 for work in process to account for. In spite of McHarg's earlier agreement to accept any loss, McHarg threatened us with a lawsuit for reimbursement of his capital account. We finally settled for an additional $100,000 to him. In retrospect, if we had been required to complete the Iranian contract as negotiated, we would have gone bankrupt. In that sense, the Iranian Revolution saved WRT.

For a while, we worried about what affect McHarg's departure would have on the firm. By 1980, when we reorganized as Wallace Roberts & Todd with three new partners, David C. Hamme, Richard W. Huffman, and Charles B. Tomlinson, Ian McHarg had become a household name for environmentalists. However, ironically and in a very real sense, he had generated—through his teaching and influence, not only in landscape architecture but also across many disciplines such as engineering, law, and real estate—an interest in his philosophy and refinement and elaboration of his methods so pervasive that his personal involvement in professional work was no longer necessary. McHarg's disciples had spread across the country and had computerized the environmental inventory process with the GIS system he had ignored. His disciples' procedures went far beyond what McHarg himself had done. Many jurisdictions had standardized them as part of land-use regulations to the point that McHarg had—except as a personality—outlived his professional usefulness. Nevertheless, his contribution to the world was well-recognized by any number of awards. His recognition culminated in the Japan Award, which he received shortly before his death on March 5, 2001.

We accomplished our firm's emancipation from McHarg during the 1970s, with Bill Robert's preparation of the award-winning master plans for the two barrier islands, Amelia and Sanibel off the coast of Florida, and for several large plantations on Hilton Head Island, South Carolina. After initially being exposed to McHarg's bombastic style at the beginning of our environmental analysis, Charles Fraser—of Sea Pines fame and the client for Amelia Island—had said, "Don't bring him down here again." Other clients also insisted that Roberts run their projects. To all intents, McHarg had been declared *persona non grata*.

McHarg's departure was a considerable personal loss to me. He and I had started out social friends as well as professional partners with a shared enthusiasm for our work that is rare. I was constantly entertained by and amazed at him. However, as time went on we drew apart, and McHarg became more preoccupied with his own approach and his growing fame and less with the firm as a firm. He says in his autobiography that I envied him and perhaps I did. Our different objectives drove us apart, but how the man could talk and write!

16

Planning New Jersey's Hudson River Waterfront

The next 20 years, from 1980 onward, brought great diversity to the firm's practice. In 1982, we were introduced to the world of New Jersey when the state's Department of Environmental Protection Commissioner, Robert E. Hughey, fired Robert Geddes of Geddes Brecher Qualls Cunningham from further planning for the 800-acre Liberty State Park in Jersey City. Geddes's wife, Eleanor, had campaigned against Governor Thomas Kean, Hughey's boss. Hughey had appointed Russell Myers as director of the state Division of Parks and Forestry. Myers had first asked Leo Molinaro and the American City Corporation from Baltimore, a subsidiary of the Rouse Company, to replace Geddes. But Myers was appalled at their standard sticker price of $150,000. Myers learned from talking to Walter Sondheim that I was the right person to hire, and when I told Myers that we would update Geddes's master plan for $12,000, Myers couldn't resist.

This was part of my foot-in-the-door marketing strategy. And for 10 years WRT implemented the new master plan with such dramatic projects as the landscape design of the two-mile Liberty Walk overlooking Lower Manhattan, Ellis Island, and the Statue of Liberty, Lincoln Harbor, and Exchange Place. Incidentally, Myers and Geddes were both Harvard classmates of mine.

In 30 years, the west bank of the Hudson River has been transformed from an almost continuous wasteland of rail yards and dumps in Manhattan's shadow to New Jersey's Gold Coast.

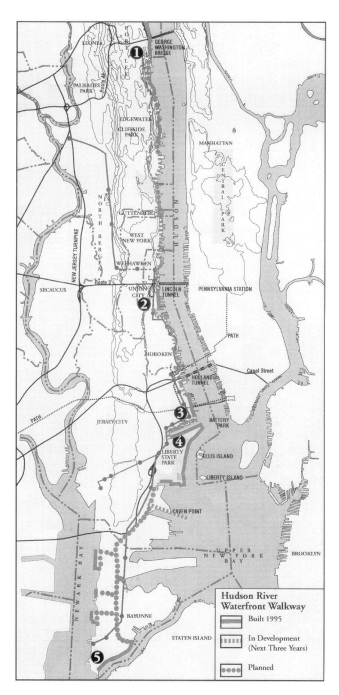

16.1 The New Jersey Hudson River Waterfront Walkway is to connect nine municipalities along the Hudson's west bank from Edgewater on the north to Bayonne on the south. It was more than two-thirds complete as of the end of 2003.

Up until the 1980s, empty factories, abandoned rail lines, and derelict piers occupied nearly 1,900 acres, close to half of this waterfront region between the cliffs of the Palisades and the water's edge.

Local redevelopment, particularly in Jersey City, Hoboken, West New York, and Weehawken, had initiated a scramble for development rights. The federal Harbor Cleanup Program implemented by the U.S. Corps of Engineers tore down the dilapidated piers, in many cases leaving the piles in place. The result was a clear opportunity and Geddes had brilliantly conceived Liberty Walk in Jersey City's Liberty State Park as a freestanding viewing platform, but it turned out to have a larger purpose. The walkway idea was one of the keys to the regional planning problem of how to link and revitalize the entire 18-mile New Jersey Hudson River waterfront.

The private response was massive. By 1985, an inventory listed more than 33 million square feet of office and commercial space in seven of the nine waterfront communities. From Edgewater on the north to Bayonne on the south, 35,000 dwelling units, 3,600 hotel rooms, and 4,500 boat slips were planned. Jersey City was one of the main targets. Liberty State Park became the center of a major redevelopment effort to eliminate areas

16.2 At Liberty State Park in Jersey City, the walkway provides an unobstructed two-mile viewing platform for Lower Manhattan and the Statue of Liberty. Ellis Island is on the near left.

blighted by the rail and industrial debris from the eighteenth and nineteenth centuries.

Each waterfront community responded separately; there was no mechanism to coordinate a regional response to the development pressure. Chaos loomed.

THE STATE ACTS

Governor Brendan Byrne responded by creating a Governor's Task Force with staff head John Weingart. The task force was the source of the estimates of growth, and recommended creation of a regional waterfront authority patterned after the Hackensack Meadowlands Commission. None of the local jurisdictions were in the least bit interested.

So the state directed two key agencies—the state Department of Transportation (NJDOT) and the state Department of Environmental Protection (NJDEP)—to develop a regulatory way of dealing with the growth that everyone wanted, but needed to be coordinated.

NJDOT hired Parsons Brinkerhoff Quade & Douglas, whose engineer Al Harf developed a transportation plan. The two most important elements of the plan are a north-south arterial highway and a light-rail transit system. Their function is to connect the waterfront areas to each other and to the two vehicular and three Port Authority Trans Hudson (PATH) tunnels to Manhattan. By doing this, the potential for development between the Palisades cliffs and the Hudson's edge maybe tripled. Along with intrinsically lower development costs and rents ($5 to $20 per square foot less than Manhattan), the Hudson Gold Coast becomes very competitive with New York City.

The waterfront highway's southern portion is already completed. It runs from Bayonne at the bridge to Staten Island over the Kill van Kull up through Jersey City with interchange connections to the Lincoln and Holland tunnels. The northern 7 1/2 mile section is built through Hoboken, Weehawken, and West New York, where it connects to a narrowed River Road at Edgewater on the north, several miles short of the George Washington Bridge approaches.

The Hudson-Bergen Light Rail Transit System (LRT) roughly parallels the highway. It runs on old rail rights-of-way from Bayonne to Jersey City's Exchange Place and the Colgate and Newport development areas. Built under an unusual turnkey arrangement for New Jersey Transit by the Raytheon Company, it is planned to extend through Hoboken and ultimately reach the Guy Lombardo Interchange of the New Jersey Turnpike for the park-and-ride customers.

I don't think there will be many park-and-riders. I hope, as development along the northern waterfront proceeds; the possibility of a waterfront branch will not be precluded. New Jersey Transit's chief planner, Al Harf, who headed the Parsons Brinkerhoff Quade & Douglas engineering team that planned the LRT, is sensitive not only to the ridership potential of people who will live along the river to commute to Manhattan via PATH stations, but also to the predominately northern areas, where people will work in Hoboken, Jersey City and Bayonne to the south.

New Jersey Transit had invested some $66 million in modernizing its three PATH stations in Jersey City prior to September 11, 2001. In the aftermath of that disaster, the agency is rethinking its whole priority with a public clientele in favor of mass transit. The first phase of LRT was only seven miles of the 22.6-mile system. I am hoping it will prove politically popular with a public support for an extension along the river to interconnect with the many ferry terminals that have sprung up after September 11.

WALKING THE WATERFRONT

NJDEP was, among other things, given jurisdiction over a 500-foot zone along tidal waterfronts, mainly intended as protection of the Jersey shore. Regulation was assigned to the Division of Coastal Resources headed up by the same John Weingart, who had worked for the Governor's Task Force on the Hudson. NJDEP was given power to approve waterfront development permits and adopt design guidelines for their preparation within this waterfront zone.

In and of itself, this approval power would not have been of regional significance except for Weingart's recognition of its potential for coordination with the transportation plan. In addition, Weingart had seen the waterfront walkway proposed by our Lower Manhattan Plan, published in *The Lower Hudson River* by the Regional Plan Association.[1] Weingart thought it was a great idea.

In 1982, Weingart issued a request for proposals for a feasibility study of a waterfront walkway from Bayonne to the George Washington Bridge and WRT was selected. Under my direction, Antoinette F. Seymour, our senior associate, re-examined the potential for development, the obstacles to be overcome, and came up with a plan.

16.3 The Liberty Walk is part of the Hudson River Walkway. Jersey City's downtown is in the distance.

To implement the plan, any development permit must have a publicly, accessible waterfront zone at least 36 feet wide, of which at least 18 feet are to be paved. The walkway is to be for pedestrians and bicycles, with connections to adjacent developments, and access links every several hundred feet to the city's street system and public transit. Construction and maintenance of the walkway is to be by the owner/developer.

In 1988, developers, and the communities who were to build the walkways, asked Weingart for explicit design guidelines, to ensure the various walkway segments would be compatible. I and Eric Tamulonis, our senior landscape associate, prepared a Design Guidelines Manual to became the basis for any NJDEP approval of a project along the shoreline.

More than two-thirds of the 18.6-mile walkway has been built, and another 3.6 miles are committed. My firm has designed three segments—at Liberty State Park and Exchange Place in Jersey City and at Lincoln Harbor in Weehawken—for more than three miles in all.

Aside from those parts of the walkway designed by WRT for various clients, the honor for getting the walkway built goes in large part to

William Neyenhouse, who for some 15 years has served as the Hudson River Waterfront Coordinator for NJDEP.

Even though it is being completed in a somewhat piecemeal fashion, the walkway has brought significant continuity to the entire waterfront. It is the linear part of a regional open space network linking the waterfront's two outstanding regional facilities, Liberty State Park on the south and the Palisades Interstate Park north of the George Washington Bridge.

OPPORTUNITIES ALONG THE WATERFRONT

The development community has not welcomed the governmental imposition of the walkway for understandable reasons. They created an organization which undertook a study of what the walkway cost. They then instituted a lawsuit claiming that the regulations constituted a partial taking without compensation. The courts ruled against them and the walkway's construction has proceeded. Opportunities abound for creating memorable urban places along the Hudson waterfront and some, such as Exchange Place directly across the river from the World Trade Center site, are among them. Liberty Walk at Liberty State Park is another.

At the north end of the walkway, the high cliffs of the Palisades stretch six miles from Weehawken north to the George Washington Bridge and beyond and are close to the river. Most of the communities along this part of the waterfront—Edgewater, North Bergen, Guttenberg, West New York, and Weehawken—have been dedicated at keeping building heights below the viewline from the top of the cliffs, which range from 150 to 300 feet. Just west of Edgewater, in Cliffside Park and Fort Lee, 30-story residential towers were built on top of the cliffs, dominating the skyline. The walkway will be, and in some places already is, a key link between these communities along the river.

In the next section of riverfront, Port Imperial North in West New York is under construction with a planned build-out of 4,360 residential units. About 1,000 units have already been built and waterfront townhouses sell for more than $1 million. And in Weehawken just north of Hartz Mountain Industries' Lincoln Harbor, the 80-acre Port Imperial South project, long in the planning stage, will include 2,000 new dwelling units, two million square feet of office and commercial space, and a ferry terminal relocating the one already in operation to Manhattan. This site is a natural for a real urban subcenter to Hoboken and Jersey City and satellite to Manhattan. The walkway is an important element in all the designs.

16.4 Exchange Place is at the center of downtown Jersey City and when the World Trade Center site is improved, it will again be the focus of satellite development.

Hoboken, at the center of the overall waterfront "opportunity zone," is another city rich in possibilities. Hoboken is very much a brownstone copy of historic Brooklyn across the East River. The city had been slow to allow waterfront development to proceed. But when it did start, as in the residential complex on the 45-acre site once occupied by the Bethlehem Shipyard, development has been rapid albeit not very compatible with its historic context. Unfortunately, Hoboken rejected the LRT route near the river, and forced it to go inland adjacent to the cliffs before connecting to the alignment for Lincoln Harbor and beyond. But it has embraced the walkway.

Hoboken officials and neighborhood activists also turned down several huge waterfront proposals, one by Hartz Mountain Industries designed by WRT, the other by the New York Port Authority, for other waterfront sites including the ferry terminal and the New Jersey Transit rail yard. In this case, the city recognized that a new master plan was needed and is carefully developing the waterfront in accordance with new guidelines. As I write, New Jersey Transit has issued a request for proposals for the 300-acre Hoboken rail yards between downtown

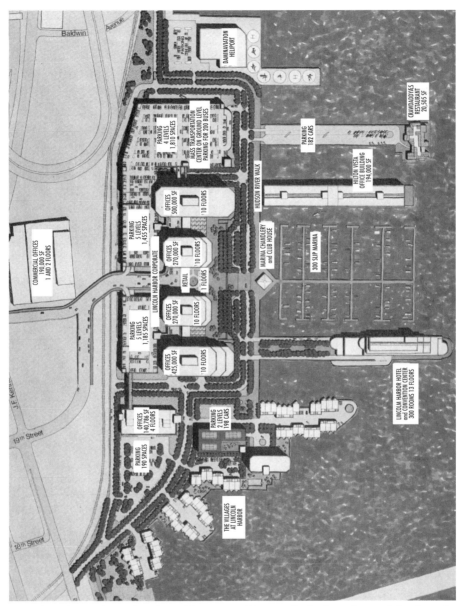

16.5 Lincoln Harbor, developed by Hartz Mountain Industries and designed by WRT, has an almost mile-long section of the walkway.

Hoboken and Newport in Jersey City. The plan is to allow development while keeping the rail yards in operation.

Jersey City to the immediate south of Hoboken also suffers from unco-ordinated and incomplete projects. But change here is already dramatic and uninhibited by height limits as the remains of the Palisade cliffs move westward away from the river. More than 10 million square feet of office development have been completed in the downtown in the last 12 years, and another 13 million are in the pipeline. Office workers and residents alike have been lured by the convenience of three PATH stations five min-utes from Manhattan. The World Trade Center disaster put the southern PATH route out of commission, but as of November 2003 it is back in operation.

Both the light-rail line and the waterfront walkway have been incor-porated into Jersey City's current development plans and have influenced the character of the designs significantly. Urban designers Andres Duany and Elizabeth Plater-Zyberk from Miami were hired by Peter Mocco, perennial non-developer of the 500-acre Liberty Harbor North redevelop-ment project to the immediate west of the old Colgate project on the river's edge, which is now in development. They came up with a mar-velous scheme for low- and mid-rise rental development, in effect repli-cating Brooklyn, at a density of more than 100 units per acre, but the market apparently still isn't right and Mocco hasn't done anything as usual. The latest word, however, is that he has prepared preliminary plans for the northwest sector.

WHAT MIGHT HAVE BEEN

It's tempting to speculate about a different outcome: What might have been, had New Jersey's waterfront had a regional authority as John Weingart wanted, an authority with the power to impose a detailed regional plan like those governing Manhattan's Battery Park City, or even Baltimore's Inner Harbor. Could there have been an overall urban design vision effective for the entire 18.6-mile waterfront?

I don't think so. In New York City and in Baltimore, only one city was involved—and no private landowners. I don't think it would have been possible to come up with a single image that included land uses, densities, design principles, policies regarding affordable housing, public facilities, open space, and the sequence and financing of development. Is it likely that an image bold enough to "stir men's blood," in the time-honored words of Daniel Burnham, could have been agreed upon by nine communities, multiple egocentric owners and developers, and the general public?

I'd like to think so, but I seriously doubt it. Elements of such a plan—in the light-rail line, the waterfront highway, the walkway, and the design guidelines—are already in place. And maybe that has been enough, although a regional authority with the development capability of Battery Park City could certainly have accelerated development and helped finance open space improvements with the proceeds from land sales.

However, a waterfront authority would surely have helped to ensure some economic diversity. As it is now, the waterfront's preponderance of luxury rental units has yielded little in the way of minority population or affordable housing. Only in Jersey City's Newport development has there been any affordable housing, and there it is mostly for the elderly. Again, except for Newport, the issue of schools has been largely avoided because of the many one- and two-bedroom apartments. But that situation could change.

I see a waterfront region that so far is more suburban than urban, with disconnected projects and pieces with few contextual connections. Except for the walkway and that, because of relatively loose interpretation of design standards, doesn't always look like the same thing everywhere. Nevertheless, the walkway comes across as the single organizing idea—the key to the kingdom—for the waterfront region.

POST-SEPTEMBER 11

The September 11, 2001, attack on Manhattan's World Trade Center changed the short-range prospects for development on New Jersey's Gold Coast to varying degrees. The PATH connection from Exchange Place to the WTC was damaged and the WTC station destroyed. Until the tubes were repaired in 2003, commuters for Lower Manhattan were required to take ferries or go by way of the remaining PATH tunnels from Hoboken to mid-Manhattan. Donald Eisen, executive managing director of Cushman & Wakefield of New Jersey, is quoted in *The New York Times* as saying that projects further north now have a considerable advantage over Jersey City. For example, SJP Properties in Hoboken is going to build a 550,000-square-foot office building on the Hoboken waterfront to match the one just completed. The first was built on speculation, rented up quickly, and the second will too, says Steven J. Pozycki, SJP's president and CEO. The two office buildings will be connected to the river and to two piers converted to parks by the Port Authority of New York and New

Jersey, with a pedestrian walkway that together with the parks is a 15-acre part of the overall Hudson River Walkway system.

Pozycki's Hoboken Waterfront Corporate Park is a short walk from the Hoboken rail, PATH, and a bus terminal, and he says there is no other place he and his partner, Newark-based Prudential Insurance, would be willing to build on speculation at a time when the economy is slowing. Emanuel Stern, president of Hartz Mountain Industries confirms this, but is ready to expand with the final phase of his Lincoln Harbor development at a moment's notice. Hartz Mountain Industries really started the redevelopment of the New Jersey waterfront in 1982, and now has in place all the approvals for its next phase, which will consist of two 450,000-square-foot office buildings. Stern says his market is overflow from Midtown, just as Jersey City's has been from Lower Manhattan, and rents are 10 to 15 percent lower than the $50 to $70 a square foot charged in New York.

The Hudson-Bergen light rail line reached Weehawken from Jersey City in the summer of 2002, adding north-south transportation to the east-west infrastructure, part of which was destroyed from Jersey City at the World Trade Center site. Meanwhile, ferry service has been increased at Jersey City, Hoboken, and Lincoln Harbor to help make up for the lost capacity.

---

1   Boris Pushkarev and the Regional Plan Association, *The Lower Hudson River,* 1970.

17

Betting Against the Odds
in Atlantic City

Our Liberty State Park client, New Jersey Department of Environmental Protection Commissioner Robert Hughey, told me that he was so pleased with working with me and WRT that in 1985, when his friend, William Downey, executive director of the Atlantic County Improvement Authority, asked him to recommend firms to prepare a hurry-up feasibility study for a new convention center and rail terminal, Hughey suggested me and WRT as the sole source. Under the gun to preserve federal funding, Downey and state senator William H. Gormley, the men behind the city's revitalization, hired us for a succession of quick preliminary feasability studies.

From this beginning, we were selected, in spite of our lack of real credentials, as the architects of New Jersey's largest public project: the $285 million Atlantic City Convention Center and Rail Terminal. It opened in 1997. While we worked on the center, we also designed multiple residential projects. Casino gaming has been in operation in Atlantic City since 1978, and it was a necessary element in the city's recovery, but reestablishing the city's convention business was crucial to the city's return to a family-oriented seaside destination resort.

Atlantic City once upon a time dreamed of itself as "America's Favorite Playground" and is working hard to realize its dream again. Major actions included establishing Atlantic City as the East Coast Las Vegas, then restore the city to its old convention center lustre with a new, state-of-the-art convention center; and to improve superior transportation access to these facilities with expressway connections to an updated local street network including a $330 million, 1.6-mile long tunnel to the city's

17.1 Atlantic City's new Convention Center opened in 1997 to rave reviews from exhibitors; it was the key to the return of conventions and tourists. The old Seaboard Rail Line to Philadelphia was restored and a rail terminal built as part of the center, now connected to the Boardwalk with a Grand Boulevard. Both the convention center and the rail terminal were designed by WRT.

Marina District, and new rail and bus terminals. The city also will finally redevelop the city's slums with money from the casinos, starting at the Northeast Inlet. New facilities, including schools and a ballpark, also would be provided as part of the new communities to be created.

The above provides a checklist against which we can see how the city is doing, and it is doing remarkably well. From 1978 when Merv Griffin's Resorts International opened its casino in the converted Chalfonte-Haddon Hall hotel on the Boardwalk to the summer of 2003 and the opening of Boyd's Borgata in the Marina District, Atlantic City has established itself as a gambling resort with 13 casinos and casino-hotels.

Rail connections have been opened to Philadelphia and New York City and a new rail terminal built as part of the Convention Center. A 300-room convention hotel is across the street.

The Northeast Inlet has been completely cleared and a new community established there. The federal Hope VI program under way south of the inlet ensures the elimination of the rest of Atlantic City's slums and the creation of a mixed-income residential community.

Since 1978, eight percent of the casino's gross revenue—amounting to $303.2 million in 1996 alone—has gone into the state's Casino Revenue Fund for statewide programs. In addition, 1.25 percent—amounting to more than $717 million since 1978—has been invested or committed to projects through the CRDA in Atlantic City alone. Another $69 million has been invested in two dozen other capital projects throughout the state, according to CRDA's 1997 annual report.

Casino gaming was always meant to be the funding source for urban redevelopment throughout the whole state, with Atlantic City given priority. In Atlantic City the current 13 casinos are doing very well, say sup-

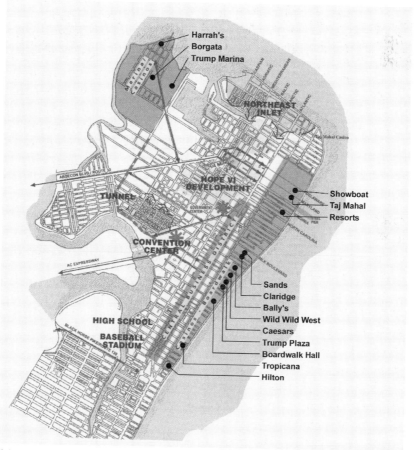

17.2 This map of Atlantic City shows the key elements in the city's strategy: the Convention Center, the casinos, redevelopment of the Northeast Inlet neighborhoods and Hope VI housing revitalizing the core.

porters, noting that the 25 years since the first casino opened should be viewed as a shakedown cruise to get the system running smoothly. The casinos, they say, have created more than 40,000 jobs, 16,000 hotel rooms, $187.5 million in 1997 property taxes, more than $1 billion a year in employee earnings, a new $268 million convention center and rail terminal, and a rebuilt Northeast Inlet community.

In its early years, Atlantic City's Casino Control Commission concentrated on keeping the Mafia out of the casinos—a task that left little time to plan effective ways to spend the 1.25 percent of the gross income dedicated to the city's urban revitalization. In 1984, the Casino Reinvestment Development Authority (CRDA) was created to focus on making appropriate investments around the state, but with a concentration on Atlantic City. By 1993, the commission officially broadened its mission to include "restoration of aging Atlantic City to its former prominence as a resort," according to its chairman, state senator Stephen P. Perskie, one of the primary players in getting the casino legislation passed.

As for the future of the Atlantic City casino industry, the gaming industry's opinion is that, although Connecticut's Foxwoods and Mohegan Sun casinos and the Delaware slot machines have cut into the gross, they and other potential competitors will not substantially affect Atlantic City's success. Business during the past years has been better than ever. Boyd's Borgata has a 1,200-room hotel and 100,000-square-foot casino; Harrah's next door has a 1,000-room expansion. The Tropicana has expanded with another 500 rooms and 200,000 square feet of retail and restaurant space along the Boardwalk. These new casinos will be similar to the latest entertainment/tourist venues in Las Vegas.

All of the above has now created a critical mass, an environment suitable as a "destination resort," as Atlantic City once was before the Great Depression. People will come to the shore on vacation, stay a week or more, and incidentally, gamble. At the same time, the new environment will help keep the retirees from Newark, the Bronx, and Long Island coming to Atlantic City in preference to Foxwoods or the Mohegan Sun, the current competition in Connecticut.

Las Vegas is the only other U.S. city in which gaming is the major industry. There, income from non-gaming activities in 1997 (the last year for which such figures are available) for the first time exceeded that from the casinos. Although for many the local scene in Atlantic City may be considered a bore unless gambling is involved, there are signs of change. While Atlantic City's non-casino income still is only a little over 20 percent of the total, the casinos and the city are adding non-gambling activity centers. A $14.5 million minor league baseball stadium and the $3.2 million Marine Life Education Center at Gardener's Basin on the Boardwalk were completed in 1996, for example. In addition, Atlantic City already offers a beachfront location that beats the southwestern deserts, plus restaurants, shows, boating, and fishing. Recently CRDA hired Los Angeles-based retail architect Jon Jerde, who prepared a plan to revitalize retail development for the tourist industry along Atlantic City's Boardwalk. It was a good plan, but it was unfortunately scuttled by the mayor. He wanted CRDA's $70 million to implement the improvements spent instead on housing, which is where the votes are.

The convention business—the city's other economic engine—always has been central to the city's economy. Its recovery has been crucial. The new Atlantic City Convention Center, first initiated by the city and county, has helped to make the city nationally competitive again. It was taken over, built and owned by the New Jersey Sports and Exposition Authority. The center opened to rave reviews from exhibitors in 1997. It has 550,000 square feet of exhibition space and has scheduled more than 300 conventions and trade shows that are predicted to draw an estimated three million attendees annually staying nearly 1.9 million hotel nights—

17.3 In the Northeast Inlet, convenience retail in the foreground serves the new townhouse and mid-rise community adjacent, all designed by WRT for Harrah's Casino as sponsor.

a number that officials expect to generate an economic impact of $1.6 billion in the Greater Atlantic City Region in the next five years. This is split between casino hotel expansion and such convention hotels as Bally's new 500-room Sheraton Atlantic City, which is connected by an elevated and enclosed pedestrian walkway to the convention center.

The old convention center on the Boardwalk has just finished a $100 million renovation as an event center with a more than 19,000-seat capacity to complement and be run in conjunction with the new convention center.

OTHER INFRASTRUCTURE IMPROVEMENTS

Meanwhile, the CRDA and New Jersey have been making large investments in infrastructure, affordable housing, and community development. The state financed construction of the new rail terminal next to the convention center and rebuilt the Seashore commuter rail line to connect it to Philadelphia and New York City. The convention center is linked by a new heavily landscaped Grand Boulevard, with a new $7.3 million bus terminal, to the refurbished Boardwalk Convention Hall where the Miss America pageant is held.

17.4 Harbourpointe Townhouses by WRT has 130 homes of the more than 2,000 developed under the Casino Reinvestment Development Authority's programs.

The CRDA, in a planning partnership with the Atlantic City Housing and Redevelopment Agency, has been instrumental in creating more than 3,000 housing units. At first this effort was concentrated in the Northeast Inlet, where a redevelopment plan for the entire area was first prepared with major input from and involvement of residents. The plan envisioned mid-rise towers near the waterfront with townhouses and garden apartments behind. Ultimately 1,200 residential units will be built there, of which 462 are now completed and 300 are in the pipeline. So far CRDA has invested $140 million and plans to put up $20 million more. Much of the money has gone into new utility systems and flood protection measures. A five-acre park has been developed next to a rebuilt Boardwalk extension.

Although the redevelopment plan's design concept called for a mix of towers close to the Boardwalk, with townhouses and garden apartments behind, the latest round of residential marketing are semi-detached and single-family detached units for homeowners, not renters. It is very suburban. The first round, completed in 1995, several hundred mid- and high-rise units were built and rented with various casino sponsorships, but it became clear that there was a strong market preference for the traditional middle-class house with a yard and a garage. "The new housing will also help draw middle- and upper-income buyers and create a balanced community," says James B. Kennedy, executive director of CRDA. He adds, "the second half of the rebuilding project is expected to be faster—five years instead of ten—because the authority owns the land and utility lines are in place."

Truly market-rate housing with no subsidy at all is still an elusive target. Several mid-rise condominium developments have turned out to be time-share hotels for New Yorkers who want a vacation *pied a terre*. This would be a viable market niche, but the city has rejected it for policy reasons. A few individual houses have been rehabbed or built anew for such devoted urbanites as local architect Thomas Sykes, but these are still the exception.

A new shopping center and health-care facility have been built as part of the revitalization of Atlantic Avenue, the spine of the central business district, but freestanding retail development is up against the competition of the massive retail developed inside the fortress-like casino hotels, which does nothing for freestanding shops and restaurants or the central business district.

MIDDLE-INCOME HOUSING AND SCHOOLS

With CRDA support, the city received a $35 million U.S. Department of Housing and Urban Development HOPE VI grant to rebuild housing in the Second Ward, eliminating what is left of the worst housing south of the Northeast Inlet. Included is a new elementary school scheduled for completion in 2009. The Ocean Community Development Corporation, a newly formed partnership, will act as the community-based developer for this $192.3 million project—leveraging nearly $4.50 for every $1 of the $35 million HOPE VI grant. In addition, 600 new affordable units are planned.

A new $83 million high school also has been built with CRDA money. If the city is ultimately to have a racially balanced population, as CRDA executive director Kennedy hopes, the schools will play the critical role. At present, the primary school enrollment reflects Atlantic City's ethnic demographics; mostly white in Upper Chelsea and south of Missouri Avenue; and mostly African-American, Hispanic, or Oriental on the north in the Second and Third wards. Many recent arrivals to the city are immigrants from Vietnam and China, attracted by jobs in the casinos that require minimal English. Middle-class white parents tend to move to Galloway or Egg Harbor townships when their children reach school age.

17.5 The Hope VI program has financed houses for sale as well as for rent.

The 1998 school board elections resulted in an evenly divided black/white school board with an Hispanic chairman as the swing vote. In 2003, the board is still divided, with a white chairperson and a new superintendent, who is also chair of the CRDA. Whether the schools can be improved sufficiently to attract white and black middle-income families remains to be seen.

Building in Atlantic City is expensive, with subsidies of from $50,000 to more than $100,000 per unit to reduce overall costs, including land acquisition, relocation, site preparation, and infrastructure, is a lot of money, requiring major subsidy to permit sales prices at affordable levels, says Kennedy. The CRDA has had to take over the role of urban renewal once played by the federal government. "The hope is that subsidies needed to build projects and keep the house prices low enough to meet the market will decrease as production proceeds, and that projects closest to the water will be built entirely with private funds," he adds. The subsidies are raised from low-interest taxable bonds based on anticipated casino income. In the Northeast Inlet, some 300-plus families were relocated, mostly within the city; 75 chose to return to new houses at the same cost as their old homes, plus the expense of moving. These costs, as well as the expense of raising ground levels some three feet for flood protection, are not necessary in later phases.

On the optimistic side, while Atlantic City's population has been increasing, it has witnessed a 54 percent decrease in welfare recipients and, based on crime statistics, it is a much safer place today than it was 25 years ago. Proponents say Atlantic City cannot lose as long as the casinos are successful. Twenty years ago, the odds against Atlantic City ever again amounting to anything were probably about 100 to 1, if a bet could be made at all. Today the odds are probably better than even that it will succeed.

THE VIEW FROM PHILADELPHIA

The *Philadelphia Inquirer* has always taken a dim view of Atlantic City. It has been 25 years since the Resorts International opened, and the *Philadelphia Inquirer*'s Amy S. Rosenberg wrote an analysis of how the casinos—now 13 with the opening of the Borgata in summer 2003—have had a mixed payoff in terms of the community. In summary, while there has been a phenomenal surge of jobs, housing and other development, "some say the benefits have not trickled down," she reports. (*Philadelphia Inquirer*, Friday, May 23, 2003.)

In point of fact, casino development programs written into the legislation mandated hotel, retail, and entertainment requirements for each minimum 50,000 square feet of gambling space. As it was built, the result has been that each casino package acts as a self-contained world, and the Borgata, copying Las Vegas's new emphasis on family entertainment, will not change that. As they say, follow the money.

It was not until the 1990s and the creation of the Casino Reinvestment Development Authority that major funds flowing from gambling began to have a real physical impact on Atlantic City itself.

Rosenberg's article has a strong slant against seeing anything good about the result. She says, "Twenty-five years after the first casino opened on May 26, 1978, amid promises of revitalization of a moribund seaside resort, many in Atlantic City are still uneasy about the impact of the gambling palaces." Paraphrasing Rosenberg's article, they acknowledge 45,000 Atlantic City jobs with an annual payroll of $1.1 billion, 1,500 new homes, major new retail developments, hotel expansion, tax dollars, and the region surging in jobs, population and new homes.

"But something still seems to be missing for many in Atlantic City," Rosenberg continues. "For all the jobs, unemployment in Atlantic City remains a stubborn problem—last year it was 11.4 percent . . . For all the innovative housing . . . few owners are families and . . . nearly 70 percent of city residents are renters . . . . For all the money in town, the casino era has created all-inclusive gaming halls and led to the closing of (local businesses) . . . there's not one black millionaire in town here . . . . For all the new attractions—minor league baseball and hockey, a ball park, refurbished Boardwalk Hall, the Ocean Life Center, a new high school, several elementary schools under construction, a Boys and Girls Club—residents complain there is little for their children to do."

Incidentally, the *Inquirer* never mentions Atlantic City's new and highly successful Convention Center if it can help it. That has always appeared to be a no-no and Rosenberg is true to form. In the meanwhile, her report on the program and the city is really quite encouraging, if you look beyond the "yes, buts."

As I write, Atlantic City's retail environment is undergoing a big change that will go a considerable way toward mirroring the Las Vegas experience. The *Philadelphia Inquirer*, in fact, has called it a "retail revolution."[1] The Baltimore-based Cordish Company is developing 60 to 70 stores, restaurants, and entertainment venues totaling 320,000 square feet along Michigan Avenue, connecting Atlantic Avenue to the new Convention Center. Fifteen hundred permanent jobs will be created.

Farther south, next to the Tropicana Casino, is a 220,000-square-foot outlet mall, offering dining, entertainment, shops, and a spa bordering Pacific Avenue, with 2,000 permanent jobs. It is being developed by the Keating Corporation of Philadelphia, and is unusual in that it is not connected to the casino. Third, Pier Developers, an affiliate of Gordon Group Holdings of Greenwich, Connecticut, is redeveloping the Ocean One Pier with 105 stores and restaurants totaling 320,000 square feet, with walkways over the Boardwalk to connect to Caesars and Bally's parking.

Key demographics behind developers's confidence in the retail potential show that Atlantic City had 33.2 million visitors in 2002, almost as many as Las Vegas's 35 million. Atlantic City's casino winnings of $4.3 billion exceeded Las Vegas's $4.2 billion. However, Atlantic City's non-casino revenue per visitor was only $12, compared to Las Vegas's $160, revealing the target potential. So, the money is there. The Borgata Hotel Casino and Spa has set the new standard, with its non-gambling revenue twice that of the average of the other 12 casinos in its three nightclubs, 10 restaurants, European spa, and high-end retail.

---

1   "Atlantic City's retail environment to undergo a big change," Suzette Parmely, *Philadelphia Inquirer,* Sunday, September 28, 2003, p. B3.

18

The Key to Downtown Norfolk

Word-of-mouth recommendations had led WRT and me from Baltimore's Inner Harbor to Liberty State Park in Jersey City, to New Jersey's Hudson River waterfront, and to Atlantic City. Our being selected to prepare plans for Norfolk, Virginia's, ailing downtown and waterfront had a parallel and even more crucially related connection to the downtown Baltimore and Inner Harbor work.

In the case of Norfolk, Dr. Mason C. Andrews's friendship with and admiration for James W. Rouse was the critical connection. Andrews, Norfolk's most distinguished obstetrician/gynecologist, was also the city's vice-mayor and a considerable politician. His former patient and close friend had become Rouse's second wife, had resigned her position as a commissioner of the Norfolk Redevelopment and Housing Authority, and had moved to Columbia, Maryland, with Rouse. She of course retained her connections and she and Andrews hoped to persuade Rouse to come to Norfolk's rescue.

It was not that Norfolk hadn't done the right things. Downtown Norfolk's redevelopment program had been both extensive and success-ful, first under the professional leadership of Lawrence Cox, who ruth-lessly practiced "urban removal." Cox had rid the city not only of most of its residential slums, but also had eliminated the famous downtown red-light district of bars and honky-tonk dance halls that gave Norfolk its bad reputation with the U.S. Navy. Cox had gone on to become assistant com-missioner of the Federal Urban Renewal and Housing Administration.

The city's cleaned-up financial district, with an Omni International Hotel on the waterfront, Granby Mall (downtown shopping), and West

Urban Design Concept

18.1 The key to downtown Norfolk's development was its waterfront, which was about to be cut off from the water by an elevated expressway. The urban design concept applied a strategy of integrating the waterfront uses into the overall framework.

Freemason area of historic buildings, restored for office and residential use, projected an image that many communities would like to emulate.

However, in 1978, when Andrews contacted me, national conditions had slowed new private investment. This temporary pause was seen by the city as an opportunity to regroup, update its development strategy, and thus ensure a coordinated, mutually supportive public and private investment program. Andrews had urged Jim Rouse to become the developer of whatever he wanted, but Rouse told him that an overall strategy needed to be prepared first. Rouse said that David Wallace, "the key planner for downtown Baltimore's renaissance," was the person to do it. Until then, architect Barton Meyers, a native son but practicing out of Toronto and Los Angeles, urban designers Ray Gindroz and David Lewis of

Pittsburgh's UDI, and economist Philip Hammer with Hammer Siler George of Washington, D.C., had been Norfolk's gurus.

THE PROBLEM

So I was to be the advance man for Jim Rouse. I almost blew it on my first trip to Norfolk as Andrews toured me around town and described the elevated expressway they had planned for the edge of the waterfront. I said I thought it was a terrible idea and that the waterfront was their most important asset. Andrews's eyes glazed and the interview was shortly terminated. However, Rouse must have insisted I was the right guy so David Rice, the redevelopment authority's executive director, hired us anyway. Andrews became a good friend and sponsor.

Elimination of downtown blight and clearing sites through redevelopment had not been enough to attract private investment beyond a certain point. Several attempts at major retail projects intended to support a flagging downtown Granby Mall and fill the central 20-acre R-8 site were aborted, most notably an effort called Norfolk Gardens in 1974. For suburban-type shopping, downtown Norfolk is "off-center" in relation to the primary Tidewater market. Long-delayed completion of Interstate 264 and expansion of bridge capacity across the Elizabeth River exacerbated downtown Norfolk's inadequate access.

Redevelopment had resulted in strong, or potentially strong, activity areas that were fragmented and unconnected. To cement them together in a cohesive interacting downtown meant that a new climate for investment needed to be recast if it was to result in the kind of private investment other cities were enjoying.

THE WATERFRONT IS THE KEY TO DEVELOPMENT STRATEGY

At first the waterfront had not been seen as the key to this new approach. In fact, the proposed elevated expressway would have used the waterfront as an opportunity to accelerate access to other areas. We pointed to the annual Harborfest celebration as evidence of the waterfront's importance for activities. Harborfest, then only three years old, brought hundreds of thousands of people to enjoy the festivities, hear music, watch "war games" by the military, and generally enjoy themselves. Clearly the area had a tremendous unrealized potential, but in spite of major public investment in infrastructure in the Freemason Harbor residential area, development had been disappointingly slow.

18.2 The annual weekend event called Harborfest focuses the region's attention on the waterfront and underscores the importance of public access to the water's edge.

The Downtown Norfolk Implementation Program was created as a joint effort of the Norfolk Redevelopment and Housing Authority, the Mayor's Ad Hoc Committee and the Greater Norfolk Development Corporation, an effort that included a new development strategy and the necessary financial support.

It had become apparent to us that the waterfront area, which had been seen by the community as a separate activity area outboard of the elevated highway, must be treated as an integral part of downtown for the strategy to succeed. The waterfront's ties to downtown were inhibited by Boush Waterfront Drive's free-flowing traffic, and an eight-foot flood wall, and its own fragmented nature. The separation from downtown would be exacerbated by the elevated expressway. The South Waterfront, which had been used as a dump for all the redevelopment debris, has only a narrow connection to Towne Point, the center of Harborfest activity, and no connection outboard of Boush Waterfront Drive to the West Waterfront or Freemason Harbor area.

The West and South waterfronts were seen to have the potential for linking together downtown's major activity areas in a two-phase strategy of development.

The first phase of our development strategy included six elements: (1) an eight-acre park at Towne Point; (2) a 150,000-square-foot Festival Market modeled after Rouse's Harborplace in Baltimore's Inner Harbor; (3) an 1,800-car parking garage in-board of Boush Waterfront Drive; (4) a 350-room hotel; (5) a 250,000-square-foot office development with 500 parking spaces; and (6) a Granby Mall Reinvestment Program to restore facades and provide amenities.

The second phase included: (1) Site preparation to fill and stabilize sites; (2) an expanded program of new housing and office/commercial development in the old Tazewell Street warehouses and the adjacent area; and (3) finally, putting the R-8 site back on the market as a major shopping mall with two, and perhaps three, department store anchors.

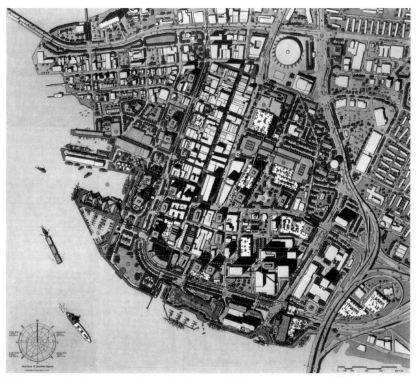

18.3 The overall plan served as the basis of development until the R-8 redevelopment area in the center of downtown was successfully completed with a two-department store retail mall.

TWENTY YEARS OF PLANNING AND IMPLEMENTATION

With this strategy agreed upon, Jim Rouse and I together worked up the first plan for the site of his festival market. Having been the planners and landscape architects for Harborplace in Baltimore, we had gotten to know his formula for success, and designed Waterside's specific elevation related to the water, the requisite waterfront promenade, laid out the building's footprint, and established the necessary relation to a nearby parking deck, in this case across Waterside Drive connected by a pedestrian walkway. Rouse then prepared a development proposal in which Enterprise and the city would be equal partners. Mason Andrews rammed it through the Norfolk City Council, and Rouse was ready to proceed.

Rouse had used Ben Thompson of Boston as architect for Harborplace and Gerry Cope of Cope Linder of Philadelphia for the retail parts of his new town, Columbia, Maryland. Rouse told me that he rejected Thompson because Thompson had taken credit for Rouse's ideas; Cope was out, because after working for Rouse, he had worked for shopping center developer Kravco in various places and Rouse accused him of giving away his ideas to competitors. I persuaded Jim that, although WRT had no experience at all in retail design, we should be his architects for that very reason. We were smart, quick learners, and would do what he

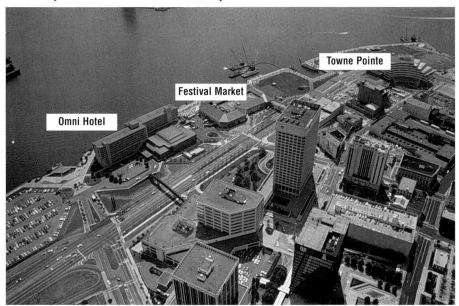

18.4 James W. Rouse's Enterprise Development Company built Waterside, a festival marketplace patterned after Harborplace in Baltimore's Inner Harbor.

told us without any argument. I remember the meeting in his office in Columbia where I brought in Tom Todd and Charlie Tomlinson and introduced them as the leaders of our team. They made a good impression, and we were selected.

Rouse's Waterside festival market became a catalytic agent for mobilizing redevelopment of the waterfront and eventually all of downtown Norfolk. Initially its program followed the format that Rouse had developed at Boston's Fanieul Hall, and further elaborated in Baltimore's Harborplace. The first phase, 60,000 square feet, was half-filled with soft goods and half with a food court and restaurants. Phillips Seafood Restaurant from Harborplace was brought in to occupy the major space. Phillips had originated on the Maryland shore and still has an extremely successful branch in the Inner Harbor. During the 1990s the Waterside has been very successful, and was expanded to double the original size.

A number of notable downtown Norfolk projects followed, energized by Waterside, and other actions of David Rice and the Norfolk Redevelopment & Housing Authority, without whom nothing much would have happened. Town Point Park was relandscaped with a design by WRT to better accommodate the annual Octoberfest fair, Marriott built a hotel/conference center across Waterside Drive from the Waterside, and Jacques Cousteau was invited to create an aquarium on the pier next to the park. Cousteau wanted total design and program control, and complete public financing of a facility that would ultimately be owned by the Cousteau Foundation. So, Cousteau was rejected, and the locally financed development of Nauticus, designed by Centerbrook Architects of Connecticut finally proceeded with an entertainment and nautical theme. It has been very successful. As I write, the battleship U.S.S. *Wisconsin*—sistership to the U.S.S. *New Jersey*, now a floating museum in the Delaware River on Camden, New Jersey's, waterfront—is anchored at the end of the Nauticus pier. Its deck is available for tours, but, unlike the *New Jersey*, the ship is being kept ready for duty on a month's notice.

Through bad staff work, WRT unfortunately lost its entree in Norfolk, and UDA from Pittsburgh was waiting in the wings. In 1998, UDA Architects, P.C., prepared a new Downtown Plan Update for the Year 2000. By then eight new office buildings had been built on or near Main Street, and the Omni Hotel, the Waterside and Town Point Park had been completed on the waterfront. A refurbished Wells Theater had opened, and east of downtown, the Chrysler Museum had been enlarged and remodeled New residential neighborhoods had developed in the Freemason Harbor and in East Ghent.

Prior to 1980, Norfolk's redevelopment program had been based on the old "urban removal" philosophy inherited from Lawrence Cox, David Rice's predecessor. The philosophy sometimes worked with a good market for land, but in the case of Norfolk's R-8 project in the heart of downtown it created 20 acres of vacant land only a block to the east of Granby Street, the city's main downtown shopping complex, which had been converted into a mainly pedestrian mall.

Jim Rouse was often quoted as saying that retail was always the last in any development sequence as it depended on all other elements to be in place. He made a supreme, but unsuccessful, effort to develop the R-8 tract with a two-anchor shopping center in the early 1990s after the Waterside and other developments had been completed, but he was unable to attract the anchor tenants. Finally, the Taubman Interests from Detroit managed to attract Nordstrom and Dillard's for the two-anchor, 1.4 million-square-foot MacArthur Center mall that opened in 1999. They are still trying to get Macy's for the third anchor, but the center appears successful without it, with such upscale stores as Eddie Bauer and Williams-Sonoma among the 200 retail stores.

In a 1995 *Update to the Downtown Norfolk 2000 Plan* by UDA, the initial concept of an electric trolley was explored as a first step toward a larger work under way, the Hampton Roads Light Rail Transit System that would stretch from the Norfolk International Airport to the Virginia Medical Center with multiple stations in downtown. NRHA's current principal emphasis is on revitalization of Granby Street and in making connections between the many successful individual development areas.

Success in urban affairs can often be attributed to talented individuals who simply stick around and continue as positive influences. Much of Philadelphia's renowned downtown planning impact is a result of Ed Bacon's continued influence, both as director of the City Planning Commission and later as a gadfly. Baltimore has had Walter Sondheim. Although he is now in his mid-90s, Sondheim still exerts influence as a special consultant to Greater Baltimore Committee. In Norfolk, Mason C. Andrews is the man to know. He has never been willing to completely abandon his ob/gyn practice and become the full-time mayor, but he continues (as perennial vice-mayor and/or city councilman) as Norfolk's *deus ex machina*, the man behind, and not very far behind, the city's success story.

19

The New Orleans Central Area

Every city is different, but New Orleans is unusually unique. It has been a possession of five different countries; its perilous and watery environment, its physical form, and its multi-ethnic population make it special among cities. Even directions are special, with the meandering Mississippi River as the landmark. From Canal Street upriver is uptown versus downtown below. Toward the river is riverside, away is lakeside (toward Lake Pontchartrain). The river flows eastward through the city, so the East Bank is north, and the West Bank is south. The normal river's elevation is 15 feet above the city, held in check by an elaborate system of canals and dikes. Constant pumping, even without hurricanes, is needed to keep New Orleans reasonably dry.

The city's Central Area is defined by the river on the south, U.S. 90 upriver, Interstate 10 lakeside, and Esplanade Avenue downtown. Its major parts include the Central Business District, the Warehouse district, the Civic Center area, HEAL (the medical center), Iberville (a public housing project), Louis Armstrong Park, and the Vieux Carre.

THE VIEUX CARRE

The oldest part of the Central Area is the Vieux Carre—or French District—that gives New Orleans much of its distinctive character. The Vieux Carre incorporates more than 2,000 buildings in its 90 blocks, over a third of which are commercial or industrial. These are concentrated on Bourbon and Royal streets, nearest Canal Street, along the river and around Jackson Square.

Most of the original eighteenth-century buildings were destroyed by fires in the late 1700s, but were rebuilt in the early 1800s in the same

The New and Uncertain City (1945 and After)

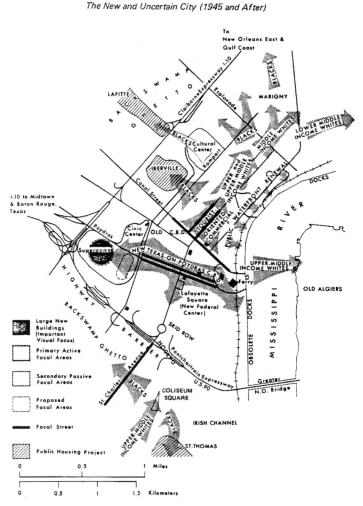

19.1 "Center City New Orleans in transition. Arrows suggest the direction of changes in downtown New Orleans, largely prompted by revival of the Vieux Carre and the symbiotic revival of lower Canal Street. Note in the Quarter: blacks ejected by middle income whites, in turn ejected by upper and upper middle income whites, in turn under pressure from tourist-oriented commercial uses—an index of who is able to pay rents at various levels. Upstream from Canal Street, the new Texan CBD is pushing into skid row, while upper income whites move into the lower Garden District from other directions. Again, blacks are pushed into less desirable areas with lower rents." Map and caption from Lewis, Pierce F., *New Orleans: The Making of an Urban Landscape*, Ballinger Publishing Company, Cambridge, MA, p.91.

French and Spanish colonial style as the originals. By the late 1920s and early 1930s artists, writers, and bohemians who had settled in the French Quarter and other private citizens began to be concerned with the increasing demolition of the Vieux Carre's buildings. It was the Great Depression and owners were tearing them down to avoid taxes and provide parking. A favorite method reportedly was to place a candle and some cheese in a combustible spot. Rats would knock the candles over to start fires so the insurance could be collected, the site also could be cleared for parking.

A new group, Le Renaissance du Vieux Carre, was formed under author Stanley C. Archer. The group successfully fought the city's plan to demolish the French Market along the river, and promoted landscaping for inner courts. In the spring of 1936, another group headed by Elizabeth Werlein and James J.A. Fortier petitioned the Louisiana legislature to put an amendment to the state constitution on the ballot, and in November 3, 1936, the voters approved the formation of the Vieux Carre Commission to preserve the district.

Unfortunately, as could be expected, members of the commission were political favorites and at first the commission didn't do very much. Buildings continued to be demolished, historic storefronts were covered by unsightly signs and architectural details that were expensive to maintain, such as delicate iron balconies and galleries, were removed. Incensed at the commission's inaction, Elizabeth Werlein and her group again mobilized and in 1939 managed to prevent the destruction of 227-33 Bourbon Street. This battle was a turning point that resulted in the appointment of new members to the commission and a public mandate for greater control for preservation.

It is interesting to read Hilary Somerville Irvin's history of the commission's first 50 years. For whatever reason, she makes no mention of the important role played by the federal Works Progress Administration (WPA). The 1930s were the bottom of the Great Depression, and the Roosevelt administration had created the WPA to put people to work on public projects. In New Orleans, the local architectural and engineering fraternity was mobilized in a number of efforts in relation to the Vieux Carre.

One such effort was the restoration of Jackson Square, the St. Louis Cathedral, the so-called Pontalba buildings that all front on the square, and the French Market along the Mississippi River. Another was the design and construction of the Iberville public housing project in 1940. Financed and managed with federal funds by the newly created New

Orleans Housing Authority, the project was used to clear an African-American slum and red-light district and through public housing to establish a stable neighborhood next to the Vieux Carre on the lakeside. Unfortunately, the displaced occupants moved into the French Quarter and for a number of years caused a high crime rate that became a threat to the increasing post-World War II tourist visitation.

I first visited New Orleans and the French Quarter in 1943. I was a captain in the U.S. Army combat engineers stationed at nearby Camp Livingston, Louisiana, and managed weekends and several weeks of leave at the city's foremost hotel, the Roosevelt in the middle of the central business district, which was also known as the American District. The Roosevelt was demolished in the 1960s to be replaced by an office building. There were few if any decent hotels in the Vieux Carre, and, though Bourbon Street was a great place to spend time, it was a pretty rough and risky environment for a serviceman. But it was exciting. I fell in with a drinking companion who claimed he was a captain in the Nicaraguan army engineers and related to the reigning dictator. We cooked up a scheme where through his influence we would be placed on detached service with him doing who knows what in Managua. We went back to our respective units and I was shipped to combat in France and I never heard from him again.

Irvin reports that the Vieux Carre Commission was relatively ineffective during the war and post-war years, and it is a marvel that the district is still more-or-less intact. Fortunately, in 1958 under the chairmanship of architect George Leake, a reformed commission conducted a block-by-block photographic survey of districts structures, and got the city council to pass a demolition-by-neglect ordinance banning that activity. A planning firm, Marcou-O'Leary (my old friend Jerry O'Leary from Charles Center days) was hired to establish a detailed survey procedure and criteria for historic qualification, which resulted in the publication of *A Plan and Program for the Preservation of the Vieux Carre* in 1968. About this time the Royal Orleans, the first large new hotel, was constructed in the French Quarter in the French colonial form and style compatible with the French Quarter. More hotels and compatible structures followed. In 1959, Anthony Downs, a leading economist from Chicago, pointed out the economic importance of the Quarter as a tourist attraction and popular pressure for preservation increased.

TEXAS TAKES OVER

After World War II, through the 1950s and 1960s, New Orleans had become the base for oil exploration and extraction in the Gulf of Mexico. Algiers in the West Bank was the center of oil rig and derrick construction, and the oil companies from Texas have had a major impact on the Central Area. Locals refer to it as the Texification of New Orleans. The city's response was a truly heroic act. Poydras Street at the uptown edge of the central business district was straightened, widened, and made into a boulevard with a landscaped "neutral ground" reaching from the Mississippi River to the Civic Center area. One Shell Square, the city's tallest office building, established Poydras Street as the top central business district address, with a new federal building at Lafayette Square. The Lykes office building near the river was developed by Anthony Canizaro. He was later to be a favorite client of WRT.

In 1968, an International Trade Center was created and at the river end of Poydras Street, the 33-story Rivergate International Trade Mart and a 60,000-square-foot Convention Center were constructed. These required demolition of a number of historic buildings at the lakeside end of Poydras Street. At the other end a site was cleared in the late '60s for the 72,000-seat Superdome designed by New Orleans premier architect, August Perez. The Superdome opened in 1975.

THE VIEUX CARRE EXPRESSWAY FIASCO

President Dwight Eisenhower's Federal Highway Act in the 1950s authorized and funded the nation's interstate expressway system. In New Orleans U.S. 90, an elevated expressway, was built at the Upriver border to the Central Area and Interstate 10 became the lakeside boundary. In 1958, the Vieux Carre Commission approved the Federal Highway Administration's plan for an extension of this network that would put an expressway along the river from Elysian Fields to an interchange with U.S. 90 where it crosses the river. This extension would have been part of the interstate system. The commission's former chairman claimed that the commission promised its approval on the basis that the highway would not be elevated.

But by 1963, the federal plan was for an elevated expressway along the river and the commission reversed its approval. A huge fight—"The Second Battle of New Orleans"—ensued. In 1965, the commission adopted national landmark status for the Vieux Carre and in 1966 Congress passed the National Historic Preservation Act. The act required prior review of all federally funded projects involving National Register listings. Finally in July 1969, U.S. Secretary of Transportation John Volpe announced cancellation of the Vieux Carre expressway plans, stating that the expressway would severely damage the "treasured French Quarter," and the 10-year battle was over.

THE CENTRAL AREA NEW ORLEANS GROWTH MANAGEMENT PROGRAM

The Greater New Orleans Chamber of Commerce—which had vigorously backed the elevated expressway—had not only lost that battle, but also had failed to get state legislative approval for creation of a special central business district tax district. Harold R. Katner, the city's director of city planning, seized this low point to suggest to the Chamber that they join with the city administration and the city council in a partnership to figure out what to do. Katner outlined a draft of a Request for Proposals (RFP) for consultants. Costs were to be shared equally and a huge steering committee was to overview the work with a seven-member executive committee to be chaired by Warren G. Moses, a consulting mechanical engineer representing the chamber. The committee really was run by Anthony Gagliano, representing Mayor Moon Landrieu. A lot was riding on this tenuous partnership.

WMRT was already working in the New Orleans area when the RFP came out in June 1973. This was an advantage in that we were familiar with the people, but also a disadvantage because our clients, Toddy Lee Wynn and Clint Murchison, big Texas oilmen, had plans for a "new town in town" in their stalled development, a 30,000-acre swamp and marshland called New Orleans East. Our planning work had been carried out under Katner's eye with many meetings in a Vieux Carre townhouse owned by Wynn as a pied-a-terre. The scheme was to create a new-town corporation, which would pay for the upfront infrastructure costs, financed by the U.S. Department of Housing and Urban Development (HUD). New Orleans would be a partner with the developers but the concept, if successful, would surely compete with the city's Central Area. If I say so, the plan was terrific, but as it turned out the Texans, HUD, and the city could not agree on the base value of the property and the deal fell through.

In the meantime, we were short-listed for the Central Area RFP. We knew that the selection committee members were soured on traditional CBD planning. As they saw it, planning had brought them nothing but

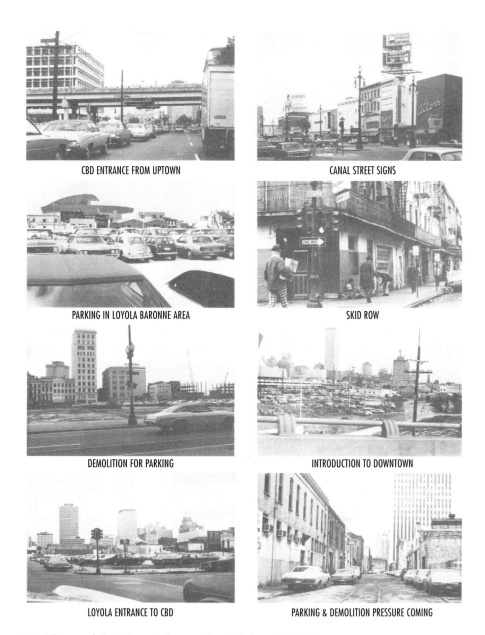

19.2 Views of the New Orleans Central Area in 1974.

trouble. So we marketed "growth management" from our Baltimore and Lower Manhattan experience, which fell right in with their aspirations for creating a tax district and doing something different.

I remember the interview well. As Tom Todd and I entered the room, Archie Rogers and George Kostritsky from RTKL/Baltimore exited smiling and wishing us luck. They thought they had won. I started with an explanation of growth management as distinct from traditional planning. I used slides from Lower Manhattan and our 1969 Baltimore MetroCenter as examples. The Growth Management Plan flow chart was complicated but intriguing, and by the end of the interview we knew we had won. Harold Katner was on our side and the clincher was that our project director would be Richard W. Huffman, our senior associate on the New Orleans East project, and later a partner at WRT. Incidentally, our first assignment was to draft our contract because neither of the two clients trusted the other to do it. It was for a total of $180,000 and provided for our having to certify we'd received payment from the Chamber before the city would pay us.

LOOKING FOR THE KEY TO THE KINGDOM

The concept of growth management was more than just a clever way to get the job. Unlike traditional planning it is an operating process; it includes planning but is more analogous to the management of a major corporation in which planning and specific action projects are seen in the context of overall operating goals. Until we prepared the database for New Orleans Central Area, there had been no proper inventory of real property assets, no bookkeeping procedure, no organizational responsibility for various programs for infrastructure, maintenance, security, marketing, and goal setting.

The Growth Management Plan was designed to determine change and the direction of trends, quickly evaluate proposed programs and policies, determine alternative public strategies as responses to new developments, encourage private response to public commitments, and open the growth management process to full citizen involvement.

The New Orleans Growth Management Plan's key features included: a "joint venture" organization; a basic information and inventory system; monitoring change and the susceptibility to change; probability of change "growth modeling;" goal, objectives, and policy development and evaluation; a focus on early action, high-impact projects and programs; and preparation of three-dimensional urban design concepts as evaluation and marketing tools.

With an August 1973 start, by March 1974 we had completed all of the above and the special tax district was in hand. In November 1974, the Louisiana Legislature had passed Act 498 enabling establishment, after a public referendum, of a special tax district to include the central business district, the Civic Center Area, and the Warehouse District. It was called the Downtown Development District.

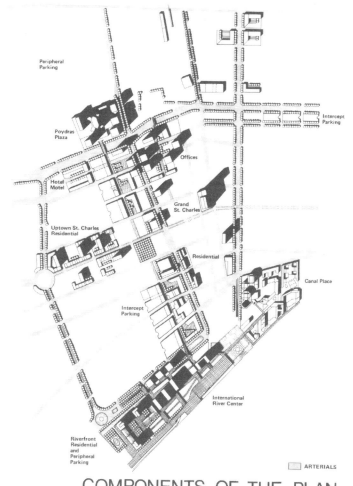

COMPONENTS OF THE PLAN

19.3 Planned developments in Category III Probability extend beyond economic or market projections to include urban design concepts giving an imageable target for future action programs.

In April 1974, the city council had voted a moratorium on further property demolition until January 1975. This gave the Growth Management Program time to prepare plans and programs for preservation of the stock of historic buildings. By April 1975, our Final Technical Report was published, and the New Orleans Community Improvement Agency was authorized as an interim management agency to adopt our central business district Community Improvement Plan and Program. In addition, the planning department prepared two Historic District ordinances (for Lafayette Square and the Warehouse District), a Draft Tax District ordinance, and a parking control ordinance. A special zoning study was also under way.

The key to the kingdom was the creation of the Downtown Development District. The Downtown Development District ordinance passed in the 1975 November referendum and went into operation in January 1976. The Technical Report became its principal guide to operation.

EVENTS IN THE LAST 25 YEARS

The Vieux Carre Commission and the Downtown Development District have worked cooperatively with great effectiveness during the last 25 years of the twentieth century. Events of special note that they have dealt with include the renovation of the Jackson Brewery at the river edge of the District on Decatur Street in the French Quarter. In 1984, New Orleans promoted a World's Fair Exposition, which became a special tourist attraction. The Fair construction was used by the city as a device to clear the riverfront, consolidate the Public Belt Line rail tracks, and create the site for the permanent New Orleans Convention Center, which opened in 1985.

Concurrent with the Convention Center, the Hilton Hotel and adjacent Riverwalk—the Rouse Company's "festival market place"—was built along the Mississippi River connecting to Moon Walk. Moon Walk, named for Mayor Moon Landrieu, was a pedestrian walkway that had opened the river to Jackson Square (where a barge had gotten out of control and had smashed the piers to bits). The New Orleans Aquarium was developed in the late 1980s between Moon Walk and the ferry terminal.

In 1986, WRT was asked to prepare a Growth Management Plan Update. My partner John Beckman managed it. The stage was set for a reassessment of growth and development in the downtown. Two more historic districts—Canal Street and Picayune Place— had been created in the meantime. Key issues in the update included new office construction that was removed from the central business district core and was weakening the traditional core and further undermining Canal Street retail, slackening of retail construction, and pressure for demolition for parking in the Warehouse District. On the positive side, hotel demand was strong, and growth along the Poydras Street corridor had been in accordance with the 1975 Growth Management Plan program.

The Growth Management Plan Update opened up new areas for housing, changed zoning in key places, provided design guidelines and modifications to historic districts, and outlined a greater management and marketing role for the Development District along with methods to finance its activities.

In the early 1990s riverboat and casino gambling became major issues. Louisiana, under Governor Edwin Edwards, first entertained riverboats, one on Lake Pontchartrain and another on the Mississippi. Then Governor Edwards went through a complicated process of selecting a casino developer for the city. Harrah's was chosen as the casino operator with the Rivergate Convention Center as its site. Under great pressure from the hotel industry, the legislation provided for stand-alone casinos as opposed to the Las Vegas/Atlantic City model: where each 50,000 square feet of casino space requires a specified number of hotel rooms. The New Orleans hoteliers had learned from Las Vegas's negative experience. Harrah's Casino in New Orleans operates independently and helps anchor the river end of the Poydras corridor. And Harrah's helps bring tourists to town, filling hotel rooms.

20

About the Form of Cities

As I write about the planning and urban design I have been engaged in around the country, I increasingly realize my involvement with the multiple projects and programs in and around Baltimore is prototypical. Today, I see these collectively as tactics in Baltimore's and other cities' long-range strategy of urban revitalization. I first reported on this in the *1970 MetroCenter Baltimore Technical Study*, and now I see it as an example for the future form of cities everywhere.

Baltimore's tactics in its long-range strategy include the Interstate Beltway that rings the city; the expressway spurs that deliver traffic to a mostly revitalized downtown; and sections of a light-rail transit system that connect the center to suburbs and to Washington, D.C. The new stadiums provide the Orioles and the Ravens with venues as part of the tourist and entertainment component. Baltimore's famous Inner Harbor attracts more than 18 million visitors a year, and employment has increased with an emphasis on jobs based on new technologies and links to the so-called "global economy" through institutions such as the University of Maryland at Baltimore, and Johns Hopkins University's Homewood campus.[1]

The investment climate in Baltimore for renovation and new development also has spread along the waterfront to the east of the Inner Harbor. There a new Marriott Hotel and office and residential towers around the historic President Street rail station in Inner Harbor East stretch on to Fells Point and all the way to Canton.

The regional long-range strategy involved building a movement infrastructure as the base for new investment; then developing a strong central core with outlying specialized employment and institutional nodes, such as the Johns Hopkins University in Homewood and Johns Hopkins Hospital in East Baltimore. These are all to be anchors for keeping and growing the employment base and for establishing a wide variety of new and rehabilitated housing ranging from luxury apartments to affordable townhouses throughout the city.

Although this strategy is clear in hindsight and was generally shared by the leaders, it was rarely articulated as public policy. In theory, long-range strategy should be the purview of the regional planners, but rarely is. Many tactical elements outside downtown—notably affordable housing and good schools—that were fundamental to the policy, never got underway or have failed. Nevertheless, Baltimore's substantial revitalization accomplishments both in and outside downtown should not be understated.

The process of implementing the strategy for Baltimore's physical renaissance involved much of the community, the power structure, many citizens groups, and politicians in learning how to solve problems, make decisions together, and get a consensus. Public servants—such as former Mayor/Governor and now Comptroller William Donald Schaefer, Robert Embry, commissioner of housing and community development, and activist now-Senator Barbara Mikulski, and their counterparts in the Greater Baltimore Committee. Martin Millspaugh headed up the Charles Center-Inner Harbor Management, Inc., and Walter Sondheim, advisor to Millspaugh, Embry, Schaefer, and many other mayors and governors—are nothing less than civic geniuses.

The list of participants is long, but rarely included African-American leaders. Blacks understandably shied away from such involvement, and were often labeled "Uncle Toms" when they did participate. The realities of race underlie the outcome of many of the strategic decisions.

In Gerald Johnson's "Toynbee" terms, Baltimore had met its fourth challenge during the 1960s through the 1980s by again overcompensating, with a responding thrust of energy and physical development. But by as early as 1970, it was fair for Johnson to say, "Today Baltimore faces its fifth challenge and has need for all the muscle it has acquired. Many cities are facing this same challenge, the challenge of a black-white confrontation and suburban indifference."[2]

Add to this mix the fact that there is no money. For while the physical renaissance was under way downtown, in the Inner Harbor, and in many isolated parts of the city, Baltimore's total population declined 30 percent from almost a million in 1950, and is projected to drop to 671,300 by 2020.

In the interim the minority population has risen from 35 percent to over 65 percent; serious and sustained unemployment and poverty increasingly characterize the low-skilled, low-income people in the densely packed inner city; and property abandonment and demolition have left many neighborhoods underdeveloped or devastated.

Residential reinvestment, the hoped-for end product of the long-range strategy, requires a viable educational system. But the public schools are in disarray, the enrollment poor and almost entirely black, and they are largely neglected by a public policy that appears to accept the thesis that black children are uneducable in spite of clear, if anecdotal, evidence to the contrary. Challenging that belief, Philip Moeller, business editor of *The Baltimore Sun*, is reported to have concluded "that the city's public-school system could become Baltimore's next Inner Harbor. Many of us, perhaps too many, simply don't believe the public schools will ever get much better, but thirty-five years ago (1955) few people in Baltimore believed the city could turn itself around" or change "the way we felt about the downtown and lots of other facets of Baltimore."[3]

Nevertheless, the city met its challenge with a vigorous responding thrust, and had an incredible run for its money, becoming an international model of revitalization with seemingly unlimited access to federal funds until the Reagan years. The November 1987 *London Sunday Times* enthused: "Baltimore, despite soaring unemployment, boldly turned its derelict harbor into a playground. Tourists meant shopping, catering, and transport, this in turn meant construction, distribution, manufacturing— leading to more jobs, more residents, more activity. The decay of old Baltimore slowed, halted, then turned back. The harbor area is now among America's top tourist draws and urban unemployment is falling fast."[4]

Baltimore's downtown and Inner Harbor renaissance has not been without its critics. David Harvey, a geographer-turned-urbanist from Oxford University who once taught at Johns Hopkins University takes a broadly critical spin in his article entitled "A View from Federal Hill."[5] He sees the initiation of Charles Center and the redevelopment program as inspired by the business community's recognizing the political danger of abandoning the symbolic and strategic center of the metropolitan area to "an underclass of blacks and marginalized whites." He charges that CC-IH was created as the first of a succession of quasi-public agencies outside any democratic control that shaped renewal efforts. But Harvey is not only against what he calls the lack of democratic process, he criticizes the results.

As to Charles Center, Harvey charges that the project is a group of "somewhat arid buildings punctuated by bleak open spaces" from which the city received little benefit. The new jobs either went to suburban residents, were temporary construction jobs, or were low-paying. Charles Center was so heavily subsidized as to be a drain on the city's finances, he alleges.

"When in the late 1960s, the Realtors and business leaders turned their attention to the Inner Harbor, there were few takers," he says, and "it took a basic shift in orientation and philosophy to bring about this new and most recent phase of construction." Harvey claims the shift was triggered by the Baltimore race riots following the assassination of Martin Luther King, Jr., in April 1968. The riot culminated in a day-long skirmish between youths and the police at the city's flower mart.

The city's response, the idea of a city-fair with each neighborhood having display booths, was initiated by a broad coalition of citizens "that included church and civil rights leaders, academics and professionals, including downtown lawyers suddenly made aware of the wretched living conditions of the majority of the city's population; city officials who had long striven to build a better sense of community; and downtown business leaders who saw their investments threatened." Harvey goes on to say that the healing process began with the first fair in Charles Center. Organized by Sandy Hillman, the fair was attended by 340,000 people of all races and ethnicities, and by 1973 the fair had an attendance of 2 million and was of necessity relocated to the Inner Harbor. As Harvey put it, "the city had rediscovered the ancient Roman formula of bread and circuses as a means of masking social problems and controlling discontent."

Harvey goes on to say, "The story of the Inner Harbor's construction is one of a steady erosion of the aims of the coalition that set it in motion and its capture by the narrower forces of commercialism, property development and financial power." He blames Schaefer, who first became mayor in 1971 as the leader in this erosion. "The turn to tourism, the creation of an image of Baltimore as a sophisticated place to live, the razzle-dazzle of downtown, the commercial 'hype' of Harborplace, have to be seen as Mayor Schaefer's (and the GBC's) distinctive solution to the problem. With the crowds pouring in, it was a short step to commercializing the city fair, first by adding all manner of ethnic festivals, concerts and spectacular events—for example, the visit of the 'tall ships' during the 1976 bicentennial celebration—to draw even more people downtown."

"Then, having proved the existence of a market, the next step was to institutionalize a permanent commercial circus through the construction of Harborplace, the Maryland Science Center, the National Aquarium, the Convention Center, a marina, and innumerable hotels, shopping malls, and pleasure citadels of all kinds. The strategy did not even have to be consciously thought out, it was such an obvious thing to try."

Harvey ends with a warning, "Like the city fair, the Inner Harbor functions as a sophisticated mask...If the mask cracks or is violently torn off, the terrible face of Baltimore's impoverishment may appear."[6]

In 1992, architects Brian Kelly and Roger K. Lewis took a less politically biased approach to the Inner Harbor in their *Planning* magazine article "What's Right (and Wrong) About the Inner Harbor."[7] After praising the Inner Harbor as a model of a successful urban renewal project, they have four complaints. The first is what they call a lack of "contextualism" caused by the "tabula rasa" approach to clearance philosophically different from that used in Charles Center. Too few of the old buildings were saved, and the city's traditional street grid was ignored, Kelly and Lewis allege, with the result that the Inner Harbor is physically cut off from the rest of downtown, and philosophically from its historic roots. The cutoff is exacerbated by the great traffic flows that inhibit pedestrian connections, the roots abandoned by the destruction of all the historic buildings. Kelly and Lewis think that today's urban planners would have done it quite differently.

I think these were cheap shots. As to the historic buildings, my response is that we proposed leaving McCormick's spice factory, the News American building, Baltimore Gas and Electric Company's old steam plant, and the Candler Building. The remainder were small and of no architectural or historic significance. All built after the 1904 fire, but before 1920, they were obsolete in design and construction materials, and either empty or occupied by unimportant activities. If we had attempted to restore them as is now being proposed in Baltimore's West Side Plan, the ultimate build-out of the area would have been substantially compromised.

As to the street grid, the authors show a map of "before and after" that supports the contrary argument, that indeed we managed to physically integrate the harbor to a remarkable degree with downtown.

Unfortunately our proposed City Hall Plaza, a linear park linking the water and City Hall, never materialized. It would have helped.

Kelly and Lewis's second allegation is that the Inner Harbor has a carnival atmosphere. They say "it's a latter-day version of Coney Island, minus the Cyclone, and without the predictability of center city streets. It is, in short, a suburban, rather than an urban, kind of place." This charge was perhaps valid in 1992 when the article was written, with the area still only partially completed, but is hardly true today.

In the third allegation, although recognizing Ben Thompson's (and James Rouse's) Boston marketplace inspiration for Harborplace as an urban festival marketplace, they say, "But there's something shallow about this shopping area. Isn't it really just the suburban mall, dressed up and brought downtown?"

Well, at night the Inner Harbor does have a somewhat carnival atmosphere, but more in the tradition of New Orleans than Coney Island, and that's not bad. To say it's suburban is, I think, undeserved. Rouse's dream of exciting urban "festive" retail has been fulfilled superbly. What I do regret was our inability to get retail frontages on all sides of the superblocks instead of just on the harbor facades in most cases. This is partly a result of the inability to break up these blocks into smaller parcels, a function of the market, and the scale of Baltimore office development.

Finally, Kelly and Lewis ask: "Where's the grand plan?" They go on to say, "These shortcomings are the result of two things: a plan that stopped conceptually at the harbor's edge, and too much site-by-site decision-making." I tend to disagree with the first, but as to the latter, many of the buildings facing the water—particularly the Hyatt Hotel with its distracting reflective surfaces—both ignore the design guidelines and weaken their function as harbor walls. Remembering how hard it was to get any hotel at all, I am grateful that at least Hyatt's designer wasn't allowed to violate the height limit.

It has been 12 years since Kelly and Lewis made their comments and much more of the plan has been implemented in the interim. While the Inner Harbor's surrounding wall of buildings will never be like those along Baron Haussmann's Parisian boulevards, they create a substantial frame to the space.

I'm glad Harvey didn't turn his attention to the results of the *Plan for the Valleys*. While the valleys themselves were saved from despoliation, the plateaus have never been sewered as we proposed. As a consequence they have been developed with large lots and expensive houses. The rel-

20.1 Cartoonist Tom Toles's view of planning and the consequences.

atively high densities and varied mix of housing units matching a metropolitan cross-section of ethnic and income groups that we proposed never materialized. Harvey could have critiqued the plan as an elitist conspiracy among the rich white landowners and the government they controlled to provide *de facto* segregation. And he'd have been right about the result, although the plan was not completely carried out.

Nevertheless, put all this together with the plans for downtown Baltimore and the Inner Harbor, and the result from Harvey's point of view would look like "The Plan" as cartooned by Tom Toles of the *Buffalo News* and reported in *The New York Times*, on Sunday, June 14, 1998. The sketch shows six stages of growth, from white dominance in the central city, then white flight to suburbs followed by minorities, then to second-ring suburbs again followed by minorities, finally whites move back into cities that have been abandoned by minorities.

Federal funds dried up under the Reagan administration, but the private market continued to invest in the Inner Harbor until the stock market crashed in 1987. By 1990, the national market for private real estate investment disappeared. In 1987, Harvard graduate and Rhodes Scholar Kurt L. Schmoke was elected as the city's first African-American mayor. He announced his slogan to be "'a city that reads,' a powerful cue that the heady days of focusing on the Inner Harbor would take back seat to long-neglected neighborhoods."[8] For the next 10 years Schmoke responded to the neighborhoods—constituents discontented with the "corporate-centered strategies bringing about Baltimore's revitalization but having little impact on citizen's lives."[9]

My impression is that much of the city's black community tends to look at the shiny downtown and Inner Harbor as an alien place populated by whites who have moved to the suburbs, using the federal highway system to commute, and as an entertainment center for tourists. Critic David Harvey tells the story of Baltimore's redevelopment and emphasizes an interpretation that downtown urban renewal has been carried out by corporate interests fueled by public funds and tax concessions. He calls Baltimore's renaissance, including Harborplace, "the strategy of bread and circuses, a distraction from, rather than a solution to, the city's continuing problems of unemployment, impoverishment, illiteracy, and social decay."[10] I disagree.

In fairness to Mayor Schmoke, he did what he could to try to get Baltimore to read, but his influence over the Baltimore City School District was so greatly diminished over the years that what he could do for the neighborhoods was limited by too little tax revenues, and too little effort. In retrospect, he was not very effective. In 1998, the State of Maryland took over Baltimore's schools and it is problematical whether there has been much improvement. Schmoke also believed that drugs were a social, not a criminal problem, and that attitude resulted in Baltimore becoming for a while the murder capital of the United States It is finally recovering under Mayor Martin J. O'Malley.

However Schmoke did not entirely abandon downtown. He supported a public/private effort from 1989 to 1991, led by Walter Sondheim, Baltimore's *deus ex machina* to involve more than 300 citizens in re-examining the city's downtown strategy. The end product was appropriate to the times: *The Renaissance Continues* was not a plan, but a collection of site-unspecified good ideas.

Today, many of those good ideas are springing to life. "The Mayor's focus is back on downtown," *The Sun* reports.[11] Baltimore's new mayor, Martin J. O'Malley, has promised to support the three major downtown development efforts under way: the Westside, the Central Business District, and the Inner Harbor.

O'Malley is a relatively recent Baltimorean, having grown up in the Maryland suburbs of Washington, D.C. He was introduced to politics as an aid to former Senator Gary Hart, and is the son-in-law of Maryland Attorney General Joseph Curran. He first came to Baltimore to help Barbara Mikulski win re-election to the U.S. Senate in the 1980s. O'Malley is supported by the Jack Pollock organization of northwest Baltimore fame and he became a councilman in 1990. After two terms on the city council, O'Malley won the majority over two African-American candidates who counterbalanced each other during the campaign. O'Malley is up for re-election in 2004. O'Malley received the nomination and is expected to win.

His central idea is called "CitiStat," providing system accountability. He recognizes Baltimore's hi-tech potential and says, "We have made recruiting, supporting and growing tech companies our highest economic development priority because the "Digital Harbor" is Baltimore's future." O'Malley's critics say he is a man who is clearly marked for state or national office and wonder whether he will stay in Baltimore long enough to make a difference. If so, Baltimore seems likely to have a far brighter future.

So far the report is good, but as to results, we can only wait and see.

---

1 David Wilson, "Preface," *Globalization and the Changing U.S. City*, The Annals of the American Academy of Political and Social Science, May 1997, p.11.

2 "Past and Future Form: Challenge and Response," *MetroCenter/Baltimore Technical Study: A Report of the Regional Planning Council and the Baltimore City Department of Planning, 1970, A Part of the Comprehensive Plan*, by Wallace McHarg Roberts & Todd, p. 109.

3 Tony Hiss, "ANNALS OF PLACE: Reinventing Baltimore" in *The New Yorker*, April 29, 1991, p.44.

4 David Harvey, "A View from Federal Hill," *The Baltimore Book*, op.cit. p. 237.

5 ibid, pp. 226-249.

6 ibid, pp. 226-249.

7 *Planning*, April 1992, pp. 28-32.

8 Robert Guy Matthews, *The Baltimore Sun*, Friday, January 23, 1998.

9 Susan E. Clarke and Gary A. Gaile, "Local Politics in a Global Era: Thinking Locally, Acting Globally," in *The Annals of the American Academy of Political and Social Science*, op.cit., p. 41.

10 "Introduction: Toward a New History of Baltimore" in *The Baltimore Book: New Views of Local History*, Temple University Press, Elizabeth Fee, Linda Shopes, Linda Zeidman, ed. 1991.

11 Robert Guy Matthews, op.cit.

21

In Retrospect

In case the reader has followed my thoughts about keys to planning and urban design kingdoms but missed my conclusions, I summarize the most relevant ones here. First, for Baltimore, the Charles Center redevelopment project became the catalyst for a downtown renaissance. It changed the city's political and civic mindset, and created a new existing situation that made the redevelopment of the Inner Harbor possible. These two actions were the necessary concomitants to broad-scale urban infrastructure revitalization throughout the city and region.

BALTIMORE SUMMARIZED

While the Inner Harbor rode on the coattails of Charles Center and then created its own market, redevelopment of the adjacent retail center didn't catch on because the conditions necessary to support a regional shopping complex had disappeared. In fact, it didn't catch on in spite of three major planning efforts: the Central Business District Plan, the Lexington Center Plan, and a plan by developer David Murdoch partially implemented by the Market Center Development Corporation under planner Robert Tennenbaum's direction. The fundamental reasons for the retail center's failure are threefold. First, the plans could not address the fundamental market conditions that had eroded. Further, they never got political support, and finally, they hung on to the increasingly obsolete concept of a major shopping center as the nucleus for the area's use. In the current effort, the key to success is to convert the area to a downtown residential neighborhood, and the city administration seems to have accepted the idea. Notice that I did not include the 1969 MetroCenter concept as a planning effort because it wasn't really a plan.

For the Inner Harbor, the key to success was a group of urban design ideas embodied in the 1964 master plan: location and character of the water's edge and use, the idea of public access and public functions adjacent to the water, and the concept of development creating a frame for the harbor by office, hotel, and retail development along the northside of the Pratt Street Boulevard. The frame became progressively persuasive as developers were persuaded or coerced into adhering to it.

Unlike the Inner Harbor, the Jones Falls Valley Plan was organized around an open space concept. Looking back on this, it was the wrong emphasis. I realize that what might have been more effective would have been to view the valley as a series of redevelopment or land development projects, each of which coincidentally had a similar element, a stream valley park. If we had approached it this way, we would have then mobilized local constituencies around community issues rather than focusing on a somewhat esoteric regional concern. In this, we failed to find the key to the kingdom. In the current effort there is the danger of making the same mistake.

For the Green Spring and Worthington Valley Plan, the key to the kingdom was the concept of the relative openness of the three valleys. This is the case of not only an idea, but also a visual identity being the catalytic element in the planning process. The fact that development of the plateaus around these valleys has not happened as we planned does not diminish the effectiveness of the overall plan or the strength of the idea.

LOWER MANHATTAN, NEW ORLEANS, AND NORFOLK

For Lower Manhattan, one could argue that the World Trade Center was the catalytic agent that triggered revitalization, but our plan guided where new development should go, and established its character as residential. Battery Park City follows the Lower Manhattan Plan concept of waterfront mixed use between the pierhead and bulkhead lines along the Hudson River. Perhaps the present planning effort in the wake of the September 11 tragedy will reaffirm similar development along the East River as well as the Hudson. Architect Frank Gehry's proposal for a second Guggenheim Museum along the East River may never happen, but if it did, I think it would be a dramatic affirmation of the Lower Manhattan Plan.

In the spate of various downtown plans that I have discussed, there are similarities and differences. For downtown New Orleans, the civic and city leaders were alarmed that any attempt to plan would discourage new development. The key concept was growth management, and the job was to convince the leaders that they could guide and control how downtown should evolve. By the time the actual plan was prepared, they had internalized the results and become convinced. The published document was almost incidental, but became the record of individual actions that they had already adopted. In Norfolk, Virginia, the key was in freeing the waterfront from a proposed elevated expressway that would have cut it off from downtown, and in its place creating development along the Elizabeth River that set the stage for now-completed redevelopment of the downtown core.

OTHER WRT PLANS

Miami's stagnating downtown received a major investment impetus from Cuban refugees and South American tourists during the years after we completed our master plan. The plan identified two major redevelopment projects: Overtown and Park West. They became successful residential anchors for commercial development in the core and along Biscayne Bay. However, the political situation was problematic and the plan has had little lasting effect. For the Central City Los Angeles Plan, we had the wrong client. It was commissioned by a group of self-designated business leaders who unfortunately never were able to ally themselves with the real power, the city's redevelopment authority. As a consequence a lot of good ideas were ignored and the plan was a failure. It takes a good client, as well as accomplished planners, to make effective plans.

We had both good clients and good planners for Sanibel Island, Florida. There the concept of a limit on environmental capacity based on the time it would take to evacuate the island across the four-lane bridge to the mainland in anticipation of a major hurricane was most important. Increasing the capacity of the bridge or building another was deemed politically impossible.

The concept of environmental capacity was based on a different, but equally compelling, measure in the Master Plan for the U.S. Capitol. The plan had to accommodate the potential growth of both houses of Congress, the Library of Congress, and the U.S. Supreme Court. George M. White, architect of the Capitol, characterized Congress as an 800-pound gorilla whose growth curve went off the chart. I remember making one presentation to a community group representing neighbors who might be displaced by expansion of the Capitol Grounds. I had noted that

Congress could expand if it wished and was faced with an outraged housewife who said, "Tell them not to."

In this case, we finally persuaded our client that the capacity of the movement system would establish the limits of development on Capitol Hill. To do this we relied on our old friends, Alan M. Voorhees and Associates with David Schoppert. Schoppert's computer model was compelling. Congressional leaders agreed that necessary growth beyond the limit we set would have to be accommodated in peripheral locations. It is interesting to note a *New York Times* article in the National section on Tuesday, May 28, 2002, reports the start of construction of a long-planned Visitor Center and additional space for both houses of Congress that together almost doubles the entire Capitol—and all underground in front of the Capitol's East Front. September 11 allowed Congress to do what it wanted to do anyway, go to underground construction as a security measure.

I rest my case.

PLANNING PRINCIPLES

"What have you learned about cities and about planning in your professional practice?" is a favorite softball question of interviewers, and I've thought a lot about my answer. I've been accused of taking on "winning" cities where the planning was easy, for example, David Harvey suggests anyone would have been able to come up with the Inner Harbor plan. I assure the reader that when one starts the planning process for a large area or project, the solution is not immediately apparent.

Far from it, which leads me to the first principle I've learned: All problems have solutions, some just take more time than others, and for many, the cost may be too high or politically infeasible. I worked long and intensely for Camden, New Jersey, and the city is just taking longer than originally expected. East St. Louis may never be resolved to anyone's satisfaction. You have to be an optimist about cities to adopt this principle.

My second principle is to rely on the professional methods that I have learned and developed. This is sort of the old adage, "when all else fails, read the instructions." But I find that a firm reliance on the rational planning model as illustrated always produces results. You can't go wrong.

My third principle is that invariably, the problem's solution, the "key to the kingdom," is inherent in the problem. The people, the ideas, the actions are there to be discovered and acted on.

My fourth principle relates to the planner as an advocate. The planner must identify with the client or client group, must for purposes of the planning process, share and understand and appreciate the clients goals. The planners should reject the assignment if that is not possible.

Finally, the best idea for any planner is to give other people, particularly the client, credit for ideas and success. That sounds so simple, but it is rarely done.

A word about the firm that I created and helped nurture for the last 40 years. Today, Wallace Roberts & Todd, LLC, is a more than 160 person firm. It is a truly inter- as well as multidisciplinary firm of architects, landscape architects, urban designers, and planners with offices in Philadelphia, Coral Gables, Florida, Lake Placid, New York, Dallas, San Diego, California, and San Francisco. No single office specializes; staff from various offices frequently combine efforts to win and do work.

In January 2002, Daniel Solomon ETC, a "boutique" firm of urban designers and architects in a San Francisco office specializing in urban residential development, merged its offices and practices with WRT into a building designed and owned by Solomon. WRT's San Francisco office has until now specialized in urban design and planning, so I expect great things from the merger. Solomon will continue to have a separate identity as Solomon ETC, a WRT Company. Dan is now a principal of WRT and is going to raise the level of our work substantially.

Jonathan Barnett, noted author and urban designer, and professor at the University of Pennsylvania's department of city and regional planning, also has joined the firm and adds a new dimension to our urban design capability.

For those interested in numbers, the latest employee census shows 47 architects, 45 landscape architects, 16 urban designers, 5 environmental planners, and 14 physical planners. In addition there are 36 support, administrative, and financial staff. Because many architects and landscape architects also act as urban designers and planners, and several of the planners are also architects and landscape architects, the above categories obscure the interdisciplinary way the firm actually works. For the bottom liners, architectural contracts amounted to slightly more than half of the firm's gross income last year.

Every firm needs a self-image that it projects to the world. WRT is no exception. I quote from one of the firm's recent publicity brochures called "Places." It is not what I would have necessarily said, but on the other hand I don't disagree with it:

Wallace Roberts & Todd LLC is an interdisciplinary practice of planners, urban designers, architects, and landscape architects dedicated to creating sustainable cities and regions, and a range of distinct places within them: communities, educational institutions, transit-related facilities, parks and open spaces, downtowns, and waterfronts.

Enough said.

Afterword

Paul M. Rookwood, AICP, ASLA, Managing Principal,
Wallace Roberts & Todd

Not least among David Wallace's many achievements is the firm of Wallace Roberts & Todd, LLC, that he helped to found and that (40 years later) is still pioneering planning and design ideas. David has asked me to summarize the firm's organizational history and outline how the legacy of philosophy, principles, methods, and experience—handed down from the four founding partners, influences the ways the firm practices today. If time is an important test of a plan, so it is also of a planning practice, and it is accurate to assert that *Urban Planning/My Way* has, indeed, become planning "our" way.

THE FIRM—THEN AND NOW

When Wallace Roberts & Todd began in 1963, four ideas captured the imagination of its founders:

- An interdisciplinary approach to resolving problems of the built and natural environments,
- An ethos of environmental responsibility that called for development to proceed in accordance with the landscape and culture of a place,
- A belief in the moral role and responsibility of the professional planner/designer as agent for the general public welfare as well as the immediate client,
- A dedication to achieving professional excellence in each of the disciplines we practice.

The ideal assignment—then as now—enables us to fully realize our commitment to those ideas through a continuous involvement, one that starts with large-scale planning, establishes goals that translate into major urban design projects creating conceptual frameworks of natural and built form, and which then evolves into specific landscape and building designs. When completed, these become the structure for further large-scale planning. As the usual project assignment deals with only segments of this continuity, it is incumbent on the professional to outline the assignment's overall context.

Forty years later, those ideas remain at the core of our firm. Today WRT practices from six offices across the nation, employs more than 160 people and has won more than 120 awards for its work. The firm has a strategic plan in place as well as a central organization that facilitates interdisciplinary efforts and inter-office collaboration. The longevity of the firm stems largely from the strength of its core principles, the continuity of its leadership and their success in grooming and passing on a legacy to younger professionals.

THE WORK

The significance of projects such as the Baltimore Inner Harbor, the *Plan for the Valleys*, and the *Plan for Lower Manhattan* transcends the major impact they've had on those particular cities, not only because their built legacy has inspired so many other communities, but also because the ideas reverberate and grow. What follows are some examples of how these ideas have continued to evolve through the firm's work.

URBAN INVESTMENT AS CATALYST

New projects have grown from the seeds of Baltimore's transformation. In Richmond, Virginia, for example, WRT's planning work for downtown and the 6th Street Market set the stage for a major civic place: Canalwalk. Here the firm worked with the public and private sectors to leverage enormous civic value from what would have otherwise been a large but mundane infrastructure investment: embedding a new combined sewer overflow (CSO) within the city's moribund historic canals. Richmond's supplemental investment of public funds for a pedestrian promenade along the newly unearthed waterways, also designed by WRT, has sparked both a popular place of pride among residents, and has resulted in more than $137 million of private redevelopment to stimulate Richmond's downtown economy.

LANDSCAPE URBANISM

Fueled by collaboration within the firm, the idea of Landscape Urbanism has emerged as an approach to integrating public parks, plazas, and civic open spaces within the urban fabric—at both a city-wide scale and that of specific places—in ways that also contribute to environmental health. As with many of our projects, the continuum of approach and perspectives—from large-scale planning to site-specific design—shapes the work. An early example can be seen in Overtown, an award-winning pedestrian plaza in Miami, an implementation project spurred by our downtown and Park West sector plans. The plaza relies on landscape and public art to knit together a neighborhood fractured by rail infrastructure. In Charlottesville, Virginia, and Dallas our designs currently under way for transit centers go beyond their functional purpose to serve greater civic ends—one creating critical mass in a downtown, the other providing a focal civic place and identity to an emerging neighborhood. WRT's award-winning general plan for the Eastshore State Park—an 8.5-mile shoreline park along San Francisco Bay—forges a new model for urban parks. Here, issues of recreation, land conservation, and environmental rehabilitation intertwine in the making of a multi-jurisdictional public park, in effect reversing decades of environmental degradation. In all these cases, meaningful public involvement has been central to the effort.

MORE LIVABLE CITIES

While one segment of our practice has focused on civic infrastructure— the "glue" of cities—another has focused on creating urban housing and better residential neighborhoods. Our goal is to make cities more viable and attractive places to live for everyone. Under the federal HOPE VI initiative, WRT has become a national leader in its work with cities and developers alike to replace distressed public housing with more vibrant mixed-use communities. The firm's ability to practice the continuum of planning through design—with an emphasis on integrated placemaking—has been a key asset to our clients. Since the HOPE VI program commenced, WRT has designed more than 14,000 units of new housing. In 2001, WRT merged with Solomon ETC, a New Urbanist firm renowned for its award-winning design of multi-family infill housing and its commitment to urban repair. Urban living is an essential ingredient of a more sustainable future, and our aim is to help cities provide residential options that are more attractive than sprawl at the urban fringe.

GROWTH MANAGEMENT: MORE SUSTAINABLE REGIONS

From its inception, the firm has recognized the symbiotic relationship between projects, cities, and their regions. History has shown that growth within regions often comes at the expense of the urban core's vitality. Unplanned growth also can compromise a region's long-term environmental health and quality of life. Hence, WRT's approach includes a tradition of innovative growth management which continues to be refined through our work.

Based on sustainable principles, the landmark Monroe County Comprehensive Plan for the Florida Keys and the plan for Sanibel Island on Florida's west coast rely on a careful consideration of carrying capacity—balancing the amount and type of development with the concurrent need to protect natural resources, public safety, and community character. Our general plan update for San Diego County, currently under way, wrestles with the same issues: how to accommodate tremendous growth pressures while protecting back-country acreage that includes more threatened and endangered species than anywhere else in the continental United States.

Sustainable practices also find expression in the site-specific design of buildings and landscapes. WRT is playing a leadership role in the development of the U.S. Green Building Council and has multiple projects moving through LEED accreditation process. WRT's Green Council assists us as we to continue to build and refine our collective knowledge and techniques in sustainable design.

Colleges and universities are in many ways microcosms of larger environments with one important exception: They can exercise more control over their environment. Another strand of our professional practice has been to apply our knowledge and ethos to suit the particular setting and aspirations of these institutions. Much of our planning work on campuses takes a systems approach to conserving and improving open spaces, and directing new campus development to repair what is often a fragmented built fabric.

WRT's projects range from planning at the campus-wide scale, such as our sustainability plan for Georgia Tech, to site-specific assignments, such as the landscape architecture for the Bren School for Environmental Management at the University of California–Santa Barbara, one of only two projects to receive a LEED Platinum rating. Our campus work also recognizes the symbiotic relationship between a university and its host community, and facilitates cooperation to yield collective benefits. WRT's master planning work with the University of Missouri–Kansas City has helped to transform the relationship between the institution and the city and will guide improvements to mutual advantage.

PLANNING AS ADVOCACY

Recently, WRT participated in an unusual assignment for the Greenbelt Alliance, a nonprofit organization that advocates land conservation in the San Francisco Bay area. Our charge was to devise and propose a viable smart-growth alternative for Coyote Valley, San Jose's largest urbanizing area. The exercise shows how the same amount of planned growth (at least 50,000 jobs and 2,000 new residences) can be accommodated using more sustainable development patterns. The result is a dynamic and flexible planning framework that envisions a dense and livable transit-oriented community that conserves significant greenfield acreage for agriculture, natural habitat and recreation. *Getting it Right*, as the award-winning plan for Coyote Valley is called, will likely influence the specific plan about to be undertaken for this area.

INTEGRATION AS MEANS AND END

The firm's position has always recognized the complexity of places, the layers and overlapping uses that contribute to the richness of environments—both natural and built. Our work seeks an integrated approach–one that joins together the full range of perspectives in environmental planning and design, as well as allied disciplines. WRT finds planning solutions and design expressions that will provide enduring value.

Because WRT has always emphasized not only what we do but how we do it, it seems important to say a few words about how the firm is organized to do its work. What began as intense, professional collaboration among the four founding principals—David Wallace, Ian McHarg, William Roberts, and Thomas Todd—has evolved today into a carefully conceived structure at the firm to facilitate collaboration and communication among 15 principals, 36 associates, six offices, and scores of professionals nationwide. In addition to the mentoring that occurs within professional disciplines, WRT is organized by what we call Affinity and Special Interest Groups, all of which correspond to a particular market or project type pursued by the firm. These groups draw professionals from different disciplines and offices, and are supported by an electronic infrastructure (network listserv, marketing budget, and the like) to foster effective collaboration. Principals and staff frequently belong to more than one affinity group, which also helps to foster cross-pollination of ideas among the groups. Similar in structure, though different in purpose, the WRT Green Council has been formed to research and refine techniques, and disseminate information that enables our work to be at the forefront of sustainable design.

The four Affinity Groups are Colleges and Universities, Comprehensive Planning, Community Planning and Design, and Urban Places. There are currently four Special Interest Groups: Waterfronts, Heritage Institutions, Parks and Open Space, and Transportation. Other

Special Interest Groups are formed from time to time as the work horizon changes.

Perhaps even more important than the firm's structure is its culture. It is one that arises from a deeply ingrained commitment to social and environmental responsibility, a creative drive that leads us both to question and to create, and a predilection for methodical self-examination. Our willingness to engage in strategic planning for the firm has enabled us to have frank and productive dialogue about our future as a company and pave the way for ownership transition.

Through the example of David Wallace and others, WRT reinforces its philosophical aims with pragmatic methods of achieving them, whether it's for the firm itself or for our clients. In the final analysis, planning—our way—continues to be a means to a greater end: We help cities and communities shape a more sustainable future.

Illustration Credits

I.1 Photos courtesy of WRT Archives
I.2 Needlepoint courtesy of the author
I.3 Diagram courtesy of Wallace Roberts & Todd, LLC (WRT)

1.1 Courtesy of WRT Archives
1.2 Courtesy of WRT Archives

2.1 Courtesy of the *News American* Photo Archive, University of Maryland Libraries, Special Collections
2.2 Courtesy of WRT Archives
2.3 Courtesy of the Thomas J.D'Alesandro Collection, University of Baltimore, Special Collections
2.4 Courtesy of WRT Archives
2.5 Photo by Marion Warren
2.6 Photo by Walter Sondheim, Jr.

3.1 Photo by author
3.2 Courtesy of WRT Archives
3.3 Photo courtesy of Downtown Partnership of Baltimore, MD

4.1 Courtesy of WRT Archives
4.2 Courtesy of WRT Archives
4.3 Courtesy of WRT Archives
4.4 Courtesy of WRT Archives
4.5 Courtesy of WRT Archives
4.6 Courtesy of WRT Archives
4.7 Courtesy of Sharon R. Grinnell, COO, City of Baltimore Development Corporation

5.1 Courtesy of WRT Archives
5.2 Courtesy of WRT Archives
5.3 Courtesy of WRT Archives

6.1 Courtesy of WRT Archives
6.2 Courtesy of WRT Archives

7.1 Courtesy of WRT Archives
7.2 Courtesy of WRT Archives
7.3 Courtesy of WRT Archives
7.4 Courtesy of WRT Archives
7.5 Courtesy of WRT Archives

8.1 Courtesy of WRT Archives

10.1 Courtesy of WRT Archives
10.2 Courtesy of WRT Archives
10.3 Photo by the Author
10.4 Courtesy of WRT Archives
10.5 Courtesy of WRT Archives
10.6 Courtesy of WRT Archives
10.7 Courtesy of WRT Archives
10.8 Courtesy of WRT Archives
10.9 Courtesy of WRT Archives
10.10 Courtesy of WRT Archives
10.11 Courtesy of WRT Archives
10.12 Courtesy of WRT Archives
10.13 Photo by Walter Sondheim, Jr.
10.14 Courtesy of WRT Archives

11.1 Photo Courtesy of William Potts

12.1 Courtesy of WRT Archives
12.2 Courtesy of WRT Archives
12.3 Courtesy of WRT Archives
12.4 Courtesy of WRT Archives
12.5 Courtesy of WRT Archives
12.6 Courtesy of WRT Archives
12.7 Courtesy of WRT Archives
12.8 Courtesy of WRT Archives
12.9 Courtesy of WRT Archives
12.10 Courtesy of WRT Archives

13.1 Courtesy of WRT Archives

14.1 Courtesy of WRT Archives
14.2 Courtesy of WRT Archives
14.3 Courtesy of WRT Archives
14.4 Courtesy of WRT Archives
14.5 Courtesy of WRT Archives

15.1 Courtesy of WRT Archives

16.1 Map Courtesy of WRT Archives
16.2 Courtesy of WRT Archives
16.3 Courtesy of WRT Archives
16.4 Courtesy of WRT Archives
16.5 Courtesy of WRT Archives

17.1 Courtesy of Matt Wargo
17.2 Courtesy of Urban Land Institute
17.3 Photo by Author
17.4 Photo by Author
17.5 Courtesy of WRT Archives

18.1 Courtesy of WRT Archives
18.2 Courtesy of WRT Archives
18.3 Courtesy of WRT Archives
18.4 Courtesy of WRT Archives

19.1 From *New Orleans: The Making of an Urban Landscape,* Second Edition, 2003, Original Map by Pierce F. Lewis, Center for Urban Places and the University of Virginia Press
19.2 Courtesy of WRT Archives
19.3 Courtesy of WRT Archives

20.1 Courtesy of Tom Toles, Universal Press Syndicate

Index